Fashion in Popular Culture

Fashion in Popular Culture:
Literature, Media and Contemporary Studies

Edited by Joseph H. Hancock, II,
Toni Johnson-Woods and Vicki Karaminas

intellect Bristol, UK / Chicago, USA

First published in the UK in 2013 by
Intellect, The Mill, Parnall Road, Fishponds, Bristol, BS16 3JG, UK

First published in the USA in 2013 by
Intellect, The University of Chicago Press, 1427 E. 60th Street,
Chicago, IL 60637, USA

A catalogue record for this book is available from the
British Library.

Cover image: Lady Gaga and Kermit The Frog, 2009 MTV Video
    Music Awards - Red Carpet. (Collection: WireImage, Photographer:
    Kevin Mazur).
Cover designer: Ellen Thomas
Copy-editor: Macmillan
Typesetting: Planman

ISBN 978-1-84150-716-3

Printed and bound by Latimer Trend, Plymouth, UK

Contents

Acknowledgements   vii

Introduction   ix
Joseph H. Hancock, II, Toni Johnson-Woods, and Vicki Karaminas

List of Figures   xvii

Fashion in Contemporary Culture

Chapter 1: Brand This Way: Lady Gaga's Fashion as Storytelling Context to the
GLBT Community   1
Joseph H. Hancock, II

Chapter 2: Navigating Cultural Anxiety: Strategic Ambiguity in Lisbeth Salander's
Style-Fashion-Dress   23
Susan B. Kaiser

Chapter 3: Australian Gothic: *Black Light Angels*, Appearance, and Subcultural Style 49
Vicki Karaminas

Chapter 4: Fashionable Addiction: The Path to Heroin Chic   67
Alphonso D. McClendon

Fashion in Media and Literature

Chapter 5: Dames and Design: Fashion and Appearance on Pulp Fiction Covers,
1950–1960   87
Toni Johnson-Woods

Chapter 6: Territories of Knowledge and Nostalgia in Modern Fashion Designer
Life Writing   103
Ilya Parkins

Chapter 7:   Looking for Mr. Benson: The Black Leather Motorcycle Jacket and
             Narratives of Masculinities   121
             Marvin J. Taylor

Chapter 8:   Fashion Photography, Phallocentrism, and Feminist Critique   135
             Louise Wallenberg

Chapter 9:   'He Can't Love Me if I'm Ugly': The Recurring Theme of Popular Beauty
             in the Television Soap Opera *Days of Our Lives*   155
             Andrew Reilly and Nancy A. Rudd

Chapter 10: Redressing the Devil's Wardrobe: Representing and Re-Reading
             the Darker Side of Fashion in Chick Lit Novels   171
             Anne Peirson-Smith

Fashion in Historical Context

Chapter 11: Redeeming the Voices of Reform   191
             Patricia A. Cunningham

Chapter 12: The Language of Luxury in Eighteenth-Century France   207
             Paula von Wachenfeldt

Chapter 13: The Devil of Fashion: Women, Fashion, and the Nation in
             Early-Twentieth-Century German and Swedish Cultural Magazines   225
             Andrea Kollnitz

Chapter 14: Rome: Eternal City of Fashion and Film   243
             Eugenia Paulicelli

List of Contributors   259

Index   267

Acknowledgements

We would like to thank Masoud Yazdani, James Campbell and Bethan Ball from Intellect for their support. We would like to acknowledge Anne C. Cecil and Roberta H. Gruber of the Fashion, Product, Design & Merchandising Department, Allen Sabinson, Dean of the Antoinette Westphal College of Media Arts & Design, Drexel University Philadelphia, as well as, Dr Joseph H. Hancock, II, President of the Popular Culture and American Culture Association (2013–2015) and the Popular Culture Association of Australia and New Zealand for their financial contributions. Thank you to Professor Lawrence Wallen, Head of the School of Design and Professor Desley Luscombe, Dean of the Faculty of Design, Architecture and Building, University of Technology, Sydney, Australia, and the University of Queensland for their unwavering support. Thanks to Bill Burmester for his editing assistance. A special appreciation to Margaret A. Miller and Edward A. Augustyn for their patience and dedication to the project.

Most importantly we are indebted to the contributors themselves who saw the worth of this project. We hope that this volume will be the beginning of many such discussions and collaborations of this caliber.

Acknowledgements

Introduction

Joseph H. Hancock, II, Toni Johnson-Woods, and Vicki Karaminas

In the opening scene of *Albert Nobbs* (2011), the American actress Glenn Close is cross-dressed as a hotel waiter who is employed at the Morrissey's Hotel in Dublin. She wears a black bowler hat, popular with working-class and civil servants, a white shirt with high upstanding collar and bowtie, and a tailored mid-calf black suit typical of the type of clothes worn by butlers and male servants in the late nineteenth century. Based on the novella by George Moore, *Albert Nobbs* is the story of a woman who dresses and poses as a man to escape economic restrictions suffered by women in Victorian Ireland. The film follows the same vein as cross-dressing film classics *Victor/Victoria* (1982) starring Julie Andrews as a struggling female soprano playing a male female impersonator to gain employment and *Yentl* (1983) in which Barbra Streisand portrays a Jewish girl who disguises herself as a boy to enter religious training that bars women. And then of course there is *Orlando* (1992), the film adaptation of Virginia Woolf's influential novel whose four-hundred-year-old hero crosses time and gender. The novel uses gender and dress to imagine what it would be like if social identities were less bound to bodies and appearance.

The cast of characters in *Albert Nobbs*, *Victor/Victoria*, *Yentl* and *Orlando* wear their stories on their backs, each garment mapping their gender and social position on their bodies. As dress historian Aileen Ribeiro writes, 'Literature conveys emotions and feelings about clothes that can highlight character and further the plot of a play or a novel…. Fashion itself can be said to produce fiction' (2005: 1). Fashion is codified and endowed with social meanings about gender, sexuality and identity. Dress frames the body. It expresses who we *are* and who we *are not* as a means of expressing identity and a way of interacting and belonging to a particular culture. Dress also plays an important part in proclaiming a person's sexual and gender identity. The adoption of what is considered masculine or feminine dress is a means of communicating membership of a particular group, the affirmation or rejection of an 'assigned' rather than 'chosen' gender or the declaration of a sexuality, be it queer or otherwise. In this way, clothes are given value as a means of making a statement about individuality and a person's place in society. If clothing is a form of the non-verbal and visual codes that communicate certain characteristics or facts about the wearer, then the dress choices of alternative genders within a culture demonstrate a desire to be seen as someone else. What makes the study of fashion so important in popular culture is the role of clothing in constructing material identity and its shaping of personal and social space. Patrizia Calefato is eloquent when she notes that

> Fashion has turned the body into a discourse, a sign, a *thing*. A body permeated by discourse, of which clothes and objects are an intrinsic part, is a body exposed to transformations, to grotesque openings toward the world; a body that will feel and taste all that the world feels and tastes, if it simply lets itself open up. (1997: 72)

Fashion is a phenomenon that exemplifies diversity across cultures. It is dependent on time and place and commonly defined as the prevailing style at a given moment or place. While the media likes to suggest that fashion is only for the wealthy it is really a commodity that is accessible to everyone at various levels of quality and distinguishable styles. Contemporary clothing items such as T-shirts, denim, khaki pants, polo shirts, sweaters and baseball caps, have become transnational garments. These mass fashion items signify most of what is bought and sold every day as 'fashion', suggesting that to define fashion only as elitist would simply be wrong (Miler and Hancock 2009: 1).

Once relegated to the field of art, anthropology and costume (dress studies), fashion now encompasses such diverse disciplines as film, theater history, and business studies. Until very recently, fashion was considered to be frivolous and was relegated to the domain of the feminine (and the 'foppish' male) and the body, as opposed to architecture, philosophy or the fine arts, which were deemed masculine and considered the domain of the mind.

Interdisciplinarity across academia has meant that scholars have approached the study of fashion and dress from a number of perspectives that challenge fashion's marginal place in traditional academic scholarship. Whilst scholars George Simmel, Thorstein Veblen and Walter Benjamin all wrote about fashion and how it was one of the principal means by which modernity manifests itself, its own identity and the zeitgeist, it has only been of late that fashion has gained critical ground in transforming our understanding of dress in popular culture as a barometer by which taste, consumption, class, and identity are measured.

Fashion scholars are not limited to the study of *haute couture* or high fashion, but also areas that relate to the dress, style, appearance, consumption, and adornment of people across cultures and in everyday society. Issues such as sexuality, gender, religion, race, ethnicity, and the various ways we construct identity have become increasingly important. Art, performing arts, history, literature, design, manufacturing, marketing and branding, merchandising, retailing, and psychological/sociological aspects of dress and body image are key disciplines in the study of fashion in the twenty-first century. Different types of methodologies are used to research and write about fashion. Art historians examine fashion from the wearer's point of view and look specifically at the actual garments depicted in painting as a source of analysis. Cultural anthropologists use qualitative methods such as ethnography to study cultures by examining elements of dress, such as the sari or the kimono. Whilst sociologists use ethnography to study subcultural styles, cultural theorists use everyday ephemera and material objects, from novels to film, photographs and so on.

Not since Patricia A. Cunningham and Susan Voso Lab's *Dress and Popular Culture* (1991) has there been an accessible 'jargon free' interdisciplinary book specifically dedicated to the study of fashion and its relationship to popular culture. As the editors of this scholarly collection, we felt it was time for another volume that builds upon previous work. While some of the chapters in this publication come from the 'Fashion in Fiction: The Dark Side' conference that took place at Drexel University in Philadelphia from 8-10 October 2010, others came from various sources including Popular Culture Association/American Culture Association (PCA/ACA) conferences.

The three sections of this book reflect the breadth of recent fashion scholarship—in both historical and contemporary settings our authors have engaged with film, photography, comics, magazines and television. They have written about the seventeenth century and the twenty-first century; about street fashion, aristocratic dress, and imagined clothing. In order to impose some structure on the book, it is divided into three sections—as with any demarcation, sometimes the chapters were suitable for more than one section.

In Fashion in Contemporary Culture, Joseph H. Hancock, II argues that in creating a relationship between Lady Gaga and her gay, lesbian, bisexual and transgender (GLBT) community fans, she has created a brand—brand-Gaga. Through a branding lens Hancock explores Gaga's deft weaving of fashion narratives into her self-fashioning. In doing so, he demonstrates that brand-Gaga is more altruistic than is traditionally associated with the commercial world of branding; Lady Gaga's unique acceptance of difference has created a political persona that translates into a brand that both sells products and benefits the causes Lady Gaga supports. And while his chapter is restricted to Lady Gaga, the implications are that this type of ethical branding has potential beyond Lady Gaga. While Lady Gaga's style is unique, Susan B. Kaiser demonstrates how Lisbeth Salander's (*The Girl with the Dragon Tattoo* books and films) style, fashion, 'dress', and body (i.e., her appearance) in The Millennium Trilogy transforms, and each transformation articulates her subjectivity through the lens of another 'creator'. Kaiser realizes that multiple Lisbeths are possible and indeed necessary for the viewer/reader to understand that the literary and visual changes Lisbeth undergoes reflects her personal journey. Lisbeth is an amalgam of many subcultures; one of which is surely the most recognizable: goth. In her chapter on gothic style, Vicki Karaminas examines the illustrations in the comic book series *Black Light Angels*. She demonstrates that the high romanticism of gothic clothing reflects a remoteness that is further mirrored in the comic's depiction of the desolate Australian landscape. Nothing is new, Alphonso D. McClendon argues in his chapter on heroin chic. He demonstrates that the 1990s fashion phenomenon for underdressed and overdepressed imagery is a distant cousin to the fashions adopted by performers of the1930s. Jazz artists were keen to distance themselves from drug addiction by appropriating aristocratic dress; but in the 1990s, fashion images celebrated the unglamorous lifestyle of the addict. McClendon argues that the penchant for semi-naked, hollow-eyed waifs has a political bias—it reflected the uptake of the drug culture as an increasing leisure activity and its consequence, the need for rehabilitation.

In the second section, Fashion in Media and Literature, books reveal a surprising focus on fashion. Toni Johnson-Woods uses the covers of 1950s pulp fiction books to demonstrate that the sexy dame on the cover was more than something to look at; she was a signifier of the increasing sexual agency of women and the growing fears of men. Ilya Parkins revisits the biographies of modern fashion designers and demonstrates their place in creative non-fiction as important. Focusing on Paul Poiret's and Elsa Schiaparelli's biographies, she shows how the biographies reveal the battle between two incompatible 'modernities': art and commerce. Underscoring their memoirs is a melancholia as the fashion industry shifts to accommodate a fast-changing world. Adopting a similarly close textual analysis, Marvin J. Taylor evaluates the BLJ—the black leather (motorcycle) jacket. Through exploration of the seminal gay text *Mr. Benson*, Taylor documents the history of the motorcycle jacket and its signification for the gay subculture of the late 1970s. Anne Peirson-Smith takes on the reviled chick lit genre; in her study of women's reading, she reveals that readers are not unthinking dupes but find fashion hints, behind-the-scenes gossip, and feminine empowerment in chick lit. What could be more fashion conscious than the middle-class, glamorous world of daily soaps? Andrew Reilly and Nancy A. Rudd look behind the glittering surfaces and demonstrate that disfiguring scarring has become a formulaic soap narrative. Through her struggle with loss of beauty, the soap star learns to love herself, regain her beauty and then she can find true love—until an alien abducts her, that is. Louise Wallenberg's chapter reminds us that the glamorous life of the fashion model can be fraught with exploitation and sexual harassment. Drawing on extensive teaching experience, Wallenberg demonstrates that the images our eyes slide over in advertisements and on the screen are in fact quite brutal—voyeurism, sadism and misogyny. She draws equally from film and fashion photography to make her point.

Fashion in Historical Context takes us on a romp through the fashion of the eighteenth, nineteenth and twentieth centuries. Patricia A. Cunningham revisits her early work on dress reform and puts the movement under a more specific microscope: that of the influence of reformers as designers, manufactures and retailers in the fashion industry. She demonstrates how these ideas were disseminated in exhibitions, lectures and shop displays. In her chapter on luxury, Paula von Wachenfeldt turns to eighteenth-century France. Comparing Rousseau and Voltaire, von Wachenfeldt shows that luxury was linked to a central concern of the Enlightenment—the effects of civilization. While Voltaire praises the new products and comfort of the Industrial Revolution, Rousseau reminds readers of the human cost of industrialization. Voltaire argues for the sensual world; Rousseau firmly believes that humans are purest in their natural state and that industrialization creates division and dissatisfaction. Fashion and philosophy make surprisingly comfortable bedmates. Swedish and German magazines of the nineteenth and twentieth century contain images of males and females that are markers of political and economic nationalism. By analyzing the images from four popular magazines, Andrea Kollnitz demonstrates how the two countries mobilized certain nationalistic values and beliefs while at the time still invoking France as the epitome of fashion. After World War II, Italy underwent considerable reconstruction, and

Eugenia Paulicelli's chapter demonstrates that fashion and film helped resurrect Rome's cultural reputation. Italian fashion houses, fashion shows and films drew Hollywood stars and attention to the Eternal City.

The study of fashion has grown to be a comprehensive and a wide-ranging discipline because of the support of this international organization. Because of Ray and Pat Browne's promotion of Patricia A. Cunningham to the area chair of fashion, fashion has blossomed into one of the largest areas of the PCA/ACA. With hundreds of participants across the globe presenting their scholarship on the many facets and methodologies that are part of the fashion discipline. The PCA/ACA continues to raise its conference standards and those who participate in all the areas, especially fashion. Over the last twenty years, fashion studies has evolved beyond the study of high or elite culture alone to include, as Ray Browne suggests in his article 'Popular Culture: Notes Toward a Definition' (1972: 5), popular, mass and folk cultures, reflecting the everyday lives of ordinary people and including everything from international and national to local cultures and traditions.

We would like to acknowledge the importance of the PCA/ACA, as it continues to foster and support the relationships between fashion and popular culture through the inclusion of this area at its regional, national and international conference venues. New international divisions of the PCA/ACA such as the Popular Culture Association of Australia and New Zealand (POPCAANZ) evolve innovations in fashion studies to both the northern and southern hemispheres. No longer is the study of fashion specific to any part of the world, but it is global and inclusive of almost all continents. The PCA/ACA's reputation as an innovative place for new scholars to present their research without the fear of ridicule fosters a culture in which academics are not afraid to make changes to their methods and views on fashion.

This volume reflects this new movement in the field of fashion studies as Intellect releases its new list of journals that reflect the diversity in the field. These include: *Film, Fashion & Consumption*, *Critical Studies in Fashion & Beauty*, *Clothing Cultures*, *Critical Studies in Men's Fashion* and *Fashion, Style & Popular Culture*. These periodicals represent the wide range of scholarship that is defining and promoting fashion as a key component of popular culture. This publication reflects this new wave of scholarship and establishes the parallax angles from which the visual and aesthetic cultural production of fashion can be viewed. Containing some of the foremost thinkers and writers in this area of study, this book establishes that fashion is a popular, mobile, and complex field in the social practices that are produced and circulated in everyday life.

References

Browne, R. B. (1972), 'Popular Culture: Notes Toward a Definition', in Ray B. Browne and Ronald J. Ambrosetti, eds, Popular Culture and Curricula, Bowling Green, OH: Bowling Green University Popular Press, pp. 1–11.

Calefato, P. (1997), 'Fashion and Worldliness: Language and Imagery of the Clothed Body', *Fashion Theory*, 1.1, pp 69–90.

Cunningham, P.A. and Voso Lab, S., eds (1991), *Dress and Popular Culture*, Wisconsin: University of Wisconsin Press.

Miler, J.K. and Hancock, J. (2009), 'Introduction', *Journal of American Culture*, 32.1, pp. 1.

Ribeiro, Aileen (2005), *Fashion and Fiction: Dress in Art and Literature in Stuart England*, New Haven, CT: Yale University Press.

List of Figures

Figure 1:1. Sanrio 'Hello Kitty'.
Figure 1:2. Examples of Brand Linkages to Popular Culture.
Figure 1:3. The Barneys New York 2011 Holiday Gaga's Workshop.
Figure 1:4. Lady Gaga poses in the pressroom at the 2010 MTV Video Music Awards.
Figure 1:5. Lady Gaga in the 2011 MTV Video Music Awards.
Figure 2:1. Swedish actor Noomi Rapace in the role of Lisbeth Salander.
Figure 2:2. Images of Hollywood's adaptation of *The Girl with the Dragon Tattoo*.
Figure 3:1. Victorian and Edwardian style dress funeral attire. *Black Light Angels*, 1999.
Figure 3:2 Graber (center) with Gothic fans, Animania Expo. Sydney 2005.
Figure 3:3. Mystik Laeke, *Black Light Angels*, 1999.
Figure 3:4. Fuck the System, *Black Light Angels*, 1999.
Figure 3:5. *Black Light Angels*, 1999.
Figure 3:6. Androgynous characters in *Black Light Angels*, 1999.
Figure 3:7. Club 77 advertisement poster *Black Light Angels*, 1999.
Figure 4:1. Billie Holiday, 1956.
Figure 4:2. A Gucci advertisement from 1996.
Figure 4:3. A Calvin Klein advertisement for Obsession cologne.
Figure 5:1. *One Live Blonde*.
Figure 5:2. *Hot Tamale*.
Figure 5:3. *Tornado in Town*.
Figure 5:4. *Dark Angel of Fire*.
Figure 5:5. *So Lovely She Lies*.
Figure 5:6. *Get Me Homicide!*.
Figure 5:7. *The Heat's On!*.
Figure 5:8. *Duchess Double-X*.
Figure 5:9. *The Hard Racket!*.
Figure 7:1. Tom of Finland.
Figure 7:2. Movie still from *The Wild One*.
Figure 9:1. The characters of Julie and Doug.
Figure 9:2. Nadia Bjorlin played Chloe Lane beginning in 1999.
Figure 10:1. Book cover for *The Devil Wears Prada*.

Figure 11:1. Peter Behren's reform dress for his wife.
Figure 11:2. Laura Lee in the Syrian reform style.
Figure 11:3. A summer dress in the reform style.
Figure 12:1. Snuffbox,1790s.
Figure 12:2. Knee and shoe buckles as example of luxury goods, 1770s.
Figure 13:1.'The Devil of Fashion' ('Der Modeteufel').
Figure 13:2. Caricature, *Strix*.
Figure 13:3. 'The Wasp Waist', Caricature, *Jugend*.
Figure 13:4. Cover, *Simplicissimus*.
Figure 14:1. Ava Gardner.
Figure 14:2. Sophia Loren.
Figure 14:3. Ingrid Bergman.
Figure 14:4. Anna Magnani.
Figure 14:5. Irene Galitzine.

Chapter 1

Brand This Way: Lady Gaga's Fashion as Storytelling Context to the GLBT Community

Joseph H. Hancock, II

Research using the cultural approach to brands and their relationships to popular culture is relatively new and developed during this century (Brannon 2005; Hancock 2009a; Hancock 2009b; Holt 2004; Holt and Cameron 2010; Schroeder and Salzer-Mörling 2006). Branding is an umbrella term for marketing as branding encompasses more than just advertising media; it also includes the context of companies, performance, merchandise, design, consumers and, most importantly, the stakeholders of the brand. Fashion branding has been defined by key scholars and professionals as the perceived message that targets customers with products, advertising, and promotion organized around a coherent image as a way to encourage the purchase and the *re*purchase of consumer goods from the same company (Brannon 2005: 406; Hancock 2009a: 4–5; Holt 2004: 2–3; Manlow 2011). Branding represents a major aim of fashion companies to produce a cumulative image that is reflective of stories, narratives, or myths common in popular culture (Vincent 2002: 15).

Pop performance stars lead some of the largest international and long-lasting brands in our global economy (Blackwell and Stephan 2004: 38–40). They influence consumers through their use of music, videos, and especially the fashions they wear and endorse (Miller 2011). Popular bands and stars such as Kiss, Madonna, Michael Jackson, Jennifer Lopez, Britney Spears, Sean 'Puff Daddy' Combs, Jessica Simpson, Beyoncé Knowles, and Kylie Minogue have all inspired, developed, and licensed their own fashion brands in collaboration with retailers (Miller 2011: 40).

Lady Gaga continuously amazes audiences with her sense of over-the-top costume and outrageous fashion, and yet studies related to her dress have been neglected in academic publication. She represents a form of self-branding. Her self-production is heavily narrative and marked with visual codes of consumption representative of mainstream popular culture (Hearn 2008: 197). Gaga's extreme self-fashioning attracts considerable media attention and builds controversy, not the least being Weird Al Yankovic's 'Perform This Way'. As well as the blog 'Lady Gaga—Cheat This Way' (gagacheat.blogspot.com), which continually accuses the performer of not being original and copying the looks of other pop cultural icons.

Regardless of these accusations, her ensembles do re-present and incorporate pop cultural icons, and in doing so generate storyline and brand meaning and extend associations to niche markets. She becomes a movement of meaning in the conveyance of fashion forms through her celebrity brand status building further connotations of meaning for both her and the iconic symbols she wears (McCracken 1988: 72). For instance, the dress she wore for a 2009 photo shoot in collaboration with the Hello Kitty wholesale manufacturing and

Figure 1:1. Sanrio 'Hello Kitty' retail store located in King of Prussia, Pennsylvania. Photo Courtesy of Joseph H. Hancock, II, All Rights Reserved.

retailing Japanese company Sanrio (Figure 1:1). For this photo shoot, Lady Gaga wore a dress made out of Hello Kitty stuffed toys and her eyelids were made up in the style of Japanese anime or manga character eyes. Each photo was taken with her eyes closed, to show the eyelids, attempting to give the performer an authentic look. Lady Gaga's co-branding with Sanrio allows her to connect with the Japanese market and with those who purchase Hello Kitty merchandise. Working with a company whose global net worth is over US$76 million dollars (Fujimura and Leung 2010) is a stroke of brilliance for both Lady Gaga and Sanrio, and the replication of manga/anime eyes embraces fans of this illustrative art form. The ties between both brands allow for a crossover between both consumer markets, strengthening Lady Gaga and Sanrio financially.

In a competitive market environment, this visual attention recognition and manipulation using popular culture icons is genius, as it allows the marketer, Lady Gaga, to link her brand to other people, places, and things as a means of improving her own brand, what this author calls *brand-Gaga* (Keller 2003: 595). Meticulously choosing each costume, as these garments represent the visual brand equity and public persona of brand-Gaga, her clothes and accessories become part of a story-like branding campaign with Gaga herself as part of the narrative to a large body of consumers.

Gaga and the Gays

One of the largest target markets for brand-Gaga has been the gay, lesbian, bisexual, and transgender (GLBT) community. With a United States net worth expected to exceed over $835 billion in 2012, marketing to GLBT purchasing power is more than worth any brand's attention to gain revenue (Witeck-Combs Communications 2007). GLBT consumers are loyal: over 71% claim they support those companies funding causes important to them (Witeck-Combs Communications 2011). Thus it is not surprising that Lady Gaga recognizes GLBT consumers as major contributors to her career (McConnell 2009); at the 2009 MTV Video Music Awards she thanked 'God and the gays' for her success.

For the GLBT community, Gaga's over-the-top camp costumes utilize symbols that transform her into homage for her gay and lesbian followers. Her garments blatantly re-contextualize GLBT iconic symbols in a benevolently based manner that produces a philanthropic image. In addition, her ostentatious style deliberately conveys a method of campiness that is identifiable by the GLBT communities through their historical association to this ideal of exaggerating visually and theatrically through fashion (Cleto 2002). This visually symbolic method of branding allows her to generate profits and achieve a sort of social dependency (Holt 2006: 300) among her GLBT followers who by consuming these images wait anxiously for her next performance or appearance. Her GLBT fashionable style inspires younger fans so much that they refer to her as their pop cultural iconic hero (Bolcer 2010).

In 2010, Greenbrier High School in White House, Tennessee, sent student Cole Goforth home on the grounds that his 'I (Heart) Lady Gay Gay' T-shirt was a disruption to classroom activities (Bolcer 2010). Goforth's mother stated that she felt this was a violation of her son's constitutional right to free speech; she noted that students who wear religious or rebel flag T-shirts are not sent home, and yet her son's T-shirt was seen as offensive (Bolcer 2010). Within hours of hearing these allegations, Lady Gaga tweeted her support:

> Thank you for wearing your T-shirt proud at school, you make me so proud, at the monsterball, you are an inspiration to us all. I love you...you just be yourself...you're perfect the way God made you. (Kaufman 2010)

But the superstar's influences go beyond high school teenagers; even younger children look to Lady Gaga as someone who understands them. In October 2011, with the recent exposé of bullying in the United States, CNN's *360* featured a young group of GLBT grade school students who had been targeted in each of their respected schools. At the end of the episode, one young student requested that he be able to sing the Lady Gaga song 'Born This Way', Anderson Cooper gladly allowed him to do so (Hadad 2010).

Purpose

By deconstructing looks that utilize iconic symbols, this chapter addresses how four of Lady Gaga's most popular media-hype wardrobe statements allow her to maintain associations to the GLBT community. These styles include her 2009 Kermit dress worn on German television; her 2010 MTV Video Music Awards meat dress; her 2011 *Good Morning America* Condom dress; and her Jo Calderone drag king look for MTV Video Music Awards in 2011. Analysis of each garment's brand story demonstrates how the GLBT communities have come to see 'Lady Gay Gay'.

Leveraging Meaning in Popular Culture to Build Brand Stories

In the twenty-first century, successful branding strategies are no longer perceived to be the quantitative-like mass demographic sales data and public-at-large studies of the past (Holt 2006: 299–302). Instead a more micro-marketed and tailored-to-individual research approach is accepted and notions that each person is unique is taken into account as consumer meaning and interpretation are viewed as crucial to successful brands (Holt 2006: 299–302; McCracken 2005: 162). By examining each person's psychographics (lifestyle preferences, descriptors, individual's attitudes, values and interests), a brand manager can compose and evolve the brand alongside changes in culture (Rath, Petrizzi, and Gill 2012: 4). Brands become attachments to lifestyles and give a perception of being personalized for each consumer. A consumer does not feel like a member of a mass population, but rather like an individual with personal attachment to the brand (Holt 2004: 218–19).

Branding adopted narratives in the fashion industry, and those companies with the ability to communicate appealing narratives, seem to be the most successful (Hancock 2009a; Manlow 2011). Individual interpretive branding through the concepts of visual storytelling allows the consumer to feel that the brand is concerned specifically with them and their needs as an individual (Vincent 2002: 15). Fashion companies aim at producing images that reflect people, narratives or myths in popular culture (Hancock 2009b). Branding allows the company to create an image that is based upon functional and hedonic characteristics that identify a product to a specific market (Brannon 2005: 405). At times this is achieved through business strategies, such as creating thematic fashion marketing, that reflect the image of the company (Schultz and Hatch 2006: 15–33).

Douglas Holt defines cultural branding as a method and a strategy utilized by businesses to sell products and services to consumers (Holt 2004: 218–19). Cultural branding is about reflecting the cultural context or the *zeitgeist*. Holt believes cultural activists and individuals who understand popular culture develop successful brands. He posits that the problem with many brands is ignorance with regard to art, history, popular culture, and trends. He calls for a new focus on consumer research that examines individuals instead of target markets. Rather than worry about traditional consumer research, brand leaders should assemble cultural knowledge (Holt 2004: 219).

As the branding relationship develops, the successful cultural branding agent will listen to and understand the consumer, producing the product a consumer desires. A successful brander will understand the historic equities of products and position them according to a strategic marketing rank toward the most advantageous customers. Brands that become iconic brands develop a reputation for revealing an appropriate narrative (Holt 2004: 219). Holt states that new brands earn higher profits when they are woven into social institutions and political awareness (Holt 2006: 300). For example, Lady Gaga's political support for gay marriage, and the controversy surrounding the repeal of being openly gay in the U.S. military, creates a brand—in this case brand-Gaga is accepted into social life because it provides customers with what Holt's called 'real informational, interactional, and symbolic benefits' (Holt 2006: 300).

In *Legendary Brands: Unleashing the Power of Storytelling to Create a Winning Marketing Strategy*, Laurence Vincent demonstrates how each company creates a brand culture through myths and brand narratives that give their products a consumer perception that their brand is the best (Vincent 2002: 25). Also, each brand situates itself within popular culture in the hopes of becoming part of the social order and cultural context. Vincent's research reveals that brand narratives must have four parts: aesthetics, plot, character, and theme. Aesthetics includes any part of the brand that stimulates one of the five senses. Vincent suggests that spectacle (what you see), song (what you hear musically), and diction (how words are constructed to convey meaning) are important elements for visual and performing arts. Brands can also stimulate taste and touch, and these are powerful narrative devices (Vincent 2002: 19). Making a connection to the consumer through brand narrative is key to success. The narrative must relate to the consumer both culturally and personally and the consumer must develop a personal attachment to the brand's narrative (Vincent 2002: 127). The brand narrative attracts customers when the audience follows the characters used in the brand advertising and marketing.

Consumer brand knowledge relates to cognitive representation of the brand. Interpretations of fashion branding strategies are necessary to understand a company's advertisements and their relationships to consumers (Heding, Knudtzen, and Bjerre 2009: 205). The cultural approach to branding relies on interpreting how brands have an impact upon consumers and how, in turn, consumers influence future meaning and branding techniques. (Heding, Knudtzen, and Bjerre 2009: 215). Increasingly competitive marketplaces demand that companies associate their brands with other people, places, things, or brands as a means of building or leveraging knowledge that might otherwise be difficult to achieve through product-marketing programs (Keller 2003: 597). Linking the brand to another person, place, thing, or cultural movement affects how consumers view the brand or 'primary brand knowledge'. A deeper understanding of how knowledge of a brand and other linked entities interact is of paramount importance. The linkages to the originating or primary brand become 'secondary' brand associations such as other brands, people, events, places, social causes, and/or other companies. To provide comparable insight and guidance, a conceptually visual model demonstrates this leveraging process (Figure 1:2).

Linking the brand (primary source) to various parts of culture (secondary source) creates new primary brand knowledge (Keller 2003: 598). The linking of brand-Gaga to other aspects of popular culture creates recognition and association with other causes and meanings, thereby creating new narratives (primary brand + secondary brand = new meanings). While a consumer may know nothing about Lady Gaga, they may be aware of secondary branding sources associated with brand-Gaga and this could entice them to become more knowledgeable about her and her brand.

Jeff B. Murray and Julie L. Ozanne argue in 'Rethinking the Critical Imagination' (2006: 46) that interpretative methods of consumer research are acceptable methods for understanding how a company is creating meaning and understandings of culture for consumers. They call for researchers to examine brands from a critical perspective. This is accomplished through analyzing the branding process where layers of multiple meanings and negotiations are created with the customer. Elements such as advertising

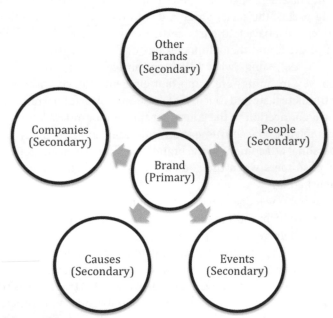

Figure 1:2. Examples of Brand Linkages to Popular Culture. Modified from Keller, K.L. (2003: 598).

are used to create such meaning (Moor 2007: 5–7). The researcher's eyes and experiences become a voice in what is possible. The researcher may examine the branding based upon life experiences that may not have been experienced by other consumers; therefore, interpretations and meaning will be different depending on the perspective. In other words, the precise meaning of the branding strategy is not so important. More crucial are the stories and narratives generated in the mind of the viewer, rather than that of the advertiser (Murray and Ozanne 2006: 51).

In order to understand and interpret the visual meanings and associations of new iconic forms, an individual must investigate the appearance of the icon, history of the icon, the evolutionary changes of the icon, iconic groups associated with that icon, and the exploitation of that particular icon. By understanding contemporary popular culture and the general history of an icon, the viewer can begin to interpret meanings and how new visual messages are generated (Nachbar and Lause 1992: 178–79). Through fashion, 'B' becomes a new context for the exploitation of historical and popular culture icons generating a new brand story (Hancock 2009a) that is seen in the GLBT community narrating to them an understandable message that allows her to make the connection.

The Brand-Gaga Story

Lady Gaga was born Stefani Joanne Angelina Germanotta in March 1986. She adopted the name Lady Gaga from the Queen song *Radio Gaga* (Anon 2011). She refers to her fans as the 'little monsters' and implies that she is an academic of the 'sociology of stardom', revealing that she uses her strategically calculated sense of fashion style to serve the multiple purposes of entertaining, publicizing her political and social agendas with many surrounding the gay community, and to hide anything she might not want the public to see (Anon 2011). According to Lady Gaga, everything she wears has a particular meaning. All of her appearances are carefully planned and executed with her team of stylists (Anon 2011).

Lady Gaga's current net worth is reported to be over US$100 million. Her second studio album, *Born This Way*, sold over 1.1 million copies in the first week of its release. She performed for over 2.4 million people in 28 countries during her year-and-a-half-long Monster Ball Tour. She has over 4.5 million 'likes' on Facebook and more than 15 million people follow her on Twitter (Robinson 2012: 60). Brand-Gaga extended into the retail sector during the 2011 holiday season when Barneys New York opened the first 'Gaga's Workshop': a shop-within-a-shop concept selling Gaga-esque products ranging from US$8 to US$4100 (Figure 1:3). The Workshop ensures that shoppers can own a Gaga-inspired consumable.

But critics have called her 'pop's newest and gayest superstar with good reason' (Stein and Michelson 2009). Her devotion to gay fans is unequal to any other performance artist.

She gladly admits that it has been the gays who supported her from the very beginning. In 2009, Gaga was reported to state:

> I'm gay. My music is gay. My show is gay. And I *love* that it's gay. And I love my gay fans and they're all going to be coming to our show. And it's going to remain gay....I very much want to inject gay culture into the mainstream. It's not an underground tool for me. It's my whole life. So I always sort of joke the real motivation is to just turn the world gay. (Stein and Michelson 2009)

Kermit Dress: The Rainbow Connection

On 22 July 2009, Lady Gaga appeared on German television while being interviewed on her latest album and music performances. Her outfit was a Kermit the Frog doll suit with green leotards, accessorized with a Kermit the Frog hat. Her makeup was very subdued which emphasized her neck area: draped by a large boa made of Kermit the Frog dolls. In this look the primary brand, Lady Gaga, uses an internationally known iconic established secondary brand—Kermit the Frog.

In relation to Lady Gaga, this fashion statement is complex and representative of the theoretical notions of cultural fashion branding (Lady Gaga + Kermit the Frog = New Meaning). In his article, 'The Performance of Nonconformity on *The Muppet Show*—or, How Kermit Made Me Queer', Jordan Schildcrout discusses the pop cultural implications and social symbolic meanings behind *The Muppet Show* (2008: 824). His research suggests that *The Muppet Show* (1976–1981) was

> a venue for rebellion against proprietary, where performers can irreverently 'play' with cultural norms. And because cultural products (e.g., songs, jokes, and fictional characters) reflect and construct our understandings of social categories and identities, the Muppets' zany performances present challenges, simultaneously gleeful and significant, to normative notions of ethnicity, gender and sexuality. (Schildcrout: 2008: 824)

The significance of *The Muppet Show* as a vehicle for radical performance is underscored by the fact that it was an independent production. Developed without network influence, it was sold and syndicated to local stations in the United States before achieving global acceptance (Schildcrout 2008: 825). *The Muppet Show* was known for its wide variety of traditional performance genres including melodrama, ballet, opera, classical music, and popular performances related to popular culture media such as pop performances, television parodies, and, of course, fashion. As Schildcrout points out, the Muppets refused to conform to culturally normative roles and the characters' *queer* categorical identities based on race, gender, and sexuality exposes them as performances rather than inherent or immutable essences (2008: 827).

Kermit first appeared in 1955 on the TV show *Sam and Friends*, produced in Washington, D.C.'s WRC-TV. He has appeared on *Sesame Street*, *The Today Show*, *The Ed Sullivan Show*, and has become so popular and well known that he became the face and voice of all the *Muppet Show* creations and still serves in this capacity today. According to Jim Henson's widow, he has become the leader that signifies the global conglomerates that include *Sesame Street* and *The Muppet Show* and is known as a global icon (Schildcrout 2008: 824). Kermit definitely understands cultural difference and uniqueness: being a green frog chased by a drag queen (Miss Piggy). While trying to calm, he orchestrates and leads the mayhem of his fellow Muppets. Kermit is also a catalyst for change and tries to get everyone to get along with each other (Abate 2009: 601–3).

Kermit has identified himself as empathetic of what it is to be different through his performances of iconic songs such as 'It's Not Easy Being Green' (1970) and 'The Rainbow Connection' (1979). Through these songs, direct connections to gays and lesbians are made: he expresses difference in appearance and adopts the gayest symbols of all—the rainbow flag. Gaga's fashionable adoption and adaption of Kermit the Frog winks at the knowing viewer.

The Kermit the Frog dress allows Lady Gaga to make connections between him and his fellow Muppets, who are often referred to as 'monsters' (Abate 2009: 589; Schildcrout 2008: 828), suggesting perhaps that the Muppets might have been brand-Gaga's inspiration for calling her fans 'little monsters'. Like the Muppets' Miss Piggy, Lady Gaga is a drag queen, since her own diva actions are highlighted as camp performance as well. Schildcrout posits Miss Piggy is a drag queen. She regularly uses drag queen shtick such as comically switching from shrill feminine voice to a masculine snarl (Schildcrout 2008: 828). The persona of Miss Piggy sends out mixed messages about the role of the female performer, since her *diva femininity* is consistently highlighted as performance. 'Miss Piggy the Star' is the creation of Miss Piggy the performer and either despite or because of her stereotypical affections, she remains one of the major icons of the Muppets.

But most notably, Miss Piggy is a female character performed by Richard Hunt and Frank Oz; she is the design and manufacture of men, and is performed by men (Schildcrout 2008: 828). This reaffirms her camp and drag-like qualities. Like Lady Gaga, she has become the star she pretends to be. *Lady Gaga the star* is the creation of Stefani Joanne Angelina Germanotta, the performer, but unlike Miss Piggy, Lady Gaga has to deal with a context of mayhem and foolishness in her own career—or what she has called the 'fame monster'.

In this context she becomes the controller and the gatekeeper of order like Kermit the Frog on *The Muppet Show*. And like Kermit, Lady Gaga continuously wants all her 'little monsters' to respect each other and get along with each other. A further connection between Kermit and Lady Gaga was established on 13 September 2009 at the MTV Video Music Awards (see book cover). As the paparazzi snapped shots of both stars giving each other an affectionate kiss, Kermit drove by in his limousine, cementing the bond between brand-Gaga and the Muppets as two popular and cultural brands.

Meat Dress: DADT

On 12 September 2010, Lady Gaga revived Jana Sterbak's 1987 'Vanitas: Flesh Dress for an Albino Anorectic' when she wore a meat dress to the MTV Video Music Awards (Figure 1:4). The dress was sewn together using prime beef; the designer, Franc Fernandez, used only the finest cuts so that the dress would not smell under heavy lighting (Vena 2010). This dress is one of the most symbolic of Lady Gaga's dresses. She explains:

> If we don't stand up for what we believe in and if we don't fight for our rights pretty soon, we're going to have as much rights as the meat on our own bones. I am not a piece of meat. (Associated Press 2010)

Her dress therefore is a signifier of *being* a *piece of meat*.

As stated, building upon this notion of being a *piece of meat*, Lady Gaga has not been the only performance artist to display this concept of actually wearing meat and is therefore just

Figure 1:4. Lady Gaga poses in the pressroom at the 2010 MTV Video Music Awards at Nokia Theatre L.A. Live on 12, September 2010 in Los Angeles, California. Courtesy Helga Esteb/Shuttershock.com.

a representative of a repetitive concept. There has been Tania Bruguera's 1998 *The Weight of Guilt, Untitled #3*, where the model wears a meat steak; Zhang Huan's 2002 run through the New York City streets wearing a muscle suit completely made out of meat; Dimitri Tsykalov's 2008 art piece, *Gas Mask II*; the 2009 Beijing 'Meat As Clothing' fashion show; and Michelle Nolan's 2010 meat blazer, signifying that this concept of being *a piece of meat* is not new.

Indicatively, since the performer Lady Gaga is wearing it, the dress also signifies the notion that pop stars are pieces of meat that are used, consumed, and discarded by their agents, their publicists, their marketers, and the public. She herself is a *piece of meat* and could thus be insulting her own fans stating how she feels she is treated. Too, this dress also has sexual overtones. In straight or homosexual lifestyles a new young person in a local bar or nightclub is sometimes referred to as *fresh meat* by more seasoned patrons. But for the purposes of this paper, this dress signifies the emotional ties that Lady Gaga has to the GLBT community when receiving her MTV Video Music Award (VMA) while thanking her 'little monsters' and the 'gays' who watched the 'Bad Romance' video, allowing it to receive approximately 278 million hits (or views) on YouTube and Vevo.

Her main focus when wearing this dress was her commitment to the Service members Legal Defense Network (SLDN). The SLDN campaigns on behalf of servicemen and women affected by the Don't Ask/Don't Tell (DADT) policy that Congress passed in 1993, which the SLDN describes as a law mandating the discharge of openly gay, lesbian, or bisexual service members (Topping 2010). This dress ties the star pop performer (primary brand) to the secondary brand of a social cause, in this case DADT (Lady Gaga + DADT = New Meaning). By signifying and publicly recognizing a social agenda (DADT) at the same time she receives an award, brand-Gaga solidifies the ties between the brand and target market.

As Shawn Trivette notes in 'Secret Handshakes and Decoder Rings: The Queer Space of Don't Ask/Don't Tell' this policy decreases the military's ability to function by harming the military's strong levels of camaraderie and cohesion within its ranks. Rather than enhancing the military and protecting the military's strong level of performance, the bond that connects members of the military are weakened by requiring gay and lesbian personnel to hide a part of themselves from fellow soldiers. In prohibiting gay identities from being openly expressed, DADT actually creates a queer space in which military gays and lesbians interact with one another and create their own form of military gay identity. This forces these men and women to create secret methods of identifying one another, a situation that is unhealthy and causes inner turmoil in many soldiers.

In his examinations and various interviews with military soldiers, Trivette found that those who were able to come out had a more positive outlook on their life as servicemen and servicewomen, while those who were forced to remain silent were not well adjusted and felt they were lying to their friends and fellow military personnel. As one interviewee, Stephen, stated,

> People know that you're lying. And when they know you're lying...that creates a problem. Because...lies are not good for relationships....And, basically, you're being asked to lie

every single day by your superiors. Now how on God's green earth can that be good for unit cohesion, when everyone in the unit knows that you're lying. And that they know that you're holding a secret. (Trivette 2010: 220)

However, on 20 September 2011, Congress officially repealed the DADT policy and this reversal was signed into law by President Obama. Lady Gaga was a huge advocate for ending the DADT policy and campaigned nationally for its repeal. Her speeches inspired many young people to support gays and lesbians in the military. Reflecting the ideology of Lady Gaga's meat dress, no longer are the men and women in the United States military going to be treated like pieces of meat. Instead, their voices have been heard as they are now allowed to serve in the United States military and be *out*.

Condom Dress: HIV Awareness and Safe Sex

Like the socially meaningful DADT meat dress, on 17 February 2011, Lady Gaga made another statement with her diaphragm hat and latex dress—worn on the *Good Morning America* show to support and raise money for AIDS research. While both dress elements reference birth control, the dress references a latex condom and Lady Gaga's notions of *covering it up* when having sex. In addition, for this appearance, Lady Gaga was promoting her new role as MAC Cosmetics Viva Glam spokesmodel for their new line of lipstick. Co-branding herself (primary brand) with a large cosmetics conglomerate, Estée Lauder (secondary brand), allows the star to reach a new line of consumers while raising awareness about a disease that greatly impacts the gay community (Lady Gaga + MAC Cosmetics Viva Glam = New Meaning).

Since 1994, Viva Glam by MAC Cosmetics has had special ties to the GLBT community, and this ad campaign has been the most successful in raising money for AIDS research. The first spokesmodel for the brand was RuPaul, the famous drag queen, followed by music performer k.d. lang. Other iconic Viva Glam spokesmodels and MAC devotees have included gay icons such as Debbie Harry, Michael Jackson, Madonna, Dita Von Teese, Eve, Lisa Marie Presley, Fergie, Miss Piggy, and Lady Gaga campaign cohort Cyndi Lauper. To add Lady Gaga to the list of fellow Viva Glam personalities seems natural.

What becomes interesting about this promotion is that MAC is using a woman's product such as lipstick to raise awareness about what was once considered a gay male disease, suggesting a crossing of sexual and gender barriers and inscribing birth control issues over the top. Lady Gaga's wearing of a flesh-colored latex dress is unique because normally this type of latex garment would be black and builds associations to the kind of fetish fashions and extreme social sexual behaviors usually aligned with sadomasochism and bondage (Cole 2000: 107–15). Furthermore, the condom is typically viewed as a male item, so the fact that Lady Gaga has wrapped herself in such an item crosses traditional gender roles and urges women to take as much responsibility for using condoms as men. The condom-style latex dress signifies the importance of using condoms and the promotion of safe sex for all individuals—but, more importantly, for the gay community that is associated with HIV/ AIDS as a major disease.

Within a week of her appearance on *Good Morning America*, the lipsticks inspired by Lady Gaga and Cyndi Lauper outsold all of the other Viva Glam lipsticks in a sixteen-year period. According to John Demsey, the president of the Estée Lauder Group, the launch day of Gaga's Viva Glam lipstick and ad campaign generated nearly 20 million hits on the company's website (Hampp 2010: 81). Her support of AIDS-related causes is instrumental. With every cent of the profits of the US$14.50 lipstick going to AIDS research, Lady Gaga is sure to make MAC's campaign a huge success for HIV awareness, which helps to build brand-Gaga. Lady Gaga's advice to 'cover it up' makes fans and others aware of her support for the gay community. Her appearance, therefore, ties her to AIDS as a secondary brand (Lady Gaga + AIDS Awareness = New Meaning); she is not only a spokesperson for a woman's product but also for GLBT health awareness. In this moment, Lady Gaga uses fashion to build relationships and at the same time to educate.

Jo Calderone: *Who's That Girl?*

On 28 August 2011, Lady Gaga appeared on the MTV Video Music Awards as her transgender persona, Jo Calderone. She performed her song 'You and I' while simultaneously maintaining the character of her macho look (Figure 1:5). Her style and show reflected that of a female performance artist who usually performs for lesbian or transgendered target audiences—a drag king. Examples of pop cultural drag kings who have popularized this ideal include such performers as the British Valentino King and the Canadian k.d. lang. Lady Gaga's costume resembles that of a young rockabilly singer sporting a pompadour hairstyle with long sideburns, black jacket and pants, and a white T-shirt.

But after delivering this new transgender Jo Calderone performance, Lady Gaga did not receive positive feedback from the entertainment community. Instead, she was criticized for being a fashion copycat.

Fashion police expert Kelly Osbourne tweeted, 'I love Lady Gaga, but I wish she would start giving credit where credit is due!' Osbourne went on to suggest that Jo Calderone was a direct replica of Annie Lennox's 'Sweet Dreams (Are Made of This)' performance at the 1984 Grammys (Maher 2011). But, ironically, Osbourne's public scrutiny and recognition of this transgendered persona strengthens both brand-Gaga and Lady Gaga's ties to the GLBT communities—perhaps even more so with lesbian communities who are usually the targets of these performances (Lady Gaga + Annie Lennox = New Meaning).

Remembering Annie Lennox's performance, Geczy and Karaminas state in their book *Queer Style*,

Annie Lennox, the vocalist for the pop duo Eurythmics (with Dave Stewart), appeared at the annual Grammy Awards ceremony as the reincarnation of Elvis Presley. Wearing

Figure 1:5. Lady Gaga in the 2011 MTV Video Music Awards Press Room, Nokia Theatre LA Live 28, August 2011. Lose Angeles, California. Courtesy S. Bukley/Shuttershock.com.

a black suit, white leather belt, silk black shirt and a gold knit lamé tie, along with Presleyesque bouffant and facial hair. (2013: 60)

Thus co-branding the Eurythmics with another icon of popular culture and thus building their careers. Lennox mirrored Presley's performance techniques by gyrating her pelvis, grabbing her crotch, and swinging her legs, reinforcing her masculinized characterization. But while Lennox was recognized for this look during the 1984 Grammys, it was really the previous year's Eurythmics' video for 'Who's That Girl?' (1983) where she first appeared as this persona. The music video took her appearance global through the popular MTV and various international music video stations. The video was risqué because, in it, Lennox is noted for kissing herself dressed as both a man and a woman. Both these performances are what Geczy and Karaminas (2013: 61) call a 'diva/camp moment…via her gender-bending performance' that allowed Annie Lennox to become an instant GLBT icon.

Over her career, Annie Lennox continued to be a major icon associated with GLBT communities and causes. She has been extremely outspoken about gay-related issues as HIV/AIDs with her 2004 'The Sing Campaign' and her 'I Am Positive' philanthropic T-shirt campaign, which was launched by her song 'Sing'. Her goal with this campaign is to remove the stigma of having HIV/AIDS in countries such as Africa (see annielennoxsing.com).

So, did Lady Gaga directly copy Annie Lennox in order to build her career or was it some mistake? As Lady Gaga claims to be in total control of her appearances and to know exactly what she is wearing and why (Anon 2011), one can only conclude that she *did* copy this fashion style. Lady Gaga borrowed one of the most successful theatrical performances of one of her most successful colleagues—Annie Lennox—and incorporated it into her own brand-Gaga to build ties to her GLBT 'little monsters' and reinforce her prominence among this target market. Additionally, this look was directed toward that same market audience as those who would enjoy drag king performances. Perhaps the whole event was a publicity stunt in order for brand-Gaga to build market share among lesbian and transgendered fans. In any case, the performance was a remarkable example of cultural branding through popular culture.

Conclusion

Lady Gaga utilizes costume as a means for branding herself to a particular target market, and particularly the GLBT community. By connecting her primary brand of brand-Gaga to secondary brands and cultural movements—such as the Muppets' Kermit the Frog, DADT, MAC Cosmetics with AIDS causes, and Annie Lennox, emulating her butch/femme appearance—Lady Gaga extends her brand beyond the borders of musical performance into other areas of performance, social agendas, and fashion-related industries. Crossing these many boundaries increases her links with popular culture and, in doing so, she becomes an iconic brand: brand-Gaga.

Further research should examine Lady Gaga's brand in other target markets and communities. How is her dress and appearance interpreted in the straight community, by different cultural groups, or by non-Westerners, who may see these iconic images differently? Do these other groups make the same associations to Lady Gaga as the gay and lesbian community? Do they see her as 'Lady Gay Gay'?

Lady Gaga's use of branding as a major vehicle to promote her own self is brilliant. She should be applauded. She is representative of the members of today's hyper-media generation, whose attention span is short, and who are constantly seeking the next look or sensation. Lady Gaga's ability to reach into her popular culture closet and pull out new looks as a means to wear new contextual fashions is remarkable. Her selections and constructions are predicated upon her wish to have influence beyond her music status, to solidify her fame, extend her social agendas, and build her business. Whether her intention is to reflect the concerns and values of a specific community or not, she is, without doubt, a pop culture fashion icon and will be discussed for generations to come.

Acknowledgements

Joseph H. Hancock, II would like to dedicate this article to his family (Peggy, Eddie, and Ruby), who continuously support him and his work; to his good friends David and Anne (Blanche) Loranger for taking the time to visit and photograph Barneys' Gaga's Workshop for this project; and, finally, to Toni Johnson-Woods for all her mentorship, feedback, and ideas, which enriched this chapter.

References

Abate, Michelle Ann (2009), 'Taking Silliness Seriously: Jim Henson's *The Muppet Show*, the Anglo-American Tradition of Nonsense, and Cultural Critique', *Journal of Popular Culture*, 42:4, pp. 589–613.

Anon (2011), 'Lady Gaga on "Mastering the Art of Fame"', CBS News, 5 June, http://www.cbsnews.com/2102-18560_162-20066912.html?tag=contentMain;contentBody. Accessed 10 October 2012.

Arvidsson, Adam (2006), *Brands: Meaning and Value in Media Culture*, London and New York: Routledge.

Associated Press (2010), 'Lady Gaga Clarifies Meaning of Meat Dress', *First Coast News*, 14 September, http://www.firstcoastnews.com/news/story.aspx?storyid=166956. Accessed 10 October 2012.

Blackwell, Roger and Stephen, Tina (2004), *Brands That Rock: What Business Leaders Can Learn from the World of Rock and Roll*, Hoboken: John Wiley & Sons.

Bolcer, Julie (2010), 'Student Sent Home for "Lady Gay Gay" T-Shirt', *The Advocate*, 7 April, http://www.advocate.com/news/daily-news/2010/04/07/student-sent-home-lady-gay-gay-tshirt. Accessed on 10 October 2012.

Brannon, Evelyn, L. (2005), *Fashion Forecasting: Research, Analysis and Presentation*, New York: Fairchild Publications.

Cleto, Fabio, (2002), *Camp*, Ann Arbor: University of Michigan Press.

Cole, Shaun (2000), *'Don We Now Our Gay Apparel': Gay Men's Dress in the Twentieth Century*, Oxford: Berg Publishers.

Fujimura, Naoko and Leung, Wendy (2010), 'Hong Kong's Billionaire Fung Family Buy Stake in Hello Kitty Owner Sanrio', Bloomberg.com, 15 October, http://www.bloomberg.com/news/2010-10-15/wal-mart-supplier-li-fung-acquires-1-stake-in-hello-kitty-owner-sanrio.html, Accessed on 9, January 2012.

Geczy, Adam and Karaminas, Vicki (2013), *Queer Style*, London: Berg Publishers.

Hadad, Chuck (2010), 'CNN Study: Schoolyard Bullies Not Just Preying on the Weak', CNN, 10 October, http://www.cnn.com/2011/10/10/us/ac-360-bullying-study/index.html. Accessed on 16 January 2012.

Hampp, Andrew (2010), 'Gaga, Oooh La La: Why The Lady is the Ultimate Social Climber', *Advertising Age*, 81:8, p. 42.

Hancock, Joseph (2009a), *Brand/Story: Ralph, Vera, Johnny, Billy & Other Adventures in Fashion Branding*, New York: Fairchild Publications.

—— (2009b), 'Chelsea on 5th Avenue: Hypermasculinity and Gay Clone Culture in the Retail Brand Practices of Abercrombie & Fitch', *Fashion Practice*, 1:1, pp. 63–86.

Hearn, Alison (2008), 'Meat, Mask, Burden: Probing the Contours of the Branded Self', *Journal of Consumer Culture*, 8:2, pp. 197–217.

Heding, Tilde, Knudtzen, Charlotte F. and Bjerre, Mogens (2009), *Brand Management: Research, Theory and Practice*, London: Routledge.

Holt, Douglas B. (2004), *How Brands Become Icons*, Boston: Harvard Business School Press.

—— (2006), 'Toward a Sociology of Branding', *Journal of Consumer Culture*, 6:3, pp. 299–302.

Holt, Douglas and Cameron, Douglas (2010), *Cultural Strategy: Using Innovative Ideologies to Build Breakthrough Brands*, Oxford: Oxford University Press.

Kaufman, Gil (2010), 'Lady Gaga Supports Teen Sent Home for "Lady Gay Gay" T-Shirt', MTV, 8 April, http://www.mtv.com/news/articles/1635666/lady-gaga-supports-teen-sent-home-lady-gay-gay-tshirt.jhtml. Accessed 10 October 2012.

Keller, Kevin L. (2003), 'Brand Synthesis: The Multidimensionality of Brand Knowledge', *Journal of Consumer Research*, 29:4, pp. 595–600.

Maher, Cristin (2011), 'Kelly Osbourne Says Lady Gaga's Jo Calderone Persona Copied Annie Lennox', *PopCrush*, 31 August, http://popcrush.com/?s=lady+gaga+annie+lennox&submit_button=. Accessed 10 October 2012.

Manlow, Veronica (2011), 'Creating an American Mythology: A Comparison of Branding Strategies in Three Fashion Firms', *Fashion Practice*, 3:1, pp. 85–110.

McConnell, Donna (2009), 'Feathers, A Red Lace Mask and a Bridal Headdress…Lady Gaga Stuns in Five Outrageous Outfits at the MTV VMA," Mail Online, 14, September, http://www.dailymail.co.uk/tvshowbiz/article-1213289/Lady-GaGa-stuns-outrageous-outfits-MTV-VMAs.html. Accessed, 28 October, 2012.

McCracken, Grant (1988), *Culture & Consumption*, Bloomington: Indiana University Press.

—— (2005), *Culture & Consumption II*, Bloomington: Indiana University Press.

Miller, Janice (2011), *Fashion and Music*, Oxford and New York: Berg Publishers.

Moor, Liz (2007), *The Rise of Brands*, Oxford and New York: Berg Publishers.

Murray, Jeff B. and Ozanne, Julie L. (2006), 'Rethinking the Critical Imagination', in Russell W. Belk, ed., *Handbook of Qualitative Research Methods in Marketing*, Cheltenham: Edward Elgar Publishing.

Nachbar, Jack and Lause, Kevin (1992), *Popular Culture: An Introductory Text*, Madison and London: University of Wisconsin Press.

Pomerantz, Dorothy (2011), 'Lady Gaga Tops Celebrity 100 List', Forbes, 16 May, http://www.forbes.com/2011/05/16/lady-Gaga-tops-celebrity-100-11.html. Accessed 18 May 2012.

Rath, Patricia Mink, Petrizzi, Richard and Gill, Penny (2012), *Fashion Marketing: A Global Perspective*, New York: Fairchild Publications.

Robinson, Lisa (2012), 'In Lady Gaga's Way', *Vanity Fair*, January, pp. 50–61.

Schildcrout, Jordan (2008), 'The Performance of Nonconformity on *The Muppet Show*—or, How Kermit Made Me Queer', *Journal of Popular Culture*, 47:5, pp. 823–35.

Schroeder, Jonathan E. and Salzer-Mörling, Miriam, eds (2006), *Brand Culture*, London: Routledge.

Schultz, Majkcn and Hatch, Mary Jo (2006), 'A Cultural Perspective on Corporate Branding: The Case of LEGO Group', in Jonathan E. Schroeder and Miriam Salzer-Mörling, eds, *Brand Culture*, London: Routledge.

Stein, Joshua D. and Michelson, Noah (2009), 'The Lady Is a Vamp', *Out*, 9 August, http://www.out.com/entertainment/2009/08/09/lady-vamp. Accessed 10 October 2012.

Topping, Alexandra (2010), 'Lady Gaga's Meat Dress Angers Animal Rights Groups, *The Guardian*, 13 September, http://www.guardian.co.uk/music/2010/sep/13/lady-gaga-meat-dress-vmas. Accessed 18 January 2012.

Trivette, Shawn A. (2010), 'Secret Handshakes and Decoder Rings: The Queer Space of Don't Ask/Don't Tell', *Sex Research Social Policy*, 7, pp. 214–28.

Vena, Jocelyn (2010), 'Lady Gaga Meat Dress Designer Tells How to Re-Create His VMA Look,' MTV, 16 September, http://www.mtv.com/news/articles/1647978/lady-gaga-meat-dress-designer-tells-how-recreate-his-vma-look.jhtml. Accessed 10 October 2012.

Vincent, Laurence (2002), *Legendary Brands: Unleashing the Power of Storytelling to Create a Winning Market Strategy*, Chicago: Dearborn Trade Publishing.

Witeck-Combs Communications (2007), 'Buying Power of U.S. Gays and Lesbians to Exceed $835 Billion by 2011', 25 January, http://www.witeckcombs.com/news/releases/20070125_ buyingpower.pdf. Accessed 10 October 2012.

—— (2011), 'LGBT Adults Strongly Prefer Brands That Support Causes Important to Them and That Also Offer Equal Workplace Benefits', 18 July, http://www.harrisinteractive. com/NewsRoom/PressReleases/tabid/446/mid/1506/articleId/835/ctl/ReadCustom%20 Default/Default.aspx. Accessed 10 October 2012.

Chapter 2

Navigating Cultural Anxiety: Strategic Ambiguity in Lisbeth Salander's Style-Fashion-Dress

Susan B. Kaiser

'It's a long, dark story', Henrik Vanger—the wealthy, elderly Swedish industrialist—tells Mikael Blomkvist, an investigative reporter, in Stieg Larsson's acclaimed best-selling novel, called *The Girl with the Dragon Tattoo* (2009) in the English translation. Vanger is talking about his own family, which obtained its wealth by industrializing Sweden through products ranging from steel and iron to textiles. During World War II, the Vanger Corporation sold fabric to the Nazis for their uniforms. In addition to some family members' histories of fascism, racism, and sexism, the Vangers have another skeleton in the closet: an unsolved, presumed murder. In the 1960s, Vanger's beloved teenage niece disappeared mysteriously from the family's northern Swedish island of Hedeby. Vanger—now in his eighties—is in the process of recruiting Blomkvist (recently disgraced in a legal scandal involving a different high-powered industrialist) to investigate the 40-year-old cold case.

Six months after moving to Hedeby, Blomkvist realizes that he needs a research assistant to track down leads he has uncovered. Vanger's lawyer recommends Lisbeth Salander: arguably the most enigmatic, troubled and yet compelling female fictional character of the twenty-first century. Larsson's Lisbeth is a world-class computer hacker and scary-smart researcher with a tragic personal and family history of her own. As a child, she had to learn how to take care of herself, and she has fashioned herself into a *sui generis* character as a young adult.[1] Lisbeth is special or unique in many ways. She fights, morally and physically, for her own and others' rights. And yet socially she puts off many other characters, we learn as readers, by the way she dresses and communicates nonverbally. She is not a talker, either. Her vigilance, intellectual curiosity, and problem-solving skills, however, serve her (and select others) well.

An important part of Lisbeth's mystique is the way Larsson describes her looks. She becomes a fascinating, revealing case study of Carol Tulloch's concept of 'style-fashion-dress' (2010). Combining style, fashion, and dress into a hyphenated complex, Tulloch notes, fosters attention to relations among ontological parts and wholes. Often, she suggests, the selection of one term or another can be somewhat arbitrary, if not uncritical. Thinking with the three as a whole sharpens an analysis of each as a part. The concept of 'style' draws our attention to visual, appearance-related statements, including those that are highly individualized and those that connect individuals with looks derived from the street and from one's own wardrobe—within and across time. As a social process, the term 'fashion' highlights themes of negotiation, norm-building and norm-deconstructing, and ongoing change as individuals collectively choose styles that resonate within an emerging present. In some ways, the term 'dress' is a bit more clinical and, simultaneously, inclusive in its reach. Helpfully, it brings us back to the body as a focal point (see Entwistle 2000). As Eicher defines 'dress', it begins with the body and then proceeds to consider modifications and additions to the body (2010: xiii). Together, all three of these terms—individually and collectively—shed light on Larsson's portrayal of Lisbeth's looks throughout The Millennium Trilogy. The term 'dress' draws attention to Lisbeth's body and what she does to modify its appearance and to articulate her subjectivity in an embodied way. The concept of style focuses upon how she mixes and (un)matches, drawing upon her own wardrobe and street-cultural references in her *milieu*. Fashion, as a concept and process, highlights social processes, including those of appropriation of individual/group style, as well as individualized 'fashion statements' that contribute to a larger collective endeavor. In turn, these statements become appropriated through processes of commodity capitalism. That is, looks can be cut and spliced back into the very pieces that everyday stylists and dressers combine to create their appearances.

Lisbeth's style draws on various subcultural looks and yet defies categorization. The commodification of her style by H&M and others (discussed later in this chapter) recalls ongoing debates regarding fashion's appropriation of street style. Lisbeth's dressing of her body's diminutive frame (4' 11" and 90 pounds) includes multiple tattoos and piercings. Her hair and makeup change continually and—along with her ongoing body modifications and primarily black, eclectically personalized clothing ensembles—propel the plots[2] throughout Stieg Larsson's Millennium Trilogy. Although I focus primarily in this chapter on the first novel in the trilogy (*The Girl with the Dragon Tattoo*), I also make references to changes in Lisbeth's style-fashion-dress in Larsson's second (*The Girl Who Played with Fire*) and third (*The Girl Who Kicked the Hornet's Nest*) novels (2010a, b).

To date, over 65 million copies of books in The Millennium Trilogy have been sold worldwide in dozens of languages. In this chapter, I argue that much of the transnational (cultural) resonance of the books can be attributed to Larsson's employment of Lisbeth Salander as an unlikely, *sui generis* teacher of possibility. The cultural themes in the trilogy are dark and provoke anxiety. Yet, as Lisbeth demonstrates through her daily actions and her style-fashion-dress, individuals can take the initiative to grapple directly with cultural anxiety and to explore its positive, open side to shape a better future. Fashion, too, has this anticipatory quality. Using her style-fashion-dress strategically and ambiguously, Lisbeth gestures toward the ethical challenges associated with taking personal responsibility. She is a character who manages to navigate cultural anxieties with 'contextual flexibility'; the situational adaptability of her style-fashion-dress becomes a metaphor for her subjectivity (Kaiser, Freeman, and Chandler 1993; Kaiser 1997).

Throughout the trilogy, Lisbeth Salander is an introverted avenger with unusual abilities to fight multiple injustices. As a chameleon, she uses style-fashion-dress simultaneously to allude to her own difficult personal and family history, to convince us of the multi-layered nature of her character and her (very few) social relations, and to open our eyes to the need to grapple openly with deep cultural problems (e.g., sexual violence, racism, corporate/state corruption) that Larsson exposes and Lisbeth tackles.

Ambiguities abound. Despite her small size, Lisbeth is strong—in an almost superheroic sort of way. Her mind, too, is almost magical. Larsson describes her as having a 'photographic memory'[3] as well as powerful analytical and research skills, especially with computers. Lisbeth's style-fashion-dress is ambiguous; it resists subcultural or other labels, just as her character does. It cuts across, for example, clothes and looks associated with punk, goth, emo, cyberpunk, rocker, and other groups. Lisbeth refuses to be associated with any particular group; she is on her own. Similarly, her gender, sexuality, age, and ethnicity are ambiguous and elude classification. Cultural discourse (e.g., book and film reviews, blogs, essays) has explored various themes, nuances, and interpretations of Lisbeth's character. Questions emerge from this discourse: Is Lisbeth a feminist? Is she genderqueer? How would she feel about becoming a commodity? She commits some illegal acts (e.g., hacking, stealing), but is she an ethical character? Why is she so compelling to readers and viewers around the world?

Complicating matters further is the fact that there are multiple Lisbeths: First, there are the various Lisbeth personae in Larsson's trilogy—the images readers conjure and re-conjure (as her looks change) in their minds. Second, there is the Lisbeth played so poignantly by Noomi Rapace (see Figure 2:1) in the 2009 Swedish adaptation of the trilogy, directed by Niels Arden Oplev.

Figure 2:1. Swedish actor Noomi Rapace in the role of Lisbeth Salander.

I actually saw the first of the three Swedish films before I delved into the books,[4] so I tended to have Rapace's image in my head as I read. The screenshot in Figure 2:1 depicts Rapace's Lisbeth in the first Swedish film, in the context of a security firm business meeting with a client (Vanger's lawyer, on the left) and her boss (Dragan Armansky, on the right). Rapace's Lisbeth is dressed in black; the spikes around her neck seem to say, 'Don't mess with me'. Her hair is short and also spiky around the edges; facial piercings are visible. Her black eyeliner is sharp and unrelenting, as is her expression. Later in the film, when she leaves Stockholm and joins (and begins to trust) Blomkvist in the more rural setting of Hedeby, her eye make-up softens, and her hair gets longer.

Most recently, there is a third Lisbeth, played by Rooney Mara—and directed by David Fincher—in the Hollywood adaptation of Larsson's first novel (see Figure 2:2 for various screen shots). Premiering on 20 December 2011, the film had been heavily marketed as 'the feel-bad movie of Christmas' (or, variously, of 'the holidays' or 'the year'). Months before, Mara was on the covers of magazines such as *Vogue* and *W*.

For the cover of *W*, Trish Summerville, the fashion designer for the film, styled Mara as Lisbeth with her last name temporarily tattooed on her chest and blood dripping from her hands. Summerville explains the tattoo, which does not exist in the book: 'I just wanted to have a bold statement piece. This was our first chance to show the world our Salander. So with the blood dripping and the jacket being pulled open, it's just kind of that really big statement of "Here I am"' (VanZanten 2011). Summerville also collaborated with H&M, the Swedish apparel company, on a 30-item clothing line inspired by Lisbeth's wardrobe in the Hollywood film. H&M introduced the line a week before the film's debut, and it sold out almost immediately. Clothes from the line—for example, black faux-leather leggings, a T-shirt with the slogan 'What is hidden in the snow comes forth in the thaw', a black zipper hoodie, and gray slouchy harem pants—have circulated for sale on the Internet through eBay and other sites. The early January 2011 version of *Entertainment Weekly* also sports Mara—this time without a visible top.

Nominated for Golden Globe and Academy Awards, Mara renders a compelling performance that is somewhat more vulnerable than Rapace's. Mara has more facial piercings and bleached eyebrows, which give her an almost ethereal quality. Her hair is layered in such a way that it—like her wardrobe—has maximum contextual flexibility, as is evident in the various screenshot images (see Figure 2:2) from the Hollywood film; note the adaptability of her hair, which somehow looks different in virtually every scene.

There is no shortage of controversy about the publicity for the Hollywood adaptation. From the film's *raison d'être* (why it was made at all so soon after the Swedish adaptations) to Hollywood's tendencies toward commercialization and appropriation, to the clothing line's potential glamorization of rape (Little 2011), to the somewhat disappointing initial box office numbers (the 'feel bad' theme seems to have backfired in the holiday season, coupled with the seriously R rating that limited the audience). However, David Fincher's version of *The Girl with the Dragon Tattoo*, like its Swedish predecessor, has received mostly positive critical reviews.

Figure 2:2. Images of Hollywood's adaptation of *The Girl with the Dragon Tattoo*, featuring a transformed Rooney Mara.

In the remainder of this chapter, I interpret Lisbeth Salander and her style-fashion-dress as offering a 'pedagogy of possibility' (McLaren 2000: 1).[5] I begin with a discussion of Stieg Larsson's background, his development of Lisbeth Salander as a character and unlikely style-fashion-dress icon, and his critique of Sweden (and other 'euromodern'[6] nations). Then I turn to a discussion of anxiety as a theme in fashion theory, as well as Larsson's Millennium Trilogy. Next I consider how and why Lisbeth's style-fashion-dress articulates strategic ambiguity, through which she negotiates cultural and personal anxieties by mixing and matching, concealing and revealing, and going on both the offense and the defense. In short, she masters the art of contextual flexibility, using articles of clothing, eyeliner, hairspray, and various accessories (along with her keen mind and strong body) to anticipate and combat evil, as well as to challenge readers'/viewers' stereotypes in an ongoing manner. Finally, I interpret Lisbeth Salander through the lens of feminist theorist Simone de Beauvoir's 'ethics of ambiguity' (1947), and consider how Lisbeth—like fashion and cultural anxiety—can offer a pedagogy of possibility, or a way to foster social change, albeit in unexpected ways.

Novelist Stieg Larsson (Feminist and Anti-Racist) and Eva Gabrielsson (Life Partner)

Stieg Larsson (1954–2004) died suddenly and tragically from a heart attack, just a few months after his trilogy had been contracted for publication (Gabrielsson 2011). Like Mikael Blomkvist, the leading male character in the trilogy, Larsson was the editor of a progressive magazine. Larsson spent his career investigating, exposing, and fighting racism (e.g., neo-Nazi groups), state/corporate corruption, and sexism. At the age of 15 Larsson had witnessed a gang rape and, for 35 years, he felt deep regret for not having intervened; he dedicated himself to the cause of exposing and fighting sexual violence and gender inequality (Gabrielsson 2011). To highlight the institutionalized nature of gender inequality and sexual violence, Larsson called the first novel *Män Som Hatar Kvinnor* (*Men Who Hate Women*) in his native Swedish language. His publisher tried to talk him into a different title, but Larsson was insistent, and his original title prevailed in the Swedish novel, published in 2004.

As the title became 'toned down' and rebranded in the English translation to *The Girl with the Dragon Tattoo*, so too—ironically—did the size of the tattoo on Lisbeth's back. In the Swedish version, the dragon covers her entire back (as seen, for example, on Noomi Rapace's back in the sex scene with Mikael Blomkvist). In the English translation, the tattoo is much smaller and on her left shoulder. Why the change? Possible explanations include the publisher's desire to curb Larsson or Lisbeth. Or, perhaps the publisher had already commissioned the cover art and needed to make the author's text fit the covers. Swedish writer and friend of Larsson, John-Henri Holmberg speculates that the latter explanation may sadly be the case and argues that 'Lisbeth Salander is not the same person in Swedish and English. The dragon tattoo is both important to her self-image and a feature striking to those she allows to get close to her' (Holmberg 2011: 37). In the Hollywood version, the tattoo grows in size but is still on Lisbeth's left shoulder blade. Larsson did not have the opportunity to explicate the significance of the dragon tattoo (or other tattoos) to Lisbeth. (Apparently he intended to do so in later novels.) *Dragon Tattoo* keeps readers wondering, and the English title adds to the ambiguity. What is very clear, however, is Lisbeth's personal history with gender/sexual violence and her commitment to help others who have been violated or abused by men who hate women.

Upon Larsson's death, his estate (which has grown to tens of millions of dollars) went to his father and brother, rather than to Eva Gabrielsson (2011), his partner of 30-plus years. They had never officially married, in part due to the fact that they would have had to record their home address upon doing so, and neo-Nazi groups whom Larsson had exposed had threatened Larsson's life. Swedish law does not recognize common-law marriages. Gabrielsson has continued to seek intellectual, editorial and managerial control of the published works and, at the time of this writing, the legal battle is still unresolved as the estate continues to grow. In 2011, Gabrielsson published her autobiography/biography, *'There are Things I Want You to Know' about Stieg Larsson and Me.*

Gabrielsson (2011: 95) believes that the greatest single influence for the development of Lisbeth as a character came from the famous Swedish fictional girl Pippi Longstocking, created by Astrid Lindgren ([1945] 2007). Years earlier, Blomkvist and colleagues had begun to speculate about what Pippi would be like as a contemporary adult character. Famously, Pippi has her own unique moral code; she does things her way and as a result does not fit in too well in social circumstances (e.g., a classroom) that demand institutionally condoned, normative behavior. Like Lisbeth, Pippi is a *sui generis* character; she lives on her own, without parents. Pippi is very small, but incredibly strong; she can lift a horse. Her appearance is rather quirky. She has bright red hair and wears braids that stick straight out sideways. She makes her own dresses from scraps, and wears striped knee socks that do not match (one black and one brown).

There are a few compelling similarities between Pippi Longstocking and Lisbeth Salander. They both have their own moral codes, have some asocial tendencies, are very smart, and are extremely strong despite their small size. We learn on page 38 of *Dragon Tattoo* that Lisbeth's hair, like Pippi's, is naturally red, but Lisbeth dyes it to a raven black. On page 48, she shows up for a meeting with her boss, Dragan Armansky, and a client wearing striped (matching) green and red striped knee socks, which undoubtedly add a Pippi-spunky spark of color to her otherwise stark, dark outfit: a black T-shirt printed with a fanged E.T. and the words 'I am also an alien', a black skirt with a frayed hem, a worn black leather jacket, a rivet belt, and heavy Dr Martens boots. (The Swedish film adaptation shows Lisbeth in the outfit in Figure 2:1; there were no striped socks in either film adaptations.) A few pages later, she says that she would give anyone a fat lip if they ever compared her to Pippi Longstocking. Armansky swallows hard, because he has often compared the two in his head. Later in the trilogy, Lisbeth, like Pippi, acquires a 'pot of gold', and she names her apartment V. Kulla (like Pippi's Villa Villekulla).

Most likely, however, Lisbeth Salander is a synthesis of Pippi and other influences. Gabrielsson notes that Larsson himself shared an acute ability to process information:

> Stieg was like a sponge, absorbing everything and without ever taking notes! For example, to come up with the clothes his characters wore, which were always described in great detail, he never consulted any catalogues or peered into any shop windows. All he did was study fashion in the street. And he loved that. Stieg had a very personal way of dressing. Unlike most people in his milieu, who generally favored sporty casual dress for every occasion, he wore tweed jackets, elegant but inexpensive, and he adapted his style to the people and situations he encountered. He had class, without ever coming across as a dandy or a snob. (Gabrielsson 2011: 63)

When asked if Lisbeth Salander was designed to be a feminine double for Larsson, Gabrielsson replied that the two shared junk-food eating habits (e.g., frozen pizzas and fast-food sandwiches), incredible memories, intellectual curiosities, and strong tendencies toward secrecy and wariness, which can be explained by their personal histories and awareness of social, cultural, and political threats. There is one other characteristic they had in common: a drive for a higher morality.

> For Stieg, Lisbeth was the ideal incarnation of the code of ethics that requires us to act according to our convictions. She is a kind of biblical archangel.... This dilemma between morality and action is in fact what drives the plot of the 'Millennium' trilogy. Individuals change the world and their fellow human beings for better or for worse, but each of us acts according to his or her own sense of morality, which is why in the end everything comes down to personal responsibility. (Gabrielsson 2011: 82)

Following months of aggressive marketing by Sony Pictures, in advance of the Hollywood release of the film, Gabrielsson indicates that Larsson would have been disgusted by the commercialization of Lisbeth Salander—especially by the 'branding' of her to sell products (e.g., the H&M clothing line). She says that Stieg and she would never have sold the rights for such commodification. Rather, he (and she) would have wanted to use the pre-debut film buzz to steer the publicity toward cultural discourse regarding gender discrimination and sexual violence (Rising 2011).

Part of the pre-debut blitz was a promotional Hollywood film poster in which Lisbeth (Rooney Mara) is topless; both of her breast nipples are pierced in such a way, according to director David Fincher, that they 'catch the light'. Blomkvist's (Daniel Craig's) arm is around the top of her chest, as if to protect her from the world. He is fully clothed. Feminist blog sites question the motivation and need for such imagery (Silverstein 2011). Adding to the feminist disappointment of the publicity surrounding the film, but not Mara's performance *per se* (which—like Rapace's—has been widely praised), is an interview by Mara, in which she interprets Lisbeth as not being a feminist, as though that would be too 'easy' for such a complex character: 'I don't think she would characterize herself as that either, you know? I don't think she really acts or does the things she does in the name of any group or person' (Cranz 2011).

Mara goes on to say that she does not necessarily regard herself as a feminist—that she is not really sure what that means—because she, like Lisbeth, does not identify with any single group or person. Blogger Alex Cranz analyzes this interview and says, 'All I can do is be disappointed. Really really disappointed' (2011). Perhaps, Cranz speculates, a publicist supplied Mara with these lines, or maybe she and the film publicists think that being feminist means that you 'have to get hung up on the hypersexual portrayal of women in the media'. Perhaps they felt it would have been too much of a contradiction to endorse feminist values, in light of the sexualization of Lisbeth in the promotional materials. Or, perhaps they believed embracing such values openly would limit their market. Or, as Cranz notes, maybe their remarks represent a failure of feminist education. At any rate, Cranz argues that Larsson created Lisbeth 'specifically to represent women and feminist ideals', which revolve around gender equality (Cranz 2011). Gabrielsson (2011), too, responds to the interview with Mara by remarking that feminism is not about a label; it is about a social movement (in Rising 2011). This movement is ongoing and involves a process of deciphering how and why the personal—and the cultural—is political.

Cultural and Personal Anxieties and Politics

Build-up disappointments aside, I was impressed with Rooney Mara's performance and with the film in general. I came away thinking that it is possible for there to be multiple Lisbeths, in different cultural contexts. I am not as interested in comparing Lisbeths as I am in multiplying them (or if not Lisbeths *per se*, then other similarly strong and fascinating female characters).

In The Millennium Trilogy, Larsson graphically (but not gratuitously, in my view) jolts readers to grapple with Salander's tragic, troubled personal story within the context of cultural anxieties associated with Sweden's past and present. Larsson wanted to let readers know that even one of the most egalitarian nations in the world has problems of neo-Nazism, gender discrimination, sexual violence, and state/corporate corruption. Typically, as the Danish philosopher and so-called father of existentialism Søren Kierkegaard (1813–1855) claimed, anxiety is a future-oriented concept; metaphorically, it can be compared to a feeling 'in one's bones that a storm is approaching' (Kierkegaard [1844] 1981: 115). Although he primarily spoke of individual or psychological experiences of anxiety, Kierkegaard did leave the door open, as I read him, to think about cultural anxiety as a concept with multiple layers: dread and fear, on the one hand, and anticipation or even hope on the other. He also ponders what one might learn by using the concept of anxiety to analyze one's cultural past. He describes anxiety as pedagogical inasmuch as it gestures towards freedom's possibilities: anxiety is the 'dizziness of freedom' (Kierkegaard [1844] 1981: 61).

However, Kierkegaard goes on to suggest that anxiety is like innocence; it is like *not* knowing what will happen next ([1844] 1981: 41). Writing about a hundred years later, Walter Benjamin (1892–1940) indicates that fashion is a compelling philosophical area of inquiry because of its 'extraordinary anticipations' (1999: 63).[7] That is, Benjamin seems to suggest that fashion fosters some vague inkling of what is to come. Perhaps we can surmise here a useful but subtle distinction between anxiety and fashion: anxiety involves anticipating without knowing what is to come, whereas fashion provides some visual, albeit ambiguous, hints about the future. We might say that fashion and anxiety are joined at the hip. Fashion does not reduce anxiety, but rather 'points to it with its finger' (to use Roland Barthes's phrase about fashion and meaning [1983: 303]).

Both Benjamin and Kierkegaard address the relation of the future to the past: Benjamin through fashion and Kierkegaard through anxiety. Benjamin also uses the 'tiger's leap' metaphor to articulate how fashion moves back in time to grab influences and to reinterpret them as fresh (see Evans 2003). Evidence of this leap emerges in the form of Lisbeth Salander's style-fashion-dress. It is not so much that it is new; it bears traces of punk, goth, and other subcultural influences from the decades since the 1970s. And yet her style-fashion-dress feels fresh in each incarnation. Kierkegaard might have described this in terms of anxiety's dreaming of the spirit, with a re-imagining of traces from the past ([1884] 1981: 41).

Fashion studies scholars Rebecca Arnold (2001) and Caroline Evans (2003) have written about fashion's expressions of anxiety, dread, and death at the end of the twentieth century. In her book *Fashion, Desire and Anxiety*, Arnold (2001) analyzes runway fashion (influenced by street style) and its articulation of desires and anxieties. She describes (now deceased) designer Alexander McQueen's dressing of models' bodies with animal skulls layers and torn leathers that reference themes of death and threat. Fashion photographers, too, introduced themes of brutality; for example, Sean Ellis featured gothic and other 'dark' fetish themes. Similarly, Caroline Evans (2003) discusses the edgy runway fashion of the 1990s as follows in her book *Fashion at the Edge: Spectacle, Modernity and Deathliness*:

> Often permeated by death, disease and dereliction, [fashion's] imagery articulated the anxieties as well as the pleasures of identity, alienation and loss against the unstable backdrop of rapid social, economic and technological change at the end of the twentieth century. (Evans 2003: 4)

Emerging as a character in the early twenty-first century, Lisbeth Salander—computer hacker extraordinaire, alienated but not victimized ward of the state, gender outlaw (Hook 2011), avenging superheroine (Rosenberg 2011), and rape survivor—literally embodies and/ or combats a complex nexus of anxiety-producing themes with transnational relevance:

- Gendered power relations and violence (including rape, torture, sex trafficking)
- Sexual difference(s) and body image issues
- Unresolved cultural histories and governmental secrecy

- Corporate and state corruption
- Immigration and racism
- Technology's potential to invade personal (or corporate) space

In an interview in 2007, Noomi Rapace was reported as saying (as translated) that playing the role of Lisbeth was especially meaningful to her because, 'I'm interested in the darker aspects of humankind, that which is not easy or well balanced. The cracks' (Anon n.d.). In many ways, the Millennium Trilogy offers a kind of post-9/11 wake-up call: threats to society are not only from outside others (e.g., transnational terrorists); very real threats emerge within our own institutionalized, cultural spaces, even in progressive, contemporary Sweden, as well as many other nations.

Let's turn to a consideration of Lisbeth's embodiment of cultural and personal anxieties. As noted earlier, she is tiny yet strong. Larsson describes her as easily passing for a 14-year-old boy, based on her height, breast size, and clothing choices. Her style-fashion-dress goes on the visual offence and provides others with a fair warning not to mess with her. If they do, she always seeks revenge.[8] She typically does so behind the scenes. As a world-class computer hacker, Lisbeth investigates and learns others' secrets, exposes corruption and violence, and moves money around the world. Lisbeth can also defend herself physically with her impressive boxing and martial art skills, combined effectively with Tasers.

Critics, bloggers, and others have debated the meaning of Lisbeth's tattoos and piercings, her makeup, spiky accessories, black wardrobe, and her combat boots. Her T-shirts with slogans, in particular, say a lot about her feelings about herself and her relation to the world:

The Girl with the Dragon Tattoo (Larsson 2009):
'I am also an alien' (a black T-shirt with picture of E.T. with fangs) (p. 48)
'Armageddon was yesterday—Today we have a serious problem' (p. 330)
'I can be a regular bitch. Just try me' (p. 505)
'Kill them all and let God sort them out' (a washed-out camouflage shirt advertising *Soldier of Fortune* magazine) (p. 550)

The Girl Who Played with Fire (Larsson 2010a):
'Consider this a fair warning' (black T-shirt worn with jeans, sandals, sun hat, and black bag) (p. 20)
'You have the right to remain silent' (p. 138)

The Girl Who Kicked the Hornet's Nest (2010b):
'I am annoyed' (p. 463)

Her anarchic and anxiety-inducing verbal messages clearly indicate: 'Don't mess with me. You'll regret it if you do.' Psychologists, psychiatrists, and various critics have described her clothes as self-protective armor (e.g., Rosenberg and O'Neill 2011: 3). If so, it seems to be an urban armor that she frequently dons in Stockholm. (Her appearance softens when on the rural island of Hedeby and—especially—in the Cayman Islands in *The Girl Who Played with Fire*.) I believe her style-fashion-dress is partially self-protective, but further would argue that it articulates and generates cultural anxieties; it makes people think twice about the stability of the social order. It questions the authority, for example, of gender and sexual categories (Hook 2011; Surkan 2012).

Lisbeth marks herself; she highlights her difference, especially on Stockholm streets and in certain situations to create social distance. Kierkegaard described anxiety as the *discrimen* of subjectivity ([1944] 1981: 197). The Latin *discrimen* translates to 'that which parts', 'intervening space', 'interval', 'distance', or 'separation' (Perseus Digital Library n.d) Some versions of Kierkegaard translate anxiety as the 'ambiguity of subjectivity' ([1944] 1981: 197). In this sense, ambiguity may be analogous to an indeterminate space in between—like a blurry gap. Perhaps Lisbeth's strong yet ambiguous T-shirt statements can be interpreted as creating a gap or distance between herself and others. Yet overall her appearance is ambiguous and, if anything, invites questioning—critical and creative thinking.

Lisbeth's tattoos, while more personal and permanent than her T-shirts, also mark her body in a way that may represent the space or distance associated with anxiety: the *discrimen* or ambiguity of subjectivity. We learn about all of her tattoos from Blomkvist's perspective when he is having sex with her. He counts them; in addition to the dragon on her back (in the Swedish version) or her left shoulder (in the English version), there is the wasp on her neck, a loop around one ankle, another loop around the biceps of her left arm, a Chinese symbol on her hip, and a rose on one calf (Larsson 2009: 420).

We never learn from The Millennium Trilogy what each of the tattoos means to Lisbeth, but we do get the impression that they function to mark (often violent) events—much like mnemonic devices—so that she will not forget what others have done to her. In *Dragon Tattoo*, after Lisbeth's guardian, appointed by the state, rapes her in a horrendously painful scene, she gets the loop tattoo around her ankle. The tattooist warns her that the tissue in that area is thin, and that it will hurt. She tells the tattooist to proceed and observes the process carefully. It appears that there are two reasons for this tattoo: (a) to mark the violent event and (b) to remind herself of the tattoo process. She manages to get some revenge and regain control over her own finances when she tases her guardian unexpectedly in a later scene; she then sodomizes him with a large dildo and, so as to hinder him from sexual relations in the future, she inflicts a tattoo across his abdomen: 'I am a sadistic pig, a pervert, and a rapist'. She marks him; she creates a permanent *discrimen*.

Had Larsson had the opportunity to complete his fourth novel (apparently he had ten planned in the series), Lisbeth's personal meanings of her tattoos would probably have been revealed. Gabrielsson writes that in the fourth novel:

Lisbeth gradually breaks free of all of her ghosts and enemies. Every time she manages to take revenge on someone who has harmed her, physically or psychologically, she has the tattoo symbolizing that person removed. Lisbeth's piercings are her way of following the fashion of others her age, but those tattoos are her war paint. To some extent, the young woman behaves like a native in an urban jungle, acting like an animal, relying on instinct, of course, but always on the alert as well for what may lie ahead, sniffing out danger. (2011: 206)

We do know from *Fire* that Lisbeth, whose online code name is Wasp, has a laser procedure to remove the wasp tattoo from the right side of her neck (Larsson 2010a). The stated reason was that it was conspicuous and marked her identity clearly. She did not want to be identified or remembered (Larsson 2010a: 19). In an essay on the psychology of Lisbeth's body dressing, Rodgers and Bui attribute the removal of the tattoo (described by them as a form of 'self-mutilation'), along with Lisbeth's surprising breast augmentation surgery (described by them as 'self-care'), to her movement away from harmful practices towards those that they see as more therapeutic or indicative of her more positive, healthy relationship with herself and with the world (2011: 43). I am afraid I cannot completely buy this argument, although it does seem to bear some resemblance to Gabrielsson's description of the fourth novel.

Somehow I feel more comfortable with the idea that Larsson uses Lisbeth's removal of her wasp tattoo strategically; it meshes with the plot and her need to go unnoticed or unmarked in *Fire*. I do think, however, that Larsson presents Lisbeth as having anxieties about her body. The reader becomes aware of this through her thoughts while looking in the mirror and through her conversations with others before or while having sex. Male characters, such as her boss Armansky and her research partner Blomkvist, seem to share her perception (or Larsson's?) that she is too skinny and too flat-chested.

Early in *Dragon Tattoo*, Armansky looks at Lisbeth and reflects on his strange, ambivalent attraction to her. He thinks that she could almost be described as attractive, if she would wear the 'right make-up' (minus the black lipstick, tattoos, pierced nose and eyebrows). He thinks that she could have been a fashion model, except for her 'extreme slenderness'. Apparently Armansky (or rather, Larsson) is not very familiar with fashion industry standards for models. Granted, she would be excluded from the fashion modeling industry, not because of her 'extreme slenderness' but rather because of her height (4' 11").[9] Armansky (or Larsson) describes her as having small, 'childlike breasts' and a wide mouth, small nose, and high cheekbones—with 'an almost Asian look'. Armansky thinks that she looks like she had 'just emerged from a week-long orgy with a gang of hard rockers' (Larsson 2009: 38).

In the cottage on the island of Hedeby, Lisbeth goes into Blomkvist's bedroom and makes it clear that she wants to have sex with him. He thinks to himself: 'Her skinny body was repulsive. Her breasts were pathetic. She had no hips to speak of' (Larsson 2009: 396). She asks him, 'Aren't I sexy enough?' (397). He counts her tattoos as he gives in to her advances. (As it turns out, this is not a new experience for Blomkvist. Women come on to him repeatedly throughout the trilogy.)

The reader learns more about Lisbeth's body image at the end of *Dragon Tattoo*, when she disguises herself as a wealthy woman named Monica Sholes in order to make a 'bank transfer'. She unmarks her own appearance by covering the wasp tattoo on her neck with a thick layer of makeup and powder. She puts on a page-boy blonde wig, false eyelashes, rouge, lipstick, pink nail polish on her fingers, and wears a sand-colored skirt with a matching blouse, black tights, waist-length jacket and beret (from Camille's House of Fashion) and black boots. She also changes her silhouette:

> For the first time in her life Salander had a bustline that made her—when she glanced at herself in the full-length mirror—catch her breath. The breasts were as fake as Monica Sholes' identity. They were made of latex and had been bought in Copenhagen where the transvestites shopped…. [She spent] five minutes examining herself in the mirror. She saw a total stranger. Big-busted Monica Sholes in a blonde page-boy wig, wearing more make-up than Lisbeth Salander dreamed of using in a whole month. She looked… different. (Larsson 2009: 560–61)

She later discards Sholes' identity, literally, in a trashcan, and flushes the (traceable) designer jewelry down the drain. But after 'a moment of anxious hesitation', she decides to keep the latex breasts.

At the beginning of the second novel, Lisbeth is in the Cayman Islands. Having come into some wealth, she has been traveling for a year. She has let her hair grow out, and she is very tanned. She is wearing khaki shorts and a black top. She's still 4' 11' and weights 90 lbs. But now her breasts are different; she has had breast enlargement surgery in one of Europe's best plastic surgery centers in Genoa, Italy. Her new breasts are moderate in size. She studies herself in the mirror and notes how dramatic the difference is, 'both for her looks and for her self-confidence' (Larsson 2010a: 19). When she left the clinic she had felt panicked—as though everyone was staring at her new breasts. It took her a while to realize that this was not the case. She had not marked herself as different with this newest modification to her body; rather, she realized that she could blend in (Larsson 2010a: 32).

In *Fire*, Lisbeth also goes to a store called Twilfit for panties and bras, and buys a drawerful of lingerie. After thirty minutes of 'embarrassed searching' (pointing again to her anxiety), she selects a sexy set that she would have 'never dreamed of buying before'. However, when she tried it on that night and looked in the mirror, she saw a 'thin, tattooed girl in grotesque underwear. She took them off and threw them in the trash' (Larsson 2010a: 95).

Several pages later, she analyzes her image again in the mirror. She has downsized her piercings. She had had the ring in her nipple removed during the breast surgery. She had also taken out the ring in her lower lip and had unscrewed the stud in her tongue. She still had rings in her earlobes, a ring in her left eyebrow, and a jewel in her navel (Larsson 2010a: 103–4).

She shares her new breasts with her girlfriend and lover, Miriam Wu (Mimmi), who says:

> They'll do…look fantastic. You're so hung up about your body…. Apart from the fact that you're not really a dyke. You're probably bisexual. But most of all you're sexual—you like

sex and you don't care about what gender. You're an entropic chaos factor…. Your breasts are luscious. They fit you. Not too big and not too small…. And they feel real. (Larsson 2010a: 120–22)

The Swedish film trilogy leaves out the breast augmentation, and it still remains to be seen if or how the second and third Hollywood Sony Pictures, film adaptations will deal with this part of the plot. However, advertising for the Hollywood *Dragon Tattoo* has certainly highlighted Mara's breasts, which she had pierced for the role. In the promotional poster described earlier with Blomkvist's arm around the top of her chest, her two nipple piercings are visible, and Lisbeth gazes into the camera, expressionless (Franich 2011). In this instance, the ambiguity of Lisbeth's sexuality slips away; a heteronormatively sexualized and commercialized version of Lisbeth moves into this promo for the film.

The following section moves the conversation back to issues of contextual flexibility associated with Lisbeth's sexual and other subject positions, as well as her style-fashion-dress.

Strategic Ambiguity through Contextual Flexibility

As the *discrimen* or ambiguity—the uncertain space in between—of subjectivity, anxiety plays out through Lisbeth's styling-fashioning-dressing of her body. She is a character who articulates her agency, or—in psychological terms—her self-efficacy and resilience (Rutledge 2011: 218) as she moves across and within gender, sexual, ethnic, class, generational, and other subject positions. Each of her subject positions is ambiguous and shifting, and taken together, their intersectionalities—in feminist theoretical terms—reveal how Lisbeth not only navigates but also fosters ambiguity: strategically, contextually, flexibly. It is hard to place her in any one subject position, and single group or subculture, or any essence of any sort. She may seem at times to care little about her appearance, but she certainly manages it with critical and creative dexterity.

A typical outfit for Lisbeth in *Dragon Tattoo* is one that she resumes upon her return to Stockholm in *Fire*. She wears old black ripped jeans (with blue panties showing through underneath) with boots, and she reunites with her black leather jacket, which is scuffed and has rivets on the shoulder (Larsson 2010a: 81).

Also in *Fire*, Lisbeth manipulates her facial piercings with considerable flexibility. She takes them off and puts them on according to the context. When she wants to pass as a more conventional woman, she slips them out. When she assumes the identity of a woman named Irene Nesser, for example, she removes the ring in her eyebrow and puts on makeup and a long blonde wig. In one scene as Nesser, she wears dark jeans with a warm brown sweater with yellow trim and walking boots with heels (Larsson 2010a: 413).

Lisbeth's body, even after her cosmetic surgery in *Fire*, could easily pass for that of a 14-year-old boy (representing ambiguous intersectionalities between gender and generation). Lisbeth knows when and how to use this ambiguity strategically to pass as a boy, using her style-fashion-dress (wearing gender-neutral attire—hoodies and jeans and such). Mara indicates, 'Before [this role], I dressed much girlier. A lot of blush-colored things. Now I literally roll out of bed and put on whatever is there. I have really enjoyed being a boy this last year' (Van Meter 2011).

Lisbeth's sexuality is also ambiguous; it intersects with her ambiguous class and gender subject positions in a complex way. At the end of *Dragon Tattoo*, when her class status increases dramatically, she experiments—primarily for undercover reasons—with more heteronormative, or conventionally mainstream, modes of femininity. In *Fire*, she goes on a shopping spree at H&M, buying separates that she can mix and match with her darker urban wardrobe. Even more surprising, though, is Lisbeth's breast augmentation surgery. Kim Surkan (2012) offers a very interesting analysis of Lisbeth's gender and sexual subject positions, and invites us to consider their intersectionalities through a queer lens. She argues convincingly, in my view, that the concept of genderqueer helps to explain these intersectionalities; this concept complicates rather than pinpoints gender and sexual identities, and opens up—rather than closes down—subjectivity. Thinking about Lisbeth's subjectivity through the lens of genderqueer enables a reading of her as not only bisexual but also as fluid in her gender identity. Rather than debating, for example, whether Lisbeth can be a feminist if she has breast augmentation surgery (as some bloggers have done), the conversation shifts to one of considering Lisbeth's desire for her body to match her self-conceptions of gender. Of course, this only becomes possible when she has the money to afford the surgery, so gender, sexual, and class intersectionalities become compelling.

We learn in *Dragon Tattoo* that Lisbeth is sexually active. She has had more than fifty sexual partners since the age of fifteen, almost always at her initiative, and often with older men. Miriam Wu (Mimmi) is the only female sexual partner we get to know in the trilogy; she is introduced briefly in *Dragon Tattoo* and then assumes a more prominent role in *Fire*. The following passage in *Dragon Tattoo* provides a clue to Lisbeth's sexual flexibility:

Salander—unlike Mimmi—had never thought of herself as a lesbian. She had never brooded over whether she was straight, gay, or even bisexual. She did not give a damn about labels, did not see it was anyone else's business whom she spent her nights with. If she had to choose, she preferred guys—and they were in the lead, statistically speaking. The only problem was finding a guy who was not a jerk and one who was also good in bed; Mimmi was a sweet compromise, and she turned Salander on. (Larsson 2009: 327)

Lisbeth's style-fashion-dress is similarly ambiguous and, as we have seen, strategic. She mixes and matches old, worn pieces (e.g., black leather jacket, distressed denim, torn T-shirts) with new articles of clothing, especially after she becomes wealthy. She styles herself in a mode that can alternately be labeled as punk, hard rocker, goth, cyberpunk, or other groups, yet she defies and resists labels of any sort. She fights against the kind of categorization that

Caroline Evans (1997) has called the futile 'butterfly' effect of pinning down subcultures that are actually more fluid.

In *Fire*, when Lisbeth goes on a shopping spree at H&M, she buys pants, jeans, tops, and socks: items that are contextually flexible. They can be mixed and matched for a range of personae and situations. Perhaps it was this mention of H&M that inspired the Swedish retailer to team up with Trish Summerville to create a 'capsule collection inspired by anti-heroine Lisbeth Salander' (Bergin 2011). Summerville explains this Hollywood 'tie-in' as follows: she took basic pieces of Lisbeth's wardrobe—worn throughout the film—and made them a little more fashionable for H&M. Summerville's goal was for women to find pieces that they could then mix with items in their own wardrobes to 'create their own personal style' (Casadei 2011). In this way, women could incorporate 'little pieces of Salander' and her 'essence', 'strength', and 'moral code' into their lives (Creeden 2011). Summerville had found some of the pieces for Lisbeth's wardrobe in 'the insane resale shops in Sweden', including ML Resale and Mix Mix Mix, which are among her favorites. Summerville also had two leather jackets custom made for Mara from a company named Cerre and by a designer named Agatha Blois, who has made clothing for rockers for over 20 years. Summerville regarded these jackets as old, comfortable shields for Lisbeth (VanZanten 2011).

Fashion bloggers reacted to the news on *Glamour*'s fashion site in advance of the line's debut in selected stores and online (Lo 2011):

WHY IS THERE NOT AN H&M NEAR ME?! I just about DIED from envy when I saw her wardrobe from the movie! She's one of my favorite characters. Although I'm not super happy about the American adaption of the movie... the Swedish version is amazing! (evelinestays)

love black everything can't wait for this line! (emmanelson96)

Here's to hoping that the leather pants don't look cheap. I'd love a pair of leather leggings, but I can't afford a proper pair. (daydream11)

Responses to a YouTube posting in late 2011 about the collection, however, yields a wider range of responses: pro, con, and ambivalent (YouTube Commentators 2011):

I think h&m is cool and I lovveeee The millennium trilogy...but i personally don't think a character like lisbeth salander should be put in the spotlight for fashion...because that's just not what her character is about...she should be put in the spotlight based on the things her character actually goes through and her abilities (joaniecheriezz)

Omg, do they have to squeeze money out of everything?! Stieg Larsson is probably turning in his grave right now. (luiza089)

I WANT EVERYTHING I SAW !!! (Technocrazify)

I;m such a huge fan of Trish Summerville!! The collections looks awesome! (SuckAFuckUToob)

Indeed, despite some obvious ambivalence about the commodification of Lisbeth, the success of the line (it quickly sold out) likely stems in part from the clothes' contextual flexibility. When Trish Summerville poses with models wearing the line, this movement from Lisbeth's wardrobe to the world of fashion reminds us just how tall fashion models are, and how different clothes look on their bodies than they do on most of ours. As various pieces (faux-leather leggings, T-shirts, slouchy gray harem pants) still circulate on eBay, the possibilities for lots of looks on various bodies multiply. So too does the potential for strategic uses of ambiguity, as individuals mix and match pieces in ways not anticipated by Summerville (or Larsson).

Speaking of unanticipated style possibilities, Lisbeth does not appear wearing red and green horizontal-striped socks in either film adaptation, as she does in Larsson's first novel on page 48, along with edgy black pieces from her wardrobe. There are no Pippi-like stripes. There is, however, what I believe to be a small nod to Pippi Longstocking in the Hollywood film. Beginning on the island of Hedeby, Lisbeth starts to fashion part of her hair (in the back) into tiny pigtails. (See the image in Figure 2:2 on the second row and to the right.) Later in the film, they even stick out a bit, like Pippi's, but in a more punkish way. Throughout the film, Mara's hair is the epitome of contextual flexibility. As shown in Figure 2:2, it is styled differently in every scene. Cut strategically with a series of jagged points, her hair looks like Lisbeth chopped it herself in a random moment of self-fashioning with a razor. In fact, her hair has been strategically styled into a kind of uneven extended shag, except for her bangs, which are cropped very short into a straight edge. The result is the potential for many different looks: On some occasions it is spiked into a mohawk. At other times it looks like Lisbeth just stumbled out of bed. And then there are the tiny random pigtails and, on some occasions a smoother look. Like her character, Lisbeth's hair is multi-layered.

Toward a Pedagogy of Possibility

Lisbeth can be interpreted as an introverted avenger with unusual abilities to fight multiple injustices; she fashions herself—and others fashion her—as an unlikely, and yet effective, teacher of possibility. By this I mean she does not give up; she has a sense of personal responsibility and she pursues what French feminist Simone de Beauvoir (1908-1986) called an 'ethics of ambiguity'. De Beauvoir (1947) was inspired not only by European existential philosophy but also by a passion to understand what allowed Nazism to rise in the 1930s. She questioned why individuals did not take more personal responsibility to resist fascism. In developing her 'ethics of ambiguity', de Beauvoir contemplated how and why individuals need to step up to circumvent oppressive uncertainties—to question and to act accordingly and responsibly for oneself and others alike. To do so, according to de Beauvoir, requires being aware of injustices, working through ambiguity (and, presumably, anxiety), and choosing and acting accordingly on a daily basis: 'Ethics does not furnish recipes any more than do science and art. One can merely propose methods' (de Beauvoir 1947: 134).

What methods can one employ? Among the everyday decisions individuals necessarily make are acts of style-fashion-dress (resources permitting and limiting). I would like to close this chapter with a brief discussion of the pedagogical possibilities of Lisbeth Salander's style-fashion-dress. That is, I am suggesting that Larsson employs her style-fashion-dress as a kind of method of inquiry. Elsewhere, I have written about 'minding appearances' as a process of embodied knowing in ways that are at once critical and creative; that include attention to issues of production as well as consumption; and that entail self-reflexivity in the interplay among style, subjectivity, and the negotiation of meaning with others (Kaiser 2001). A pedagogy of possibility takes the process of minding appearances a step further by embedding style-fashion-dress in the context of entangled cultural anxieties in a transnational world. As a case study and unlikely teacher of possibility, Lisbeth Salander— as a character in the book trilogy, the Swedish films, and the Hollywood film—keeps us on our toes. She reminds us that it does not make sense to judge by appearances or to stereotype. She challenges us to think beyond labels or essences of any kind. She fosters ethics of ambiguity that enable her to disrupt conventional expectations and to grapple with—indeed to embody—cultural and personal anxieties. Lisbeth's style-fashion-dress and its appropriation by Hollywood and H&M alike challenge us to embrace the possibilities, as well as the limits, of subversion in the context of capitalism.

One of the final scenes in *The Girl Who Kicked the Hornet's Nest* (Larsson 2010b) gestures artfully and strategically towards Lisbeth's pedagogy of possibility. As she hopes to 'take down' state corruption along with gender violence and other sources of cultural anxiety that have been surreptitiously stifled through acts of secrecy and denial, Lisbeth enters the courtroom as the defendant. Blomkvist gasps when he sees her. What was his sister (Lisbeth's attorney) thinking? Lisbeth wears a black leather miniskirt with frayed seams. Her black T-shirt says 'I am annoyed' and barely covers her tattoos. She has a ring through her left eyebrow and ten piercings in her ears. She is wearing gray lipstick and the heaviest and darkest eye makeup he has ever seen her wear. In the Swedish film adaptation, her hair is spiked into the most striking Mohawk imaginable. It is sticking straight up.

Then Blomkvist realizes that her look is a strategic parody of the decadent way in which the media had been labeling her throughout the last two novels. If she had appeared in the courtroom 'with her hair smoothed down and wearing a twin-set and pearls and sensible shoes', she would have been interpreted as 'a con artist trying to sell a story to the court'. Rather than stifling anxiety, she articulates it through exaggerated self-fashioning that is both ambiguous and 'way over the top—for clarity' (Larsson 2010b: 463).

I believe that Simone de Beauvoir would have liked Lisbeth as an existential teacher of possibility. In the spirit of strategic ambiguity, however, I just have one minor regret: I would have liked to have seen some striped socks in the film adaptations. Maybe in black and gray?

References

Anon (n.d.), 'Noomi Rapace as Lisbeth Salander', *The Literary Magazine of Swedish Books and Writers/Stieg Larsson*, http://www.stieglarsson.com/noomi-rapace?page=40. Accessed 10 October 2012.

Arnold, R. (2001), *Fashion, Desire and Anxiety: Image and Morality in the Twentieth Century*, New Brunswick, NJ: Rutgers University Press.

Barthes, R. (1983), *The Fashion System* (trans. Matthew Ward and Richard Howard), New York: Hill and Wang.

Benjamin, W. (1999), *The Arcades Project* (trans. Howard Eiland and Kevin McLaughlin), Cambridge, MA: The Belknap Press of Harvard University Press.

Bergin, O. (2011), 'H&M Brings "The Girl with the Dragon Tattoo" Look to the High Street', *The Telegraph*, 26 October, http://fashion.telegraph.co.uk/article/TMG8849972/HandM-brings-The-Girl-With-The-Dragon-Tattoo-look-to-the-high-street.html. Accessed 29 December 2011.

Casadei, M. (2011), 'Trish Summerville for H&M', *Vogue*, 14 December, http://www vogue.it/ en/magazine/daily-news/2011/12/trish-summerville-lisbeth-salander-for-hem. Accessed 29 December 2011.

Cranz, A. (2011), 'Rooney Mara Wouldn't Call Herself a Feminist', *Fempop*, 21 December, http://www.fempop.com/2011/12/21/rooney-mara-wouldnt-call-herself-a-feminist/. Accessed 21 December 2011.

Creeden, M. (2011), 'Breaking Out: Trish Summerville on Her New Collection at H&M—and Dressing *The Girl with the Dragon Tattoo*', *Vogue*, 13 December, http://www.vogue.com/culture/article/breaking-out-trish-summerville-on-her-new-collection-at-hmand-dressing-the-girl-with-the-dragon-tattoo/. Accessed 29 December.

de Beauvoir, S. (1947), *The Ethics of Ambiguity* (trans. Bernhard Frechtman), Secaucus, NJ: Citadel Press.

Eicher, J.B. (2010), 'Encyclopedia Preface', in J.B. Eicher, ed., *Berg Encyclopedia of World Dress and Fashion: Global Perspectives*, Oxford: Berg, pp. xiii–xiv.

Entwistle, J. (2000), *The Fashioned Body: Fashion, Dress, and Modern Social Theory*, Cambridge: Polity Press.

Evans, C. (1997), 'Dreams That Only Money Can Buy…or, the Shy Tribe in Flight from Discourse', *Fashion Theory*, 1:2, pp. 169–88.

Evans, C. (2003), *Fashion at the Edge: Spectacle, Modernity and Deathliness*, New Haven, CT: Yale University Press.

Franich, D. (2011), "The Girl with the Dragon Tattoo" Poster Features Nude Rooney Mara, Curiously Upset Daniel Craig (NSFW)', *Entertainment Weekly*, 8 June, http://insidemovies. ew.com/2011/06/08/girl-dragon-tattoo-nude-poster/. Accessed 25 February 2011.

Gabrielsson, E. (2011), *'There Are Things I Want You to Know' about Stieg Larsson and Me'* (trans. L. Coverdale), New York: Seven Stories Press.

Grossberg, L. (2010), *Cultural Studies in the Future Tense*, Durham, NC: Duke University Press.

Holmberg, J.-H. (2011), 'The Novels You Read Are Not Necessarily the Novels Stieg Larsson Wrote', in D. Burstein, A. de Keijzer and J.-H. Holmberg, eds, *The Tattooed Girl: The Enigma of Stieg Larsson & the Secrets Behind the Most Compelling Thrillers of Our Time*, New York: St. Martin's Griffin, pp. 29–41.

Hook, M.K. (2011), 'Lisbeth Salander as a Gender Outlaw', in R.S. Rosenberg and S. O'Neill, eds, *The Psychology of the Girl with the Dragon Tattoo: Understanding Lisbeth Salander and Stieg Larsson's Trilogy*, Dallas, TX: Smart Pop, pp. 47–64.

Kaiser, S.B. (1997), *The Social Psychology of Clothing: Symbolic Appearances* (2nd ed., revised), New York: Fairchild Publications.

—— (2001), 'Minding Appearances: Style, Truth, and Subjectivity', in J. Entwistle and E. Wilson, eds, *Body Dressing*, Oxford: Berg, pp. 79–102.

Kaiser, S.B., Freeman, C.M. and Chandler, J.L. (1993), 'Favorite Clothes and Gendered Subjectivities: Multiple Readings', *Studies in Symbolic Interaction*, 15, pp. 27–50.

Kierkegaard, S. ([1844] 1981). *The Concept of Anxiety* (trans. Reidar Thomte), Princeton, NJ: Princeton University Press.

Larsson, S. (2009), *The Girl with the Dragon Tattoo* (trans. Reg Keeland), New York: Vintage Crime/Black Lizard.

—— (2010a), *The Girl Who Played with Fire* (trans. Reg Keeland), New York: Vintage Crime/Black Lizard.

Larsson, S. (2010b). *The Girl Who Kicked the Hornet's Nest* (trans. Reg Keeland), New York: Alfred A. Knopf.

Lindgren, A. ([1945] 2007), *Pippi Longstocking* (trans. Tiina Nunnally), London: Viking.

Little, L. (2011), '"The Girl with the Dragon Tattoo" H&M Clothing Line Under Attack', ABC News, 16 December, http://abcnews.go.com/Business/girl-dragon-tattoo-clothing-line-launches-criticism/story?id=15165315#.TwNoY5jlBUQ. Accessed 20 December 2011.

Lo, D. (2011), 'The Girl with the Dragon Tattoo's Lisbeth Salander-Inspired H&M Collection Will Launch December 14th', *Glamour*, 26 October, http://www.glamour.com/fashion/blogs/slaves-to-fashion/2011/10/the-girl-with-the-dragon-tatto.html. Accessed 20 December 2011.

Matheson, L. (2011), 'Divinely Attired', Ph.D. diss., University of California, Davis.

McLaren, P. (2000). 'Paulo Freire's Pedagogy of Possibility', In S.F. Steiner, H.M. Krank, P. McLaren and R. E. Bahruth, eds, *Freirean Pedagogy, Praxis, and Possibilities: Projects for the New Millennium*, New York, NY: Falmer Press, pp. 1–22.

Perseus Digital Library (n.d.),www.perseus.tufts.eduhttp://www.perseus.tufts.edu/hopper/r esolveform?redirect=true&lang=Latin.

Rising, M. (2011), 'Larsson's Partner: "Girl with the Dragon Tattoo" Merchandise Masks Novel's Points', *The Christian Science Monitor*, 21 December, http://www.csmonitor.com/World/Latest-News-Wires/2011/1221/Larsson-s-partner-Girl-with-the-Dragon-Tattoo-merchandise-masks-novel-s-point. Accessed 21 December 2011.

Rodgers, R. and Bui, E. (2011), 'The Body Speaks Louder Than Words: What Is Lisbeth Salander Saying?', In R.S. Rosenberg and S. O'Neill, eds, *The Psychology of the Girl with the Dragon Tattoo: Understanding Lisbeth Salander and Stieg Larsson's Trilogy*, Dallas, TX: Smart Pop, pp. 29–44.

Rosenberg, R.S. (2011), 'Salander as Superhero', in R.S. Rosenberg and S. O'Neill, eds, *The Psychology of the Girl with the Dragon Tattoo: Understanding Lisbeth Salander and Stieg Larsson's Trilogy*, Dallas, TX: Smart Pop, pp. 253–70.

Rosenberg, R.S. and O'Neill, S. (2011), 'Introduction', in R.S. Rosenberg and S. O'Neill, eds, *The Psychology of the Girl with the Dragon Tattoo: Understanding Lisbeth Salander and Stieg Larsson's Trilogy*, Dallas, TX: Smart Pop, pp. 1–5.

Rutledge, P. (2011), 'Resilience with a Dragon Tattoo', in R.S. Rosenberg and S. O'Neill, eds, *The Psychology of the Girl with the Dragon Tattoo: Understanding Lisbeth Salander and Stieg Larsson's Trilogy*, Dallas, TX: Smart Pop, pp. 214–31.

Silverstein, M. (2011), 'The Pornification of Lisbeth Salander', *Indiewire*, 8 June, http://blogs.indiewire.com/womenandhollywood/the_pornification_of_lisbeth_salander#. Accessed 20 December 2011.

Surkan, K. (2012), 'The Girl Who Turned the Tables: A Queer Reading of Lisbeth Salander', in Eric Bronson, ed., *The Girl with the Dragon Tattoo and Philosophy: Everything Is Fire*, Hoboken, NJ: John Wiley & Sons, pp. 33–46.

Tulloch, C. (2010), 'Style-Fashion-Dress: From Black to Post-Black', *Fashion Theory* 14:3, pp. 361–86.

Van Meter, J. (2011), 'Rooney Mara: Playing with Fire', *Vogue*, 17 October, http://www.vogue.com/magazine/article/rooney-mara-playing-with-fire/. Accessed 20 December 2011.

VanZanten, V. (2011), 'Creating Lisbeth: Five Minutes with Costume Designer Trish Summerville', *W Magazine*, 14 February, www.wmagazine.com/w/blogs/editorsblog/2011/02/14/creating-lisbeth-five-minutes.html. Accessed 20 December 2011.

YouTube Commentators (2011), Comments posted in response to Stateofstylechannel (2011), 'ENGLISH: H&M Dragon Tattoo Collection by Trish Summerville', November, 2011, YouTube, www.youtube.com/all_comments?threaded=1&v=1e3OfLUV-Kc. Accessed 10 October 2012.

Notes

1 I am very grateful to Elizabeth (Liz) Constable, my friend and colleague in Women and Gender Studies, for suggesting the *sui generis* terminology to capture Lisbeth Salander's

one-of-a-kind quality. Liz made many other insightful and constructive comments on an earlier draft of this chapter.

2 Many thanks go to Linda Matheson for all of the conversations we have had about clothing's 'plot propelling' role as she was working on her dissertation (Matheson 2011).

3 In an essay on Lisbeth Salander as a superhero, psychologist Robin Rosenberg discusses how the more accurate technical term is 'eidetic imagery'—'the experience of, after looking at a scene or object, being able to conjure up accurately and vividly in the mind's eye an image of what was previously seen'. No memory, she argues, is truly photographic (Rosenberg 2011: 262).

4 I am indebted to my friend and colleague in Women and Gender Studies, Anna Kuhn, for introducing me to Stieg Larsson's novels and the Swedish adaptations, and for many helpful conversations and suggestions throughout this project.

5 McLaren uses 'pedagogy of possibility' to characterize and expand the ideas of Paulo Freire (1921–1997), the Brazilian educator and theorist of critical pedagogy (2000: 1). Such a pedagogy enables a philosophy and politics of liberation through resistance to oppression in everyday life (McLaren 2000: 5).

6 I use 'euromodern' here in the cultural studies sense, as articulated by Lawrence Grossberg. He uses the term to include 'western' European nations and other 'western' nations with European colonial roots (e.g., the United States, Australia, Canada) which share entangled cultural histories and processes of modernization and industrialization. By this usage, he acknowledges that euromodernity is only one of many forms of modernity around the world (Grossberg 2010: 264–65).

7 It is evident from notes in Benjamin's uncompleted book, *The Arcades Project*, that he read Kierkegaard's work. Because Benjamin died before he was able to finish his project, it is impossible to know if Kierkegaard's writing on anxiety influenced Benjamin's thinking about fashion. There are some intriguing parallels, however. Colleagues of Benjamin compiled and edited his notes into the published volume that continues to fascinate and itself serves as a pedagogy of possibility.

8 Larsson also had this quality, according to his life partner, Eva Gabrielsson (2011).

9 This discrepancy between Lisbeth's height and that of fashion models becomes especially evident when considering an image of H&M models, wearing Lisbeth-inspired clothing prior to the release of the Hollywood film. The models surround, and tower over, Trish Summerville, fashion designer/stylist of the Dragon Tattoo clothing line for H&M (Lo 2011).

Chapter 3

Australian Gothic: *Black Light Angels*, Appearance, and Subcultural Style

Vicki Karaminas

A good deal of work has been done on subcultures since Dick Hebdige's landmark *Subculture: The Meaning of Style* ([1979], 1988) situated it as a viable social and aesthetic category. In this seminal text, Hebdige argues that dominant forces of mass media and commerce work to incorporate, regulate, and negotiate subcultural fashion or 'style'. His argument is that subcultures are not authentic because once a 'look', style, or fashion is co-opted into mainstream culture, it loses its resistance through a particular style. According to Hebdige, authenticity of subcultures is to be found at the level of fashion and style. Similarly, in *Resistance through Rituals* ([1975,] 2006), Hall, Jefferson, and Clarke et al. examine and critique themes of negotiation, resistance, and struggle connected to youth subcultures. Subcultures are formed mostly around common leisure-time activities, social rituals, and cultural spaces and are supported by an expression of a subcultural style. This special 'authentic' style consists of dress, music, argot, and rituals, which creates the meaning, forms the identity, and expresses the values of the subculture. Goth identities are fashioned through performance and dress, masks, veils, and disguises, and are a form of subcultural rebellion expressed through style. As Rob Latham wrote of the film *The Lost Boys* (1987), 'consumption…becomes for teens both an avenue of self-expression and also of objectification in the form of fashion' (2002: 67). Although other aspects of gothic subculture, in particular novels and films, are crucial in the formation of gothic identities, visual appearance is perhaps the most important feature.

This chapter examines the work of Sydney-based comic artist Louise Graber, whose fashion illustrations and gothic comic series *Black Light Angels* has been influential among teen goths in Sydney, Australia. Graber (b. 1958) is widely considered to be one of Australia's most intriguing illustrators and icons of fashion. Over the span of thirty years she has produced hundreds of illustrations of pop or rock stars dressed in subcultural styles and eleven self-published comics about an Australian gothic rock group called *Black Light Angels* which have influenced Sydney's gothic subculture for the last nine years. Since childhood, Graber cultivated a distinct illustrative style from watching television involving bold, black character outlines and block colored fills she calls moving stained-glass images. Later, in school, she drew animation-inspired cartoons of her friends in the margins of her books and continued her passion at art college where her interest in the genre was often criticized. During a long period working for Australian music magazine *Countdown* in the 1980s, Graber became intrigued by pop and rock stars and their styles of dress. Graber learned quickly to respond in illustration to requests she received by readers to draw cartoon versions of stars such as Tom Cruise, Spandau Ballet or Madonna. It is this era of her life where, as a comic artist, she became commercially popular and refined her attention not just in identifying the markers of narcissistic and androgynous rock stars but also to the signifiers of fashion that sets rock and pop musicians apart from the everyday and the production of characters or personas that have a chaotically activist, subcultural sense of themselves. Stardom itself is a trope throughout *Black Light Angels* and Graber tentatively admits that one of the characters (Edward) is based on Hollywood actor Johnny Depp while another scene within the series depicts a character mocking another for imitating Robert Smith, lead singer of The Cure.

Throughout her time at *Countdown*, Graber began moving toward a physical style for herself. Half Japanese, half German, Graber favored wearing gothic fashion, including black material, fluorescent nails, and crosses and chains. She frequented Sydney's Club 77 in King's Cross and various Newtown gothic underground clubs and established a reputation as a style social influencer, which continues today.

In 1997 Graber created the set of X-rated comix, which she referred to as B.L.A.cK (*Black Light Angels*), following a group of gothic musicians touring Australia with a vampire as the lead, a dingo drummer, and a Tasmanian devil guitarist as band members. The characters themselves—vampires, mortals, fairies, and half-human creatures—clearly draw on Graber's knowledge of the fantastic and fictitious lives of pop stardom, and at the same time, epitomizes the elite, immortal allure of gothic fantasy. Much of the storyline is based around the bored antics of the group and their relationships with fans and the road crew while the vampiric lead singer takes 'groupies' and turns them into 'the living dead' after consensual sex.

The plot of *Black Light Angels* is, of course, familiar to narratives of gothic literature: The hero, Damien Violette, is the charismatic lead singer of the musical band Krucifiction; he has a group of devoted and faithful followers (Sapphire, Amethyst, and Emilye Blackthorn); he undergoes various trials and tribulations, only to escape mortality and live among earthlings as a vampire, crossing the lines of gender and blurring the boundaries of heterosexuality. Damien Violette is thus *divine*.

Gothic Subcultural Style

Although it is difficult to place when the term *gothic* as a subcultural identity emerged, it is evident that it began to gather currency in the 1970s and the early 1980s with the 'underground' successes of music bands such as Bauhaus, Siouxsie and the Banshees, and Joy Division. Gothic subculture is anchored in music and dress, both equally 'melancholic and haunting' in their styles and characteristic themes: sensibility, imprisonment, spectrality, haunting, madness, and the grotesque. The most notable feature of the subculture is the various styles of dress worn by its adherents. Gothic fashion can be characterized by artificiality and ornament rather than naturalism. Garments are restrictive, heavily layered, and often accompanied by elaborately twisted or styled hair. The color-ways tend to be

Figure 3:1. Victorian and Edwardian style dress funeral attire.
Black Light Angels, 1999.

predominately black or violet and are associated with mid-Victorian and early Edwardian funeral attire (Figure 3:1).

In her book *Seeing through Clothes*, fashion theorist Anne Hollander argues that the Romantic man wore black to establish his remoteness. It was a style with strong literary connections, which marked him as a 'fatal man'. For Hollander the fatal man was 'specifically connected with spiritual unrest and personal solitude [and in league with]…a dark power that exempted him from the responsibilities of common feeling and experience' (1993: 56). Red was also a popular color in the construction of gothic sartorial identities because of its association to blood and sexuality. The Victorian era style detailing on masculine and feminine garments include boning in corsets, lace-up bodices and 'pirate' shirts, hook-and-eye fasteners, cone hats, top hats, and long, mid-length capes. The shapes created by women's attire in particular echo those of Gothic Revival architecture, almost suggesting that it is compiled from parts of a church. Cosmetics are also used to achieve the particular 'death look' associated with the gothic mode—pale, white skin, black kohl eyeliner, and black nail polish.

Like all subcultural styles, the gothic genre constitutes a *bricolage* of objects and signs appropriated from commodities symbolically reassembled to erase and subvert its original meaning. In this way, gothics, or 'goths' can be said to be functioning as *bricoleurs* when they appropriate a long evening coat and top hat, the conventional insignia of Victorian middle-class respectability with objects from other subcultures, such as metallic studded belts and wrist cuffs from punk and rock culture, dreadlocks from Rastafarianism, or hair feathers and 'pirate' shirts from the New Romantics of the 1980s. In this way, the original meaning of respectability and compliance with authority is erased and replaced by resistance to middle-class values. Similarly, what qualifies as gothic fashion changes, depending on the historical context—gothic style in the early 1970s differs in various ways from the gothic mode of the twenty-first century, which tends to fuse elements of a futuristic, cyber warrior sensibility (Figure 3:2). As Robert Mighall has argued in a different context, 'Gothic cannot be an essence, for what is Gothic, constantly changes' (1999: 25). In a similar vein, in an interview with the *New Musical Express*, the musician Nick Cave emphasized the longevity of the

Figure 3:2. Graber (center) with gothic fans, Animania Expo, Sydney, 2005.

gothic genre and its ideas, predicting that goths would be only one of two surviving species following a nuclear war, the other being the cockroach, known for its radiation-proof body.

Gothic fashion trends and style features heavily in *Black Light Angels* and Graber's illustrations are meticulous and innovative in design; from one character's court jester headwear to the striped socks, loop-knitted tops, and safety-pinned outfits of others. 'There is a lot of reference through the series on Goth fashion and accessories,' says Graber, describing her resources in creating the outfits for her characters, 'It was like a Toulouse Lautrec situation, where you sit in a corner of a club and observe this wonderfully rich scene to play in' (Karaminas, 2006). Graber spends close to three hours illustrating each frame, focusing on the feeling and paying high priority to the details of the garments, hearkening back to her days as an illustrator for *Countdown*, where fashion was one of the defining features of a rock star. At the end of each booklet in the series, Graber includes several fashion illustrations; dramatis personae, which serve as fashion editorials and have been treated as such by Sydney's gothic scene, many of whom write to Graber and profess their love for a character or ask her questions on the origins of her fashion ideas. Indeed, the intricate cloth patterns she interpolates between illustrations, the chain details, woolen sweaters, and flannel shirts brings to mind a cross between Australian grunge, slick 1980s pop fashion and '*Blade Runner*' gothic style.

In terms of a subcultural style, the flannel shirt, or the 'flanny' as it is called in the Australian vernacular, has always been associated with being a 'Westie', a label used to describe someone who has grown up in the outer western suburbs of Sydney in a working-class family. The flannel shirt also has its roots in the anti-fashion Grunge look of the early 1990s, considered a harsh, understated reaction by disaffected youth to the grandeur of the 1980s. The depiction of the flannelette shirt in *Black Light Angels*, influenced by Graber's youth spent in Canberra, is intended to evoke the sexless and studiously nonchalant attitude of its characters. 'Yes, the "flanny" probably comes from my teenage years spent in Canberra,' she says,

> It was suburban and we always tied our shirts and jumpers in knots around our waist. I didn't own a 'flanny' for a long time until I picked one up. I realized that it was a classic dress item. I believe that when the 'ie' is added to an item of dress then it becomes a classic, like the knitted woolen cap known [in Australia] as the 'beanie'. (Karaminas, 2006)

The Australian Sublime

It is the second part of the series that is arguably the closest to Graber's experimental style, depicting the group driving their tour bus which accidentally drives off the side of a cliff into a dry riverbed, initiating within them complete sexual abandon and the awakened realization that the afterlife is episodic and incessant.

The dry riverbed scene—called 'Mystik Laeke'—is pivotal to the storyline due to the characters emerging from the afterlife facing, as vampires must, the endlessness of eternal life and bringing to mind the heightened need for pop stars to chase amusement as well as the darker, more disquieting understanding of the gothic subculture in which Graber is immersed. Traditionally associated with grotesqueness, savageness,[1] and enclosed spaces, such as caves, burial vaults, and ancestral homes, the term 'gothic' itself seems to bear no initial relation to the desert. Gothic was once a style of medieval architecture [2] and gave its name to an eighteenth-century fictional genre typified by a fascination with darkness, horror, sexuality, tragedy, and the supernatural. Yet, the dismay evoked by being killed yet alive, or otherwise interpreted as being 'buried alive' in the salt plain of 'Mystik Laeke' (Figure 3:3) serves for Graber's readers, to heighten the scene's claustrophobia and acts as a landscape of imprisonment for the rest of the series.

Figure 3:3. Mystik Laeke, *Black Light Angels*, 1999.

The visual interpretation of the 'laeke' is, as Graber indicates, based on a combination of influences such as Lake George in Canberra, which is now dry; winding roads from her memory through lakes and mountains, and the morning mist in the Blue Mountains of New South Wales, which acts to enhance the deadening panic caused by being stranded in the Australian outback. In his introduction to *The Oxford Book of Gothic Tales*, Chris Baldick cites as important aspects of gothic, 'a fearful sense of inheritance in time with a claustrophobic sense of enclosure in space, these two dimensions reinforcing each other to produce an impression of sickening descent into disintegration' (2001: 89). In one particular scene (issue 7), the reader encounters Edward, a young apprentice from the Department of Death whose job it is to place a Post-it note on the foreheads of the deceased with the word 'DEAD' written on it. With a clear play on 'black irony' and 'comedy noir', Graber injects humor into the scene, without utterly removing the readers' sense of trepidation and conflicted reality. In another scene (from issue 7), two featured characters—'Gabe' and 'Joolz'—are shown draped over each other, lifeless. The two never make it to the afterlife and the reader is left wondering why, after a joyful courtship and partnership, the apprentice did not tag the two. As a literary form or, in this case, graphic novel form, the gothic mode emphasises the horror, uncertainty and desperation of the human experience, often representing the solitariness of that experience through characters trapped in a hostile environment, or pursued by an unspecified or unidentifiable danger.

Graber describes the experience of the Australian desert both in *Black Light Angels* and in reality 'as open yet alienating spaces with this incredible emptiness and blinding light. The thought of being lost is very powerful' (Karaminas, 2006). Her emphasis on intense light is a major theme of the entire series, indicated primarily in the light that spasms from the thoughts of the characters. Intense light is also in Graber's barren Australian outback, which makes *Black Light Angels* a distinctly Australian gothic tale. Such intense light is not uniquely Australian as such, but signifies as Australian if placed in a binary relationship to the less intense English and northern European light. This is the case with many claims of art or objects considered uniquely Australian, even without direct comparison: the dry scorching heat, the dust, the red desert earth, flatness and wide, open spaces. This apparent distinctiveness could be considered a binary function that prioritizes the English and European construction of a gothic imaginary as cold and dark. In his examination of Australian Gothic culture, Turcotte states that 'The Antipodes was a world of reversals, the dark subconscious of Britain. It was for all intents and purposes, *Gothic par excellence*, the dungeon of the world' (1998: 22). It is precisely this sense of isolation, of being imprisoned by the desert's spatial immensity, that Graber successfully traps her characters and creates, for the reader, an unpredictable world as horrific as being imprisoned by walls.

Since colonization, or even before British settlement in 1788, Australia had been constructed and imagined as a place that contained fear and the unknown. To explorers and botanists, it was a land occupied by exotic fauna and flora, populated with strange and bizarre creatures. As the early settlers struggled to domesticate the wild shores, their European gaze considered Australian land a *terra nullius*[3]—a land awaiting their inscription. In their eyes, the eucalyptus and gum trees were empty signifiers in a bleak and indeterminate landscape. Bushrangers, devils, and witch doctors lived in the bush, spirits and ghosts dwelt in the trees, and with the transportation of convicts[4] its darkness was confirmed. It is perhaps for this reason, argues Turcotte, 'that the Gothic as a mode has been a consistent presence in Australia since European settlement' (1998: 2).

To Graber, the landscape of Australia is gothic. As she describes it, miles of black bitumen roads wind and wrap themselves like serpents around arid mountains. Cliffs drop into bottomless sandy lakes and the characters themselves—a rock band consisting of half-human hybrids, a vampire lead singer, a dingo[5] drummer, a Tasmanian devil,[6] and a fellatio-loving horse—reflect the darker aspects of gothic sensibility as they traverse and transgress the boundaries of hetero-normative behavior. 'Naturally, neither gender ambiguity nor being dead in any way inhibits more or less continuous sexual activity by virtually all the characters in any of these strips', writes Joan Kerr about *Black Light Angels*, and points out, that 'androgyny is just one more sign of the artist's refusal to conform to any known ethical, moral, sexual, or other standard imposed by conventional society' (1999: 89).

In some respects, Graber's work can be read as within the framework of resistance to middle-class values and the means of production (Figure 3:4), but also to dominant forms

Figure 3:4. Fuck the System, *Black Light Angels*, 1999.

of representation and appearance—gender, race, age, and ethnicity (Figure 3:5). Graber intentionally sets out to subvert the power invested in these traditional discourses by blurring the boundaries between masculinity and femininity, young and old, white and black. 'Real life is weird enough', she says, 'but genders, names, hair, clothes or subcultures have been changed to protect the innocent' (Karaminas, 2006).

Figure 3:5. *Black Light Angels,* 1999.

In her analysis of Graber's work, Kerr comments on the innocent sexless look of most of the 'living dead' characters in *Black Light Angels*. 'The fact that [there is a] male protagonist may suggest that the archetype hasn't changed, but it is worth noting, that [its] representation [is] actually quite androgynous' (1999:55) (Figure 3:6). In this dark utopia, Graber creates an imaginary space where hybrid characters, mixtures of human and animal, become so entwined that they cannot be split. In this way, *Black Light Angels* challenges and breaks down the old dualisms of Western thinking like the mind/body split, Self/Other, male/female, reality/appearance, lightness/darkness, and life/death, and produces a reality void of the systems of myth and meanings structuring Western culture.

Figure 3:6. Androgynous characters in *Black Light Angels*, 1999.

Graber's Descent

In some ways, *Black Light Angels* could be described as a visual interpretation of aspects of Sydney's gothic culture as its narrative comprises three key elements found in the majority of subcultural formations: a style of music, a mode of dress, and a geographically located 'scene'. In Sydney, goths meet at Wake the Dead, or Die Maschine in the inner city suburb of Surry Hills. DJ's Slaughter, Voodoo and Ether focus on goth music, deathrock, industrial, and electrogoth, with a hint of dark alternative. There are no live bands and plasma screens show music video clips as crowds of goths lounge on comfortable couches, play pool, or grind their bodies to popular gothic beats. The boundaries of *Black Light Angels* are also set around familiar goth locales in Sydney such as Enmore, Newtown, and Glebe, with favorite 'scenes' like Black Market Night Club, Mortuary Station and Wentworth Park. In a one sense, the precincts serve to legitimize the construction and maintenance as a gothic comic for its readership. This is also achieved by Graber's experimentation with different methods, such as German woodblock and the use of 'splash panels'. There is also a subtle anime and shojo sensibility in her graphic style and the lightness and thickness of the lines tend to lean toward a more manga aesthetic that merges with Japanese woodblock art.

Graber herself is a gothic character, delighting in wearing the 'dark' melancholic styles of fashion and listening to the hard-driving sound of Australian goth/pop band Effigy, and dark Britpop bands Placebo, Manson, Suede, and Blur. Having self-published the eleven issues of the *Black Light Angels* series, she continues to involve herself in influencing fashion's underground both in wearing and overseeing the graphic branding of Sydney's Serpentine fashion store in Newtown. Her website depicts a few of her illustrations but it is her *Black Light* series which has recently and perhaps unwittingly emerged as Sydney's critical guide to gothic street fashion. The comics are subsequently only available at comic conventions and subcultural manga and animation events like the Artists' Alley at the Supanova Pop Culture Expos held throughout Australia.

She favors the offbeat, quirky style of American film director, writer, and designer Tim Burton and the exaggerated style of his characters, which always retain their serious human characteristics. She values all things fluorescent and enlightened with ultra-violet radiation which, although unable to be successfully depicted in a black-and-white comic, is part of the surreal environment she creates throughout the series. Subjective experience is paramount for Graber, though she adamantly rejects the belief that everything has an inherent meaning. Any existential angst is dealt with by partaking of liquorice and ice cream. *Black Light Angels* is Graber's manifesto as a comic artist. 'Inspired by the punkiness of *Sick Puppy Comix*', says Graber, 'terrified by my slow descent into the unconsciousness of daytime television and disgusted with the grunge that surrounded me, I decided to fuse everything that I ever fancied into one small, personal, obsessive, indulgent wank of a comic' (Karaminas, 2006).

Regarding the characters themselves, the faces of Graber's 'angels', as she calls them, are innocent and dreamy, pale and translucent, yet sexually charged and erotic in their playfulness. Eternally hovering between realism and fantasy, the androgynous characters converge onto nightclubs and bars (Figure 3:7), ready to dance, talk, drink, and have sex. The array of styles goths identify as 'gothic' can be applied to *Black Light Angels*: it is dark (although there is humor, optimism, and insight), the characters court a vampiric aesthetic and they portray the 'death look'—pale, white skin, black eyeliner, and black nail polish. In his analysis of the Australian small press, comic artist and academic Michael Hill states that many Australian comic artists situated in Sydney, Melbourne, and Brisbane have chosen to represent subcultures in their work. Drawing on the dark humor of Louise Graber's *Black Light Angels*, Hill comments on her style as, 'gothic romanticism drawn in bold but elegant form with considerable attention to costume details' (2000: 45). It is perhaps clear then that Graber's desire for alternative ways of being takes expression in her characters appropriation of gothic attire as a means of producing nonconformist identities through oppositional dress.

Figure 3:7. Club 77 advertisement poster *Black Light Angels*, 1999.

Conclusion

Black Light Angels is a tale where Australian landscape, fashion, architecture, and climate bleed into one. Dark forests and salty lakes, winding tunnels, misty mountains, moonlight, and towering cliffs—from such materials does Graber frame her gothic fable. In her work we encounter vampires and hybrid creatures obsessed with death and morbidity, eroticism and decay, and possessing a predatory sexuality. They remain, however, innocent and optimistic in their dealings. Despite the series popularity, B.L.A.cK continues to play an active role in the underground gothic scene, balancing on the creative edge of mainstream commercialism and the Australian 'small press'. As an admired comic among young Sydney goths, *Black Light Angels* marks a discursive space where subcultural identity and its products (music, fashion, argot) are negotiated and redefined.

References

Baldick, C. (2001), *The Oxford Book of Gothic Tales*, Oxford, London.

Cave, N. 1996. Interview, *New Musical Express*, January 27.

Graber, L. (1999), 'Black Light Angels Review', *Stu*, 3, Goodwill Festival Productions.

—— (1998), *Black Light Angels*, 1, Graber Hill, Gravity Press, Sydney, Australia.

—— (1999a), *Black Light Angels,* 2, February, Graber Hill, Gravity Press, Sydney, Australia.

—— (1999b), *Black Light Angels*, 3, September, Graber Hill, Gravity Press, Sydney, Australia.

—— (1999c), Black Light Angels, *Black Light Angels Comik*, 4, October, Graber Hill, Gravity Press, Sydney, Australia.

—— (1999d), 'Black Light Angels', *Black Light Angels Comik*, 5, November, Graber Hill, Gravity Press, Sydney, Australia.

—— (1999e), 'Long Black Shorts', *Black Light Angels Comik*, 6, Graber Hill, Gravity Press, Sydney, Australia.

—— (1999f), 'Angst and Ankhs', *Black Light Angels Comik*, 7, Graber Hill, Gravity Press, Sydney, Australia.

—— (1999g), 'Little Black Book', *Black Light Angels Comik*, 8, Graber Hill, Gravity Press, Sydney, Australia.

—— (2000), 'Black Light Angels', *Black Light Angels Comik*, 9, December, Graber Hill, Gravity Press, Sydney, Australia.

—— (2002), 'Black Light Angels', *Black Light Angels Comik*, 10, October, Graber Hill, Gravity Press, Sydney, Australia.

—— (2003), 'Black Light Angels', *Black Light Angels Comik*, 11, April, Graber Hill, Gravity Press, Sydney, Australia.

Hall, Jefferson, and Clarke et al. ([1975,] 2006), *Resistance through Rituals*, London: Taylor and Francis.

Hebdige, D. (1988), *Subculture: The Meaning of Style,* London: Routledge.

Hill, M. (2000), 'Outside Influence/Local Color: The Australian Small Press', *International Journal of Comic Art,* 2.1, Spring, pp. 117–32.

Hodkinson, P. (2002), *Goth: Identity, Style, and Subculture,* New York: Berg.

Hollander, A. (1993), *Seeing through Clothes,* Berkeley: University of California Press.

Karaminas, V (2006), Interview with Louise Graber Sydney, Australia, July 22.

Kerr, J. (1999), *Artists and Cartoonists in Black and White: The Most Public Art,* Sydney: Southwood Press.

Latham, R. (2002), *Consuming Youth: Vampires, Cyborgs, and the Culture of Consumption,* Chicago: University of Chicago Press.

Martindale, A. (1974), *Gothic Art,* London: Thames and Hudson.

Mighall, R. (1999), *A Geography of Victorian Gothic Fiction: Mapping History's Nightmares,* Oxford: Oxford University Press.

Myrone, M, ed., and Frayling, C., consultant ed. (2006), *The Gothic Reader: A Critical Anthology,* London: Tate Publishing.

Ruskin. J. (2005), 'The Nature of Gothic', in *On Art and Life,* London: Penguin.

Smith, B., ed. (1975), *Documents on Art and Taste in Australia: The Colonial Period, 1770–1914,* Melbourne: Oxford University Press.

Turcotte, G (2009) *Peripheral Fear: Transformations of the Gothic in Canadian and Australian Fiction,* Peter Lang Australia.

Westwood, C. (2005), 'Japanese Manga Artist Vivienne To Is but One of Many Females Now Working in a Previously Male Dominated Medium', *Pavement,* Autumn.

Notes

1 See Ruskin, J, 'The Nature of Gothic', in On Art and Life, London: Penguin, p.5.

2 Ruskin believed that the signs of Venetian spiritual decline appear in the city's movement from Gothic to Renaissance architectural styles. In 'The Nature of Gothic', which provides the ideological core of *The Stones of Venice* (1853), Ruskin argues that because the Gothic style permits and even demands the freedom, individuality, and spontaneity of its workers, it both represents a finer, more moral society and means of production and also results in greater architecture than does the Renaissance style, which enslaves the working man.

3 The Latin expression '*terra nullius*' derives from Roman Law and means 'no man's land', i.e., 'empty land'. When European colonizers first arrived in Australia they encountered an unfamiliar land occupied by people and a land 'ownership' system that they didn't understand. As such, Australia was deemed to be '*terra nullius*' and the British sovereign crown claimed the land. *Terra nullius* was recently overturned by the Australian High Court through the Native Title Act of 1993, commonly known as the 'Mabo' decision.

4 After the loss of the American colonies in the 1780s, Britain needed to take the population of its overcrowded prisons (full mainly due to the unemployment created by the Industrial

Revolution) to a penal colony. As such, the British Crown colony of New South Wales started with the establishment of a settlement and penal colony at Port Jackson by Captain Arthur Phillip on 26 January 1788.

5 The 'dingo' is commonly described as an Australian wild dog, but is not restricted to Australia. Modern dingoes are found throughout Southeast Asia, mostly in small pockets of remaining natural forest, and in mainland Australia, particularly in the north. They have features in common with both wolves and modern dogs, and are regarded as ancestors of modern dogs. The word 'dingo' comes from the language of the Eora Aboriginal people, who were the original inhabitants of the Sydney area. Another name for the dingo is 'warrigal'.

6 The 'Tasmanian devil' is a carnivorous marsupial now found only in the Australian island state of Tasmania. The size of a small dog, but stocky and muscular, the Tasmanian devil is the largest carnivorous marsupial in the world. It is characterized by its black fur, offensive odor when stressed, extremely loud and disturbing screech, and viciousness when feeding. It is known to both hunt prey and scavenge carrion and although it is usually solitary, it sometimes eats with other devils. The Tasmanian devil became extinct on the Australian mainland about four hundred years before European settlement in 1788. Because they were seen as a threat to livestock in Tasmania, devils were hunted until 1941, when they became officially protected. Since the late 1990s devil facial tumor disease has reduced the devil population significantly and now threatens the survival of the species, which may soon be listed as endangered.

Chapter 4

Fashionable Addiction: The Path to Heroin Chic

Alphonso D. McClendon

Introduction

At the end of the twentieth century, drug use was accentuated as a cultural influence in mass media channels including print, television, film, and radio. The convergence of narcotic representations gave birth to heroin chic, an extreme appearance and manner of dress appropriated by sectors of the fashion industry. Models exhibiting blackened eyes, disheveled coifs, and loosely draped garments characterized the emaciated aesthetic. The allure of the shocking style was disseminated in fashion magazines and runway presentations. Programmed in this visual identity were stereotypical traits of a heroin addict. In his scholarship on heroin, Francis Moraes (2000: 39) argued that attributes of being thin, dazed, and unkempt were misleading accounts of a junkie. Nonetheless, these traits were blatantly featured in fashion advertising of the 1990s as suggestive of heroin chic. Thus the trend, which countered the 1980s 'Just Say No' anti-drug campaign, was subversive in the eyes of local government officials and the president of the United States (Wren 1997). In an effort to calm the tide, Fern Mallis, executive director of the Council of Fashion Designers of America, stated that 'drugs are not fashionable and we want to make sure that nobody in the fashion industry thinks that it's the case' (Wren 1997). The debate around heroin chic style and the realities of drug use in the United States established a discourse concerning the relationship of fashion and drug addiction.

There has been a narrative of narcotics in American popular culture. Narcotics are one of the five classes of drugs regulated by the Controlled Substances Act (CSA) in the United States. Classified as a Schedule I substance under the (CSA), 21 U.S.C. § 812, heroin has 'a high potential for abuse, no currently accepted medical use in treatment in the United States, and a lack of accepted safety for use under medical supervision' (Drug Enforcement Administration 2012a). Fifty years prior to heroin chic, the consumption of heroin was shrouded by users and demonized by the law. Jazz performers, such as Billie Holiday, Charlie Parker, Miles Davis, Gerry Mulligan, Chet Baker, and Anita O'Day, navigated a decade of heroin popularity during the 1940s bebop and 1950s cool jazz movements (Spencer 2002: 124). 'There was a lot of dope around the music scene and a lot of musicians were deep into drugs, especially heroin,' asserts Miles Davis in his autobiography (Davis and Troupe 1989: 129). Contrary to the 1990s fashion trend of imitating the effects of heroin, jazz artists of the mid-century rejected associations to heroin use. Newspaper headlines named and shamed. In 1947, one news service heralded 'Singer Billie Holiday Jailed as Dope Victim' (Associated Press 1947), and the *Long Beach Independent* declared 'Anita O'Day Convicted'

(Anon 1953). O'Day described the enduring label: 'Once you have the reputation of being an addict, it's hard to shake' (O'Day and Eells 1989: 124). More so, those convicted of drug offences were subject to supervision, which threatened their ability to perform. Following a guilty plea of possessing narcotics, Holiday was warned by a Philadelphia judge that any violation of probation would result in her return to Philadelphia for penalty (Anon 1958). The early regulation of heroin in the United States created a stigma that was intensified by the legal system and news coverage. Hence, the avoidance of heroin association was in contrast to the heroin chic style that amplified a relationship. The style adoption of heroin traits demonstrated 'fiction in fashion', where the production of fantasy in images had powerful meaning with social implications (Gledhill 2007: 342).

Historical Background

The linking of drug use to fashion, whether it be clothes or music, is nothing new. In the 1940s the *New York Times* published stories that claimed that listening to bebop music fostered drug use. An article on hearings of proposed 'drug' clinics states: 'instances of narcotics used had been detected in the hall during the past year when concerts of "bebop" music were held there' (Weaver 1951). On 26 April 1955, the *New York Times* reported that a member of a Commission on Narcotic Drugs 'remarked that there seemed to be a definite connection between increased marijuana smoking and "that form of entertainment known as bebop and rebop"'. These early accounts reflect the treatment that would be apparent with heroin chic and fashion, where underlying circumstances triggering drug consumption are underrepresented in the negative coverage.

Bebop possesses another parallel with heroin chic, that being, its birth and maturity during a time of political conflict. World War II was followed by the African-American struggle for social equality—it was an era of frustration and anti-establishment attitude. American optimism of the 1980s turned to fear and cynicism in the 1990s after the U.S. involvement in the Gulf War, and the bombings of the World Trade Center and the Murrah Federal Building in Oklahoma City. The fashion world's adoption of illegal substance imagery suggests the need for escapism and reflects a culture's pessimism and despair. As Patrizia Calefato's work on body transformations posits, heroin chic is a 'grotesque image' containing exaggeration and multiple meanings (2004: 30).

Fiction in Fashion

Jazz artists such as Anita O'Day, Billie Holiday, and Miles Davis utilized dress to shield their heroin habit. Dress is defined as 'an assemblage of body modifications and/or supplements displayed by a person in communicating with other human beings' (Roach-Higgins and Eicher 1992: 1) According to French philosopher Roland Barthes, dress is 'a strong form of meaning' that informs a 'relation between a wearer and their group' (2006: 10). Davis described how his use affected his clothing during his years of heroin addiction: 'where I used to be a fashion-plate dresser, now I was wearing anything that would cover my body' (Davis and Troupe 1989: 143). Concealment was essential for the addict: 'policemen routinely would make me roll up my shirtsleeves, looking for fresh needle marks' (Davis and Troupe 1989: 163).

Since the nineteenth century, tuxedos, suits, and elegant evening gowns were established stage fashion for entertainers. Such formal attire dress reflects that 'clothing could signal social distinctions' as practiced by aristocrats, who altered their dress to distinguish them from the middle class (Barthes 2006: 23). The fashionable dress of the upper class was heightened by pre-Code Hollywood films, swing orchestras, and Harlem nightclubs. From 1910 to 1950, 'wearing one's wealth on one's back' became an elite status aesthetic imitated by less affluent segments of the population (Davis 1994: 58). Formal dressing among jazz artists negated the drug-addict media representations. In recounting his dress and appearance on stage, Miles Davis alluded to the desire for admiration, also the requisite of formal clothing. 'We were up there in our processes (chemically straightened hair) and I had my suits out of the pawnshop, so you couldn't tell me we weren't doing it' (Davis and Troupe 1989: 158). This statement demonstrates Hurlock's thesis that recognition from the stage offers 'widespread popularity and prestige' (1929: 115), especially when buttressed by fashion.

Billie Holiday wore long gloves during the 1940s—it is commonly believed the gloves concealed heroin track marks (Kliment 1990: 77). Pianist Carl Drinkard described another of Holiday's concealment tactics: 'She carried a kerchief on stage, chiffon in a colour to match her gown, to cover the needle marks in her hands…' (Clarke 2002: 391). Thus, the gloves and kerchiefs were both disguise and upper-class fashion accessories. Holiday was meticulous in her appearance; she wore fur coats, turbans, embellished gowns, and ornate jewelry. These expensive and striking adornments reinforced a jazz star's status, and distanced them from the tag of narcotic user. On 22 January 1949, following an arrest on narcotics charges, Holiday was photographed at the San Francisco booking wearing a shawl collar mink, high-knotted turban, and aviator sunglasses (Kliment 1990: 89). This representation included two components of a sign established by Swiss linguist Ferdinand de Saussure, according to Roland Barthes (1973: 35). The signifier or material thing in the photograph consists of Holiday's fur coat. Affluence and refined behavior are the 'mental representations' or signifiers of this item (Barthes 1973: 42–47). The fashionable appearance of Holiday contested the drug arrest and exhibited the merger of celebrity-fantasy and narcotic involvement. When Holiday was recorded in the mid-1950s with her arms visibly marked and her face bloated, the perception of fame and glamour was directly challenged (Clarke 2002: 148–49). The peak of heroin trouble for Billie Holiday was recognizable in a photo of her leaving a Philadelphia jail in February 1956 (Kliment 1990: 97) (Figure 4:1). In the image, Holiday, with a leashed Chihuahua leading the way, exits a holding area with her head hung low. A cigarette accents the hand that camouflages her anguished face. Holiday wears a stylish suit with poet sleeves, shawl collar, and narrow skirt; all have been

Figure 4:1: Billie Holiday, 1956. Holiday and her Chihuahua leaving a
Philadelphia jail after her arrest for possession and use of narcotic drugs.
Note the merger of fashion and distress. Corbis Images.

rumpled during the detention. In the background, an official traces her footsteps. The photo
demonstrates the concept of heroin chic style, where unnatural glamour is presented in a
shadowy setting and drug-related distress is expressed by the subject.

Through colorful quotes in her autobiography, Anita O'Day exemplifies a comparable
approach: 'Going the glamour route—long white gloves, champagne-blonde hair, etc.—
was my way of countering my reputation as a user' (O'Day and Eells 1989: 160–61).
Hurlock posits this behavior in *The Psychology of Dress* as an avoidance of social

disapproval (1929: 41), performed here by concealing attributes of drug addiction. More so, the singer's statement attests to the deception necessary to perform in music venues of the 1940s, as O'Day declares: 'I may have looked straight to casual observers, but three quarters of the time I was higher than a kite' (O'Day and Eells 1989: 160–61). O'Day and Holiday were users of heroin, an opiate that 'is processed from morphine, a naturally occurring substance extracted from the seed pod of certain varieties of poppy plants' (Drug Enforcement Administration 2012b). For efficiency, heroin is injected into the circulatory system for quick delivery to the brain. Its effects include euphoria, constricted pupils, and respiratory depression (Moraes 2000: 3–6).

Male musicians such as Charlie Parker, Miles Davis, Dexter Gordon, and Gerry Mulligan experienced the narcotic trend that influenced the genre of modern jazz. In the 1940s, Parker, an innovative alto-saxophone player with a well-known heroin habit (Giddins and DeVeaux 2009: 317), and other male members of the Earl Hines band observed the law of clean and tidy dress (Gourse 1994: 23). With particular attention to fashion, Parker sported a wavy coif and wore bow ties and stylish business suits—as documented by the photography of Herman Leonard (Houston and Bagert 2006: 130–33). Made in stripe or Glen plaid patterns, his suits had broad shoulders, peak lapels, and tapered pants. Parker, despite his heroin addiction, attempted to maintain the integrity of traditional men's dress. Miles Davis recalls the time Parker 'pawned his suit to get some heroin' (Davis and Troupe 1989: 65), and so he had to borrow Davis's suit for a performance. As Colin McDowell (1997: 158) ascertained in *The Man of Fashion*, the striped suit was a 'symbol of reliability and conformity'. Reasonably, the wearing of the suit on stage cloaked Parker's action of forfeiting clothes related to his heroin addiction. Attractive and formal fashion had the ability to shield artists from drug demonization. On the other hand disheveled hair, messy clothes, bruised limbs, excessive sweat, and nodding were markers of dependence. Frederick Spencer succinctly notes that 'the thread of substance abuse is inextricably woven into the fabric of jazz' (2002: 247).

Regardless of the appearance techniques that artists used to conceal addiction, the dangers of heroin and alcohol were unavoidable, as evidenced by the deaths of Charlie Parker, Lester Young, and Billie Holiday in the 1950s. Artie Shaw notes that, 'jazz music… was born in the whisky bottle, nourished on the marijuana cigarette, and is now dying from heroin' (Atwood 1953: 22).

Demonizing Drug Addiction

In 1949, following confiscation of narcotics on airplanes and ocean liners, the *New York Times* declared 'Seizures Reach Peak in Heroin and Cocaine'. This headline summarized the outcome of governmental laws that commenced at the start of the century. Primarily, the Smoking Opium Exclusion Act of 1909, the Heroin Act of 1924, and the Marihuana Tax Act of 1937 were instrumental in curtailing drug practice in the United States (Keel 2010). These laws controlled or banned the manufacture, distribution, and use of specific substances.

Prior to the 1900s, a less regulated period demonstrated the circulation of opium and cocaine, with little federal oversight. These substances were included in patent medicines that offered cures for numerous ailments (Anon 2010). Around 1899, Bayer, a German pharmaceutical company, manufactured diacetylmorphine and sold it under the brand name heroin (Askwith 1998). Heroin was advertised to relieve and sedate coughs in Bayer product materials. This benefit came from the chemical's ability to depress the respiratory system (Moraes 2000: 6). It is acknowledged that consumers were not fully educated on the 'potentially addictive and deadly ingredients' contained in these formulas (Anon 2010). The regulation of narcotics and the restriction of certain substances for medical purposes contributed to a negative association of heroin by designating it harmful.

Societal fear around substance addiction was strongly contextualized by President Franklin D. Roosevelt in the 1930s. Warning of America's crime problem that was leading to social disorder, Roosevelt explicitly commented on weak laws that were unable to impede the trafficking of illegal drugs (Anon 1934). This danger was further discussed four months later. To persuade states to pass uniform anti-narcotic legislation, Roosevelt invoked the words 'narcotic drug evil', as detailed in the *New York Times* on 22 March 1935. The letter read over the radio described a nation that was not being fully protected from the illegal drug trade. Roosevelt argued that legislative support would prevent the nation's 'ravage' from narcotic drugs. In 1936, the film release of *Reefer Madness* directed by Louis Gasnier heightened the drug peril, equating marihuana to 'a violent narcotic, an unspeakable scourge'. Heroin was mentioned in the propaganda loaded introduction as one of the drug menaces. These occurrences added to the nervous tone of narcotic discourse in America.

Even with legislative restrictions, by the late 1940s, heroin had become a drug of choice with a number of modern jazz performers. Miles Davis recalled in his memoir, '... all of us, started to get heavily into heroin around the same time' (Davis and Troupe 1989: 129). The culmination of labeling drugs 'evil' and aggressive enforcement resulted in the arrest and confinement of several jazz artists. In 1947, Billie Holiday served time in prison after pleading guilty to receiving and concealing a narcotic drug (Nicholson 1995: 158). Reports released by the Federal Bureau of Investigation illustrated the incessant surveillance that was placed upon jazz performers. For example, this teletype letter addressed to Inspector John Mohr from Harry Kimball, special agent in charge of the San Francisco FBI office:

> The source states that because of the importance of Holiday it has been the policy of his bureau to discredit individuals of this caliber using narcotics. Because of their notoriety it offered excuses to minor users. Source states that raid was a legitimate raid based on above and that claimed quote frame up unquote was as much for publicity purposes as it was to avert the suspicion of guilt from her inasmuch as she was caught in possession of the makeshift pipe. (Anon 1949b)

Such haste to find narcotics and arrest users negatively impacted the reputations of performers that used heroin. Davis cited the reason for his aloofness during his years of addiction: 'when I was a drug addict, the club owners had treated me like I was dirt and so had the critics' (Davis and Troupe 1989: 180). This declaration proposed that a change in behavior, including isolation from others, was a response to being associated with narcotics. In the 1940s, the assault on heroin and demonization of addicts planted an ideology that drugs were evil and parasitic, prompting a reaction in society among users and straights.

Manifestation of Heroin Chic

Fifty years later heroin chic influenced the fashion industry, polarizing the nation between disputes of artistic freedom and protective censorship. The style was visible in magazine editorials, fashion advertisements, and runway shows. *Elle*, a women's magazine, contained fashion ads in the mid-1990s that illustrated the range of brands showing attributes of heroin chic. In February 1996, *Elle* contained fashion advertisements (Gianfranco Ferre, J&ANS by Dolce & Gabbana, G Gigli by Romeo Gigli, and Istante by Versace) with subjects who appeared to be affected by depressants that eradicated their joy and liveliness. This representation was achieved with disheveled hair, ultra-thin limbs, darkened eye sockets, and blank stares and body postures that included heads hung low and tilted, hands that emphasized erogenous zones, and legs spread wide, signaling unsuitable behavior, conceivably of an individual using heroin (*Elle* 1996: 101–75). In this issue, the gloomy aesthetic was countered by cosmetic and fragrance ads featuring smiling models in bright floral settings. L'Oréal, Revlon, and Estée Lauder were the antithesis of heroin chic—happiness, healthy beauty, and high energy were foregrounded in their ads.

In November 1997, *Elle* featured an ad by bebe, an American clothing retailer that epitomizes the heroin style. The layout presents a model draped in a clingy evening dress sitting on the tiled floor of a bathroom or shower (*Elle* 1997: 109). The subject stares downward, her dress is crumpled around her thigh and a thin arm clutches her ankle. Her eyes are heavily painted and broad shadows complete a visual that signifies the controversial trend. Likewise, a 1996 Gucci advertising campaign identified the characteristics of heroin chic with seemingly semi-conscious models strewn across a sterile room (Figure 4:2). The layout consisted of three female models in mini-dresses of black Chantilly lace that exposed the bare skin of the upper torso. Along with provocative nudity, the subjects appeared dazed and unresponsive, particularly the model on the floor with twisted legs and sunken head. The central figure who directly confronts the viewer with messy hair and a lack of emotion intensifies this scene that implies the intoxication of a substance. Fashion editors and stylists drew upon the myths of a street junkie, replicating the darkened eyes, frail limbs, and sexual proclivities of an addict seeking another fix. In the late 1990s, the *New York Times* raised the question of the industry's 'complicity in beaming seductive images about the thrills of drug use' (Woodward 1997).

Kate Moss, featured in Calvin Klein underwear and denim campaigns that started in 1992, was most associated with the glamorization of heroin (Elliot 1992). With waifish

Figure 4:2. A Gucci advertisement from 1996 reflects the new fashion aesthetic. Note the exposed skin, delicate limbs, and blank facial expressions. Courtesy of Advertising Archives.

features and suggestive poses, the British icon amended set definitions of model beauty. This aesthetic was obvious in a 1995 Obsession fragrance ad for Calvin Klein taken by Mario Sorrenti (Figure 4:3). In the image, Moss, with upper body nudity, slicked back hair, and wide pupils, engages the viewer with a lethargic gaze, seemingly resultant from substance use or indecent behavior.

The black background heightens the shadows on Moss's skeletal frame. 'In the taste for the emaciated, hollow-cheeked look, some social critics see an allusion to hard drugs,' argues Gabriel Trip (1994) in her article mapping heroin's link to the prevailing style.

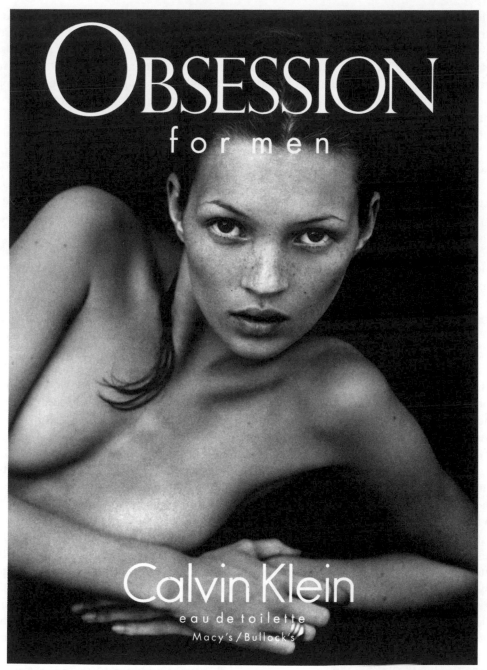

Figure 4:3. A Calvin Klein advertisement for Obsession cologne from 1995 illustrates the use of nudity, shadows, and an affected gaze. Courtesy of Advertising Archives.

The heroin chic of the 1990s was not new; in fact, the visual imagery was derived from the early art of Larry Clark and Nan Goldin. These photographers deliberately captured raw attributes of their subjects, often conveying sexuality, violence, and substance abuse. As Brian Wallis, Curator of the International Center of Photography, has written, 'Clark produced remarkably intimate and beautiful pictures of his drug-shooting coterie from 1963 to 1971' (2005). In his use of black-and-white images, shadowy backgrounds, drug paraphernalia, and provocative nudity, Larry Clark's work drew attention to drug use and adolescent sexuality (for instance, the untitled 1963 snapshot of a young man in a tub injecting a syringe in his forearm). The perspective places the viewer above the man's shoulder, so the viewer literally and figuratively looks down on the drug addict. Clark's *oeuvre* of drug use and open sexuality demonstrates a new, youth-inspired attitude about drugs. 'I took pictures in the Seventies and Eighties, when I was a junkie, of my friends and myself when we were high…a lot of us got sober,and my pictures showed that' (Lockwood and Ramey 1997). Nan Goldin indicates that the spread of AIDS and the growth of recovery programs lessened the drug-related characteristics in her work (Lockwood and Ramey 1997). Goldin's and Clark's anti-concealment approach highlights the drug use among young people and inspired a future fashion trend (Spindler 1997). In the 1990s, photographers including Davide Sorrenti, Vincent Gallo, Herb Ritts, Richard Avedon, and others extended this graphic portrayal of the effects of narcotics. Disputes surfaced when a correlation was made between the severe appearance of models and the reality of heroin addiction among celebrities.

A decade earlier, the death of Gia Carangi did little to halt the wave of drug chic. Gia, a top fashion model, had died in 1986 from AIDS complications following addiction to cocaine and heroin (Elias 1998). Transitioning from obscurity to fame and succumbing to the pitfalls of success, Gia's life is an exemplar of drug use and its outcome. Apparently, track marks were visible on her arm in photographs appearing in a November 1980 issue of *Vogue* (Anon 2007). This pop culture legend was a prelude to heroin chic. Gia refers to the narcotic trend in fashion during a *20/20* interview on the ABC television network in the United States. 'When you're young…it's hard to make the difference between what is real and what is not real,' commented Carangi (1982) in response to being young and vulnerable in the modeling business, and falling prey to drugs. The high-fashion clothes that Gia wore during photo shoots and runway presentations eclipsed the working-class, Philadelphia neighborhood from which she came, as well as obscured her early drug use. Further in the interview, when asked if she got into the drug scene, Carangi (1982) replied, 'Yes, you can say that I did. It kind of creeps up on you and catches you.' As noted by Hurlock (1929: 35), dress has been a method that individuals have used in America to alter class status. Thus, Gia's status as 'girl of the moment', along with the designer garments and exclusive cosmetics she wore in photo shoots and on the runway, rebuffed any identification of her as a heroin user by the audience (Fried 1993). The idea of fantasy and the reality of addiction were juxtaposed in the fashion industry, when heroin chic appeared in the 1980s and was labeled 'the dark side of modeling'. As Stephen Fried wrote in *Thing of Beauty*, a tale of Gia's life, 'her drug problems have been so acute that if she didn't have that incredible look, she might never work at all' (1993: 3).

Hooked on a Feeling

Visual attributes of heroin chic have qualities of the early art movements of expressionism, surrealism, and cubism. In contrast to the soft, airiness of impressionism, artists in the latter movements distorted reality, depicted dream-like conditions, and placed an emphasis on the subject's suffering (Cleaver 1988). *The Scream* (1893) by Edvard Munch forecasted the aesthetic condition of heroin chic. In this painting, Munch positioned the frail subject in the foreground, where the viewer is confronted by the distressed nature represented in the artwork. *Les demoiselles d'Avignon* (1907) by Pablo Picasso boldly exhibited nudity, distorted faces, and the twisted limbs of prostitutes to engage the viewer. Picasso's cubist treatment highlighted 'the African idea of abstraction and emphasis of body parts', consequently going 'beyond strict representation of natural forms' (Davidson 1966: 165). A similar context is demonstrated in advertising appearing in a September 1997 issue of *W* magazine. An ad for Donna Karan New York features model Linda Evangelista kneeling foreground with only a kimono-style coat concealing her nudity. The subject's troubled disposition is conveyed through interlocking limbs, hunched posture, and guarded eyes. In the same way, a Prada advertisement shows a model asleep or unconscious on the floor gripping a leather handbag. The perspective of the photo places the limp hand and slender wrist at foreground, while the model's head and bag are out of focus. A black-and-white Giorgio Armani image on the back page of the September issue presents Stella Tennant with tousled hair, an exposed breast, and a menacing gaze, mimicking the affective qualities of expressionist and cubist art.

Similar impressions of distress are notable in the modern work of Walt Kuhn. His paintings of circus performers blend happiness and sadness. Kuhn achieved this quality through the use of color, straightforward poses, and despondent facial expressions (Peltakian 2010). For instance, Kuhn's 1946 *Roberto* has a structural likeness to a 1995 Calvin Klein underwear campaign featuring Joel West. The Klein ad with heroin chic traits featured the model, clad only in a low rise brief, with legs fully extended to accentuate the male crotch and physique. Adding to this sexuality, the subject displayed a dejected gaze heightened by dark shadows around the eyes and jaw line. In Kuhn's painting, the circus performer is positioned forward with brawny lower limbs spread apart, equivalent to the Klein ad. The doleful expression projected straight at the viewer was realized by white ghostly clown makeup and dark-rimmed eyes. Both representations framed the scene in darkness and shadows, whereby fantasy yields to an unsettling reality. In a *New York Times* article on the fashion trend, Richard Woodward (1997) describes heroin chic as 'a somber, quasi-realistic style that seems to equate dressing down with being down'. Indeed, heroin chic images contained subjects with a hooked appearance that had roots in the austere work of modern artists such as Munch, Picasso, and Kuhn.

Aesthetic Exploitation and Criticism

In its most visual form, heroin chic caused alarm on fashion runways. Here, the representation was brought to life by emaciated models who moved awkwardly and displayed unresponsive expressions. The gloom of the aesthetic transformed the vivacious catwalk style of the 1980s into a lethargic, careless stagger. Although the trend did not dominate all presentations, it was instrumental in establishing a severe, military style of modeling, where individuality was obsolete and conformity ruled. Stylists promoted the most prolific traits of pale foundations, darkened eyes, and messy hair on runways and in magazines. This element was part of deconstructionism in fashion that defined new forms of beauty through contorted garment designs and doleful appearances. The Ann Demeulemeester and Helmut Lang Fall 1993 shows featured garments that hung on the body in a twisted manner, worn by models who were pedestrian and unemotional (Klensch 1993). The deconstructionist approach had an unmerited association to heroin chic because it was less romantic, devoid of bright colors, and embraced a severe, solemn posture. James Danziger, a Soho gallery owner, in a *New York Times* article on the changing face of fashion editorials asserts, 'Not all downbeat, muted color photography glamorizes heroin chic' (Woodward 1997).

Fashion and drugs were further linked by branding strategies and consumer behavior. Comparable to the retailing of clothes, heroin has been trademarked with names that identify the quality of the product. Street names, including Superman, Adidas, Al Capone, and E.T., have been utilized to generate interest and establish a symbol of the high (Volk 2011: 16; Kowalski 1984). Furthermore, fashion is marketed in creative ways to connect emotionally with the customer. The appropriation of brand and celebrity names to sell illegal street narcotics amplified the problematic connection. Steve Volk in analysis of the Philadelphia narcotics trade declares 'drug dealing is, at heart, competitive retailing of a rare and precious commodity: Feeling good' (2011: 10). Arguably, the merchandising of fashion and drugs aims to satisfy and transform the end user, as well guarantee a zealous demand for additional purchases. This economic objective draws parallels between two diverse businesses, oddly united by product aspiration and imitation.

With his familiar quote, 'you do not need to glamorize addiction to sell clothes', President William J. Clinton established a debate in the fashion industry concerning the responsibility of advertising (Lockwood and Ramey 1997). The merger of distress characteristics, provocative sexuality, and famous models in fashion ads produced concern, particularly among the Family Research Council (Lockwood and Ramey 1997). Marc Jacobs offered the following rebuttal: 'I don't think someone gets interested in taking heroin because there's a picture of a junkie in a magazine' (Lockwood and Ramey 1997). This said, fashion scholarship has identified forces of dress that support its ability to persuade: 'It is from their clothes that we form a first impression of our fellow-creatures as we meet them' (Flügel 1950: 15). In simplest terms, individuals dress to attract or repel the attention of others. Distinctions , related to gender, cultural, and social roles, are generated by the viewer based on this visual representation (Barnes and Eicher 1992: 1–2). Thus, a fashion advertisement with heroin chic qualities induces the observer to react in approval or displeasure. If an observer admires the advertisement, psychologists have argued that conformity or imitation in dress would likely follow (Flügel 1950: 138). The fact of self-expression was marked in this equation, through which individuals merged their style with external stimuli. Heroin chic thrives when fashion channels, specifically glossy magazines and fashion shows, promote affluent lifestyles. Models and celebrities, as arbiters, sway mass market purchasing decisions. Therefore, consumers, who copy the dress and appearance 'gain some of the pleasure of prestige' of the trendsetters (Hurlock 1929: 39).

History has illustrated the variability of fashion where newness is essential and extremes are habitual. The heroin chic trend is part of a style cycle that stirred debate by challenging standards of dress and appearance. For example, the raised hem lines of the 1920s challenged Victorian sensibilities by establishing a modern, active, and socially liberated woman. The amount of exposed skin on the legs was striking compared to the floor-sweeping silhouettes of previous decades. Equally, the thigh-high hemline and androgynous traits of the 1960s contrasted with the voluminous, petticoated skirts of the 1950s. Fashion shifts are often abrupt, contentious, and represent a moral conflict. The addition of war, social rebellion, and economic uncertainty raises the level of public concern.

With great effect, the aesthetic of heroin chic stressed the significance of elements beyond the garment's style. Clark and Goldin engaged the observer to experience the subject's disturbing predicament. These artists employed uninhibited elements to record environment, establish meaning, and initiate dialogue. The heroin chic trend focused attention on the mental and physical condition of the model, attempting to account for the visual. As such, the fashion design was secondary to the hyper-marketing of the drug extremity. Kate Moss, with gaunt frame, androgynous features, and discarded glamour, became the poster child for society's crisis with substance abuse and sexuality. Hence, a cultural revolution was evident in heroin chic that challenged socially acceptable forms of expression. Accounting for the audacious movement can be likened to John Dewey's theory on human voices: '... when they are suppressed and oppressed will in time rebel and demand an opportunity for manifestation' (1989: 100).

A path to heroin chic has been established based on four areas: drug demonization, fashion association, historical pattern, and exploitation. Forceful drug legislation was a catalyst for individuals to develop a means of defiance. Cumulative narcotic regulations placed significant pressure on drug users. The manipulation of dress and appearance became connected with substance use, when jazz artists stylishly negotiated the two elements. By evoking attributes of high glamour, these performers attempted to avert the drug link. Their reaction gave birth to a fashion motive that would later resonate. Along a similar line, art history had provided thorough experimentation with dark subject matter and human plight. This distorted visual style of self-centered themes, controversial material, and dim settings cultivated the characteristics of heroin chic. The fourth area revolved around the necessity for change in the fashion industry. It was most persuasive when the alteration from one period to the next was thrilling. Rupert Skinner's comment on the heroin chic debate showed this viewpoint: '...the frailty, that is en vogue at the moment, and some people don't mind that association, because it lends a certain kudos, it's something risqué' (Lockwood and Ramey 1997).

Fashion shifts that were originally based on artistic innovation had evolved into mechanisms for brand positioning via hyper-marketing and product sensationalism. Gucci strikingly demonstrated this concept in their advertising throughout the 1990s. Cropped photos, male and female bodies layered, states of undress, and affected behavior of subjects became attributed with the brand. Joseph H. Hancock, II describes this 'cinematic' approach where companies like Dolce & Gabbana and Abercrombie & Fitch produce marketing campaigns with fantastic themes, nudity, and homoeroticism (Hancock 2009: 55). In a competitive business environment, successful branding required the creation of a memorable identity and an emotional relationship to the product, aptly achieved through racy advertisements.

Conclusion

A narrative between fashion motives and signs of drug use has been posited. This manifestation was discernible years before it was lionized as heroin chic. It was arguable to state that fashion glorified drug addiction. Through this analysis, the complex relationship has been defined in a historical and symbolic context. The fashion industry's adoption of traits directly related to heroin use established an associative position. It was disseminated via marketing of clothing, accessories, and fragrances to a mass media audience. The role of fashion was dependent upon the wearer and the observer, where meaning was elastic. Further complicating the issue was that the correlation changed over time, dependent on political, economic, social, and artistic variables.

Since the narcotic concept was identified years earlier, its attributes conveyed a diverse subtext, when placed in a new period. A percentage of the contemporary audience found the audacious heroin style dangerous to young people, who were highly influenced by fashion. Dress theory had shown that clothing provided acceptance or exclusion, thus wielding authority. The environment of heroin chic was critical to its downfall. Occurring in an uncertain period of war and terrorism, the nation repudiated an arrogant, creative hazard. Concurrently, ultra-realistic drug films were trending: *Pulp Fiction* (1994), *Kids* (1995), *The Basketball Diaries* (1995), and *Trainspotting* (1996). *The Basketball Diaries*, starring Leonardo DiCaprio, portrayed Catholic school boys falling prey to heroin. In addition, the prominent deaths of Gia Carangi, River Phoenix, Kurt Cobain, and Davide Sorrenti— all in their twenties, added to the heroin peril.

In the twenty-first century, qualities of fashionable addiction have resurfaced. The contemporary habit embraces prescription medicines, accentuated by the contribution of drugs to the deaths of celebrities including Heath Ledger, Anna Nicole Smith, Michael Jackson, and Whitney Houston. Prolific drug advertisements on network television and in print media have offered remedies to treat every thing from depression to sleep disorder.

A byproduct of greater prescribed medicine has been a growing problem among teenagers taking unauthorized prescription drugs (Harris 2010). Also, high unemployment and a weak global economy have defined this volatile period. The fashion industry has responded with opulence, flawless beauty, unimaginable garment construction, and self-branding references. Fifteen years beyond the decline of heroin chic, the fashionable narrative of narcotics in America has shifted from models imitating opiate consumption to the recurring path of drugs in society, where actual narcotic and prescription abuse among celebrities is anticipated.

References

Anon (1934), 'President Demands Drive by All Forces of Nation to Solve Crime Problem', *New York Times*, 11 December.

—— (1935), 'Roosevelt Asks Narcotic War Aid', *New York Times*, 22 March.

—— (1949a), 'Bebop Doesn't Make Child Musical Moron, Says Expert Here with a School Project', *New York Times*, 25 July.

—— (1949b), 'Billie Holiday', Federal Bureau of Investigation, Communications Section, http://foia.fbi.gov/foiaindex/billieholiday.htm. Accessed 19 July 2010.

—— (1949c), 'Seizures Reach Peak in Heroin and Cocaine', *New York Times*, 4 March.

—— (1953), 'Anita O'Day Convicted', *Long Beach Independent*, 26 August.

—— (1955), 'Alter-Proof Order for Drugs Sought', *New York Times*, 26 April.

—— (1958), 'Billie Holiday Guilty', *New York Times*, 13 March.

—— (2007) 'Gia in Magazines', GiaCarangi.org, http://giacarangi.org/magazines.html. Accessed 10 October 2012.

—— (2010), 'Balm of America: Patent Medicine Collection', http://americanhistory.si.edu. Accessed 24 July 2010.

Askwith, R. (1998), 'How Aspirin Turned Hero', *Sunday Times*, 13 September, http://opioids.com/heroin/heroinhistory.html. Accessed 8 January 2012.

Associated Press (1947), 'Singer Billie Holiday Jailed as Dope Victim', 28 May, *Billie Holiday: The Ultimate Collection*, DVD, 2005, Produced by Multiprises, Universal Music Enterprises.

Atwood, N. (1953), 'They Pay Off…with Death', *Confidential Magazine*, pp. 22–23.

Barnes, R. and Eicher, J.B. (1992), 'Introduction,' in R. Barnes and J.B. Eicher, eds, *Dress and Gender: Making and Meaning in Cultural Contexts*, Oxford and New York: Berg, pp. 1–7

Barthes, R. (1973), *Elements of Semiology* (trans. A. Lavers and C. Smith), New York: Hill and Wang.

Barthes, R. (2006), *The Language of Fashion* (trans. A. Stafford, ed. A. Stafford and M. Carter), Oxford and New York: Berg Publishers.

Calefato, P. (2004), *The Clothed Body*, Oxford and New York: Berg Publishers.

Carangi, G. (1982), 'The Dark Side of Modeling', *ABC 20/20*, Interview with Gia Carangi, http://www.youtube.com/watch?v=605nMZ2xmGk. Accessed 25 September 2010.

Clarke, D. (2002), *Billie Holiday: Wishing on a Moon*, Cambridge: De Capo Press.

Cleaver, D. (1988), *Art: An Introduction*, Boston: Houghton Mifflin Harcourt.

Davidson, B. (1966), *African Kingdoms*, New York: Time-Life Books.

Davis, F. (1994), *Fashion, Culture, and Identity*, Chicago: University of Chicago Press.

Davis, M. and Troupe, Q. (1989), *Miles: The Autobiography*, New York: Simon & Schuster.

Dewey, J. (1989), *Freedom and Culture*, New York: Prometheus Books.

Drug Enforcement Administration (2012a), Controlled Substances Act, http://www. deadiversion. usdoj.gov/21cfr/21usc/index.html. Accessed 8 January 2012.

Drug Enforcement Administration (2012b), Controlled Substances Act, http://www.justice. gov/dea/pubs/abuse/drug_data_sheets/Heroin.pdf. Accessed 8 January 2012.

Elias, J. (1998), 'A Chic Heroin, but Not a Pretty Story', *New York Times*, 25 January.

Elle (1996), vol. XI, number 6, no. 126, February.

—— (1997), vol. XIII, number 3, no. 147, November.

Elliot, S. (1992), 'Calvin Klein Turns to Television', *New York Times*, 23 October.

Flügel, J.C. (1950), *The Psychology of Clothes*, London: Hogarth Press.

Fried, S. (1993), *Thing of Beauty*, New York: Pocket Books, Simon & Schuster.

Gasnier, L. (1936), *Reefer Madness*, directed by L. Gasnier, United States: Motion Pictures Ventures.

Giddins, G. and DeVeaux, S. (2009), *Jazz*, New York: W.W. Norton & Company.

Gourse, L. (1994), *Sassy: The Life of Sarah Vaughan*, New York: De Capo Press.

Gledhill, C. (2007), 'Genre and Gender: The Case of Soap Opera', in S. Hall, ed., *Representation: Cultural Representations and Signifying Practices*, London: Sage, pp. 337–384.

Hancock, J. (2009), *Brand Story: Ralph, Vera, Johnny, Billy, and Other Adventures in Fashion Branding*, New York: Fairchild Books.

Harris, D. (2010), *ABC World News Sunday* (television broadcast), 9 September, New York: American Broadcast Company.

Houston, D. and Bagert, J. (2006), *Jazz, Giants, and Journeys: The Photography of Herman Leonard*, London: Scala Publishers.

Hurlock, E. (1929), *The Psychology of Dress: An Analysis of Fashion and Its Motive*, New York: Ronald Press.

Keel, R. (2010), 'Drug Law Timeline', http://www.druglibrary.org/schaffer/history/drug_ law_ timeline.htm. Accessed 23 July 2010.

Klensch, E. (1993), 'New Direction: Fall 1993', on *Style with Elsa Klensch*, CNN, http://www. youtube.com/ watch?v=DONJCsm_5rg. Accessed 24 July 2011.

Kliment, B. (1990), *Billie Holiday*, New York: Chelsea House.

Kowalski, L. (1984), *Story of a Junkie*, directed by Lech Kowalski, New York: Troma Entertainment.

Lockwood, L. and Ramey, J. (1997) 'Industry Reacts to Clinton's Criticism', *WWD*, http:// www.wwd.com. Accessed 31 May 2010.

McDowell, C. (1997), *The Man of Fashion: Peacock Males and Perfect Gentleman*, London: Thames and Hudson.

Moraes, F. (2000), *The Little Book of Heroin*, Berkeley: Ronin Publishing.

Nicholson, S. (1995), *Billie Holiday*, Boston: Northeastern University Press.

O'Day, A. and Eells, G. (1989), *High Times Hard Times*, New York: Limelight Editions.

Peltakian, D. (2010), 'Walt Kuhn (1877–1949), American Modernist', http://www. sullivangoss. com/walt_Kuhn/. Accessed 29 July 2010.

Roach-Higgins, M.E. and Eicher, J.B. (1992) 'Dress and Identity', *Clothing and Textile Research Journal*, 10.4, pp. 1–10.

Spencer, F. (2002), *Jazz and Death: Medical Profiles of Jazz Greats*, Jackson: University Press of Mississippi.

Spindler, A. (1997), 'A Death Tarnishes Fashion's "Heroin Look"', *New York Times*, May 20.

Trip, G. (1994), 'Fast-Lane Killer: A Special Report; Heroin Finds a New Market along Cutting Edge of Style', *New York Times*, 8 May.

Volk, S. (2011), 'Top 10 Drug Corners: A Look at the City's Drug Trade in 2011', *Philadelphia Weekly*, 24–30 August, p. 10–16.

W (1997), vol. 26, issue 9, September.

Wallis, B. (2005), 'Larry Clark', International Center of Photography, http://museum.icp. org/museum/exhibitions/larry_clark/. Accessed 28 July 2010.

Weaver, W. (1951), 'Narcotics Clinics Proposed Upstate', *New York Times*, 1 December.

Woodward, R. (1997), 'Whither Fashion Photography?', *New York Times*, 8 June.

Wren, C.S. (1997), 'Clinton Calls Fashion Ads' "Heroin Chic" Deplorable', *New York Times*, 22 May.

Chapter 5

Dames and Design: Fashion and Appearance on Pulp Fiction Covers, 1950–1960

Toni Johnson-Woods

Mr. Brady wants to change *The Scarlet Letter* to *I Was an Adulteress*.... Mr. Brady understands the 25-cent book field.... The cover will be a picture of Hester Prynne with a cigarette hanging out of her mouth. She'll be in a real tight, low-cut dress. Our big problem is—if the dress is cut low enough to sell any copies, there won't be any space on the front for a big red letter. (Dialogue from George Axelrod's play *The Seven Year Itch* [1952])

Mr. Brady's plan for repackaging *The Scarlet Letter* summarizes the pulp fiction industry and products of the 1950s. He wants to give the book a more provocative title and an even more provocative cover in order to compete in the expanding cheap fiction market. In the post-World War II period, a handful of rogue U.S. publishing companies (Dell, Avon and Gold Medal) had broken from publishing tradition and printed books that contained original fiction rather than to reprint books from hardcover publishers. They sought ways to effectively market their original fiction (usually but inaccurately labeled 'pulp fiction'[1]) by presenting the public with covers that promised exciting and entertaining reading. They hired artists to create eye-popping covers that could compete with all the other books on the crowded paperback stands. Publishers knew that a successful cover translated into sales. Novelist Malcolm Cowley recalls a publisher boasting, 'give me the right cover...and I could sell two hundred blank pages. I could sell *Finnegan's Wake* on Skid Road as a book of Irish jokes' (1954: 120). One of the standard covers became a female who promises, but rarely delivers, literary thrills. She is easily recognizable, even in the twenty-first century: she has a lush body and wears skintight, revealing clothing. Her appearance is a signifier of narrative function, social class and sexual power—basically they tell the reader something about her and possibly something about the narrative. In this chapter, I examine the clothing of these most iconic females, the demure, dizzy, and dangerous 'dames' of 1950s detective fiction.

Literary scholars have, by and large, ignored book covers. Recently, however, book historians have started to consider the paratext that frames and informs. Twenty-five years ago Gérard Genette posited that

More than a boundary or a sealed border, the paratext is, rather, a threshold. [It is] a zone between text and off-text, a zone not only of transition but also of transaction: a privileged place of pragmatics and a strategy, of an influence on the public, an influence that...is at the service of a better reception for the text and a more pertinent reading of it. (1997: 1–2)

Despite the potential power of book cover semiotics, recent research has focused on covers' marketing and publishing issues rather than the actual cover art or images. For example, nearly all of the chapters of *Judging a Book by Its Cover* have devoted considerable space to marketing, but very few lines to visual analysis of the covers. Furthermore, most academic research focuses on literary fiction, and literary books favor *avant-garde* or high art wrappers (as most literary texts are published as hardcovers in the first instance). Yet the most imaginative covers, to my mind, are those that grace cheap paperbacks. In the recent past, several books crammed with colorful reproductions of trashy covers celebrate genres, artists, or publishers (*The Look of Love: the Art of the Romance Novel* by Jennifer McKnight-Trontz ; *The Paperback Art of James Avati* by Piet Schreuders, Kenneth Fulton, and Stanley Meltzoff; *Great American Paperback: An Illustrated Tribute to the Legends of the Book* by Richard Lupoff). Despite the increased interest in visual culture and the growing research into popular fiction, precious little work has been done on visual analysis of arguably the book industry's most enduring legacy: the book cover.

Since the nineteenth century, the world has become increasingly saturated with images: advertisements, films, television shows, magazines, photographic images, and book covers. As the covers have to summarize a book's sensibility, each genre developed a visual shorthand: science fiction books preferred large, colorful monsters, westerns had energetic gun fights, romance fiction relied on a romantic clinch, and crime stories largely depended upon voluptuous women. But my particular favorites are the trashy girls. While crime fiction seems to have the monopoly of the come-hither female; another subgenre is particularly redolent of the 1950s paperback market—the 'hillbilly hoyden'. The females who adorn these covers are squeezed into denim shorts and ragged revealing dresses and offer the potential of an Edenic sexualized liberality.

Viewers and readers have come to learn the truism that a picture does say a thousand words and have learned to 'read' images at a glance. But we are still amazingly inept at explicating what those images convey as they are embedded with so many cultural cues. We look *through* costumes in films and television shows as if they are just what people wear. In her article on Cleopatra, Suzanne Osmond notes that 'in the visual and performing arts, ideas about gendered and racial identity are framed and made manifest by the way in which the body is dressed' (2011: 58). And Stella Bruzzi (1997) reminds us, we must stop looking *through* the costume of historical dramas and look *at* them.

As no image exists in a vacuum, the 1950s cover women are the descendants of centuries of female 'beauty'. These women inherited the artistic beauty of Venus de Milo and thousands of years of a beauty aesthetic plus the more recently evolved pinup girl. The pinup girl comes from the wholesome but highly sexualized art of George Petty and Albert Vargas,[2] who took their poses from real life burlesque artists. The burlesque artists of the nineteenth century achieved notoriety for they posed 'nude' in classical *tableaux vivants* for the gaze of their appreciative audiences; the nude effect was achieved by fleshings (nude-colored body suits). Over decades burlesque artists moved from the theater to the sideshow and eventually to nightclubs where they evolved into strippers. Thus the females who dominated the covers of the 1950s crime fiction had a complex visual journey. They were purveyors of body image, ideals of beauty, draped in garments that spoke to readers.

The women on crime fiction covers are part-art, part-advertisement and part-narrative. The clothes they wear transcend fashion and appearance—they signal to the reader the type of women they are. These women have become so firmly embedded in popular consciousness that sixty years later they are still emblematic. In the animated feature *Who Framed Roger Rabbit?* (1988), the female protagonist, Jessica Rabbit, is a curvaceous redhead with a proclivity for sexy clothing. For the knowing viewer, Jessica Rabbit is the cartoon embodiment of the 'dangerous dame' of pulp fiction. Her opera gloves, tight red lurex dress, and high heels function as a costume—a costume that summarizes her character.

The Case Study

My cover database is restricted to Australian crime fiction covers of the 1950s for three reasons: it avoids national differences, generic demands, and fashion changes. Crime fiction was selected because it is most often associated with pulp fiction and because its images are among the most culturally visible. It also has the most complex relationship with its depiction of women. Crime fiction covers embrace a wide spectrum of females; from those seeking help or needing protection to gun-toting women blasting their way out of trouble. The cover women in this study, therefore, are not simply 'good girls' or 'bad girls' but offer a range of female possibilities. And these possibilities are inscribed on their bodies, their appearances, and their clothing.

Fashion, Appearance, and the Cover 'Girls'[3]

Drawing on my collection of 800 books; I selected only those books written, illustrated, and published in Australia between 1950 and 1960 by 'pulp' fiction authors such as Carter Brown, Larry Kent, K.T. McCall, and Carl Dekker. These authors were chosen because they were the most prolific and popular authors of the period—they produced a title each month for several years and, more importantly, their covers are visually arresting and focus on females. I visually examined them and divided them into two basic groups: 'good girls' and 'bad girls'. The groups were further defined by (in descending order of importance): clothing, appearance (hair color, silhouette, body type), accessories, pose, and background. From the two groups, the following genres emerged: 'good girls' became 'demure dames' and 'playmate pals', and 'bad girls' became 'dangerous dames' and 'hoochie coochie mamas'. For the covers that have elements from more than one category, the dominant sensibility was selected. The two ends of the visual spectrum, the 'demure dames' and the 'hoochie coochie mamas', were the rarest.

Not surprisingly, the cover women reflect the fashions and appearance of the times and change across the decade. For example, skirts get shorter and one-piece swimsuits give way to bikinis. Indeed, it can be argued that the covers form a visual archive of the decade's looks. What is most striking is that while the garment styles (such as long evening dresses) remain relatively stable, it is their silhouette, color, and fabric that differentiate the 'good girls' from the 'bad' ones. Some generalities were also observed: 'good girls' wear more clothes, less jewelry, and their hair is natural; 'bad girls' smoke cigarettes, wear tight, low-cut evening gowns, and dye their hair. However, while 'looks' matter, fashion and accessories alone are not enough, essential visual signifiers are her pose and the setting that alert the viewer to the 'type' of woman she is.

The 'demure dame' is perhaps the rarest female, she appeared briefly around the mid-1950s. Culturally she is the housewife or girlfriend caught in a dangerous situation; subtextually she has strayed from the home and as a result is caught up in a dangerous man's world.

The drab appearance of the 'demure dame' underscores her ordinariness. She wears 'realistic' clothes that cover her body; twin sets, sensible skirts, and even hats and gloves. Twin sets had been fashionable since the 1920s but by the 1950s they had become the uniform of the middle-class housewife; as Colin McDowell notes, twin sets responded to the needs of the 'average' woman who 'didn't work, almost always lived in a house with no central heating, and had time on her hands' (2002). The woman on the cover *One Live Blonde* (Figure 5:1) wears an 'abbreviated' twin set—cardigans were a 'formal' addition to the twin set and her short-sleeved top reflects a suburban outing (McDowell 2002). Her full skirt mirrors Dior's New Look; as an antidote to the uniforms of World War II, this new style, according to Dior, was 'molded upon the curves of the feminine body, whose sweep they would stylize' (quoted in Harris 1992). Thus the skirt of the 'demure dame' is feminine and floaty, gliding over her frame; its fullness makes it practical and the colors are rather dull. The outfit could be worn to church or in the home; the outfit is that of the suburban housewife. Even her jewelry is

Figure 5:1. *One Live Blonde.*

practical: she may wear a watch but not diamonds. If her hair is blonde, it is a natural blonde and not the vibrant (dyed) colors of her trashier sisters. If, however, her clothes are torn, the visual narrative is not one of body display but of violence and helplessness; she has been attacked. She is subservient to the male. She is the fashion embodiment of the girl, or, more precisely, the wife, next door.

One Live Blonde depicts a situation in which a woman has been thrown to the ground, placing her in the most subordinate position—a position from which she cannot defend herself. Even though she is splayed on the ground, her legs remain covered. The male protagonist protects and shields her. Because she does not court sexual desire, she fails to meet the male reader's gaze; she looks down or away and often her face is obscured. If her face is visible, her expression is benign—not threatening. Artistically, she is often blurred and rarely achieves visual clarity; it is as if the artist has Vaseline-coated her or perhaps they did not know how to draw a female without an apron in a kitchen.

Thus the 'damsel in distress' is an acquiescent female who has strayed from home, lands in trouble, and needs rescuing. A male protector acts as her 'knight errant'. She is rarest on the covers because the fantasy of helping the woman next door is the domain of romance fiction. What the intended male reader wants is a fantasy woman, the sexy playmate.

The 'playmate pal' is the *Playboy* Playmate who is so-called for a specific reason—she is someone with whom the 'playboy' can 'play' (euphemistically, sexually play). She is the most common cover girl. She is the girl next door with fewer clothes. First and foremost her outfits expose breasts, hips, and legs. Swimsuits (Figure 5:2), quasi-swimsuits (Figure 5:3), and lingerie (Figure 5:5) are the garments of choice for the 'playmate pal'. Subtextually, the lack of covering signifies a lack of protection. Swimsuits had evolved from the neck-to-ankle costumes of the nineteenth century; by the 1920s women wore figure hugging but rather baggy wool jersey suits. In the 1930s, latex meant swimsuits could be even more figure defining; boning and zips gave 1950s one pieces more structure and body-flattering features. By the 1950s Hollywood stars such as Esther Williams and Ava Gardner had glamorized the swimsuit. Many of the earliest cover swimsuits have ruffs, frills and furbelows (*Hot Tamale*) that signal that the swimsuit is not really a swimsuit but simply a method of body display.

Though Louis Reard had patented a 'bikini' in 1946, variations had existed since Greco-Roman times. In the twentieth century, two piece swimsuits continued to decrease in size, and the showgirl on *Tornado in Town* wears not a two piece but a bikini (Figure 5:3). The passion-red bikini is transformed by the addition of a feathered headdress and flowing drapery. The wispy layers frame her hips and legs; they play hide and seek with the viewer's imagination. The headdress frames her face and highlights her brightly dyed red hair. What is often at odds with the swimsuit on book covers is the background: whether a showgirl and rural setting or the bikini at a Ku Klux Klan meeting (Figure 5:4), she is a creature out of place. Her clothing then becomes a signifier of inappropriateness and it undermines her 'executive function' (Goffman 1976: 56).

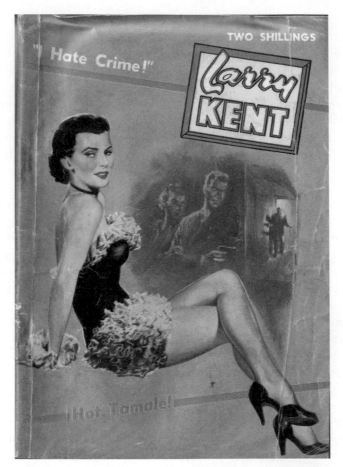

Figure 5:2. *Hot Tamale.*

The slip (Figure 5:5), negligee/nightgown, towel, and sheet suggest undress and bedroom fantasy. They are not functional garments nor is the body protected. Gone is the controlling girdle; the cover woman who wears a towel or sheet is only a tweak away from total nudity. Nightgowns might cover more of the body, but their transparency barely shields nudity and by extension the potential of sexual activity. Creators were careful to avoid censorship and thus women in night attire were allowed to sit on stools and stand in telephone boxes but not to recline on beds. These women are unconfined—they do not wear corsets or girdles—but they do wear high heels—another fetishized object.

Of all cover outfits, the evening dress is the most iconic. Silhouette is all and the silhouette is curvaceous. The material is luxurious, not practical, and the colors are bright. The dresses are strapless or halter-neck and, because the focus is the breasts, they are highlighted

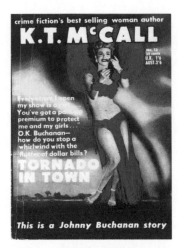

Figure 5:3. *Tornado in Town.*

Figure 5:4. *Dark Angel of Fire.*

through judicious daubs of white paint. It positions the wearer as a creature of the night—the *habitué* of nightclubs, casinos, places of drink, fun and all things not domestic. The tighter and shinier and therefore sexier the dress, the more likely she slides from 'playmate' into 'dame'. *Get Me Homicide*! (Figure 5:6) shows the 'playmate pal'. Her dress is red and she wears black opera gloves, but the focus is not her breasts or her body but the situation.

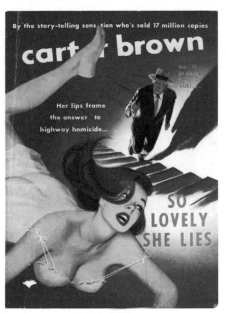

Figure 5:5. *So Lovely She Lies.*

Figure 5:6. *Get Me Homicide!*   Figure 5:7. *The Heat's On.*

The cover narrative is of a blonde who is clearly in trouble but is being saved (note the outsized phallic phone). She might have strayed into the twilight world of the nightclub, but she is clearly out of her depth. However, the woman in *The Heat's On* (Figure 5:7) is a 'dame'; she too wears a red dress but her voluptuous silhouette, smoking cigarette, and air of independence differentiates her from the 'damsel in distress'. The females might both wear red dresses, but the compositions send different social messages.

The 'playmate pal' also does not wear expensive jewelry—she presents as a low-maintenance female and therefore more aligned to a working-class culture. Most striking is her playful head toss and head cant. She is flirting because though she is in power, it is a playful power. She adopts classic cheesecake[4] poses that are familiar to the knowing male reader, and they show off her erogenous zones. She is turned slightly off-center for admiration, not domination. Often she is presented akimbo, which not only indicates playfulness but also a lack of physical ability, because though she might have sexual power, reassuringly she still needs a male's protection. Erving Goffman postulates such playfulness and invites the viewer not to take the female seriously and this can be visually represented as falling down, being thrown about, or depicted in a messy room or office (1976: 50). Furthermore, the women are infantilized (e.g., Marilyn Monroe's 'little girl' breathy voice); this is captured by the women posing on rugs and often with fingers to their mouths as if in wonder (aside from the obvious phallocentric implication). While some are captured in domestic settings, reclining on couches or in chairs, the majority are in chorus lines, singing in nightclubs, and other public spaces. The girl is a plaything unfettered by domestic duties. Still she has the potential of domesticity and thus her appearances in domestic spaces that suggest apartments rather than homes. Occasionally she faces the reader, however, in order to offset the threat of a direct gaze, she invites her viewer into her world under lowered lashes. She is a sexually alluring fantasy woman—as such, she is placed in fantastic situations and has an unrealistic body that is clad for maximum exposure.

Figure 5:8. *Duchess Double-X.*

Figure 5:9. *The Hard Racket!*

Of all the cover girls, the 'playmate pal' is the best known; she is the one most associated with paperback fiction. She is more glamorous than the 'demure dame' but her childlike wonder and blatant sexuality make her fabulous but potentially accessible for a male rather than a female readership.

The final two types of females are related but subtly different. The 'dangerous dame' (Figure 5:8) presents a physical danger to the male character. She is bad to the bone. Her clothing is always transgressive. Her evening dress is tighter and more revealing than those of the 'playmate pal'. Her aberrant appropriation of high culture clothing, evening dress, fetishized stiletto heels, and opera gloves gesture to burlesque artists. Her dresses are even tighter and though the small waist mimics Dior's New Look, her clothing does not float in femininity; they mold to her breasts and legs. Black and red are preferred colors; the fabrics are more akin to latex and leather than to cotton and silk. Indeed, she appears more like an avaricious black widow or a succubus; she is Madam Lash rather than a Duchess. She wears diamonds and other expensive jewelry because they signify gold digger, a kept woman or someone who makes her own way in the world—illegally, of course. She is high maintenance. Her most important accessories are her cigarette and her smoking gun. Her face is hard and she glares at the viewer, daring them to respond. She does not pose in supine positions; she stands as a man's equal and confronts him. Her smoldering look challenges rather than invites; her unapologetic stare reeks of power—the *über femme* offers impertinence and a subtle inversion of traditional femininity. Her power refers to her physical threat which, though unnerving, is not as unsettling as the blatant sexual aggression of the 'hoochie coochie mama'.

The 'hoochie coochie mama', like the 'demure dame', is a rare cover female. She takes her name from the slang for private parts, and a provocative belly dance made popular at the end of the nineteenth century. The lyrics and rhythm of Elvis Presley's song 'Little Egypt' summarizes the performance and appearance of the hoochie coochie. By 1954 Dior had replaced the full skirts and cinched waists of the New Look with a boxier silhouette; skirts were shorter and slimmer but 'bad' cover girls ignored this fashion transition. *The Hard Racket* (Figure 5:9) retains the cinched waist but her pencil skirt wraps around her hips and clings to her knees, emphasizing her hips. Her off-the-shoulder top barely covers her breasts and her strappy wedge shoes complete an outfit that screams sexuality. Her glamour is that of the night and of public spaces. But it is not a high-fashion glamour; her costume tends to be tawdry and positions the wearer as working class. The look is street hooker and not suburban housewife.

Often she stands with her hands on her hips, pelvis thrust forward. Her ripeness suggests fertility and, by association, sex rather than sexuality. Thus the focus is more intimate— her vagina rather than her breasts. Hers is the most powerful female representation. Males can deal with pointed guns—there is the possibility they can physically disarm the 'dangerous dame'—but the fully sexualized female scares them. She is bold and hard, but not dangerous in a physical sense; her danger is the threat of the sexually uncontrolled female. She faces the viewer but she refuses to engage with them. Her body and her head are held high 'stereotypically a mark of unashamedness, superiority and disdain' (Goffman 1976: 40). In *The Heat's On*, the dark background accentuates the lone female, the spotlight hits her breasts and thighs, but her most telling accessory is the smoking cigarette that signals danger. She is a woman of power who looks down at the viewer.

The 'bad girls' offer a selection, albeit a smallish one, of women who actively occupied men's spaces both figuratively and literally. Unlike the 'good' cover girls, they do not drape across furniture, chatting on the phone, nor do their clothes drape on their bodies. Their garments slither over their curvaceous forms, giving a hyper-sexualized silhouette that, paradoxically, is both available and yet unattainable. For when women enter male spaces, they are de-feminized; the waspish waists and floating skirts of suburbia are replaced by sleek garments which slither on the body. She is seen in urban streets, in offices, gambling dens, and nightclubs actively participating in a public world and rejecting the private space of the home. So while she is in male places (and thus potentially available), she is independent enough to choose her mate and not vice versa.

The four broad categories reflect different cultural heritages and influences. The 'demure dame' and 'playmate pal' have their historical roots in courtly love, the male romance and the boy's adventure story where women have little if any social agency. They are potential partners and offer the male reader the fantasy female—sexually available but still demure enough to be domesticated. The 'dangerous dame' and the 'hoochie coochie mama' reflect the sexual agency of the 1920s and the 1930s flapper and vamp—whose rejection of marriage and domesticity were reflected in their jazzing, partying, bobbed hair, and rolled-down stockings. They are linked to nightclubs and strip joints, but they are not there earning their living as singers and actors; they are the business women who run the gin joints and are gangster molls rather than wives.

To revisit Judith Butler, if gender is performance then fashion is performance too. What we wear is part of that performance. Thus, the clothing on the covers of these books is not merely a covering (is clothing ever merely covering?) but an inactive performance. Clothing is an active signifier of a 'type' of woman and subtextually a positioning of that woman.

Book Cover Design: Case Study—Carter Brown

It is a mistake to dismiss book cover designs as incidental. Culturally and industrially, publishers deliberately create a visual metonymy that speaks to the readers. When Australian detective author 'Carter Brown'[5] was taken up by American publishers Signet, the editorial team's first priority was a marketing strategy and that strategy focused on the covers. They hired America's most sought-after softback cover artists—Bayre Phillips, Ronnie Lesser, and Robert McGinnis—to execute the covers. The artists were given detailed instructions as to what cover treatments were appropriate for each of the three detectives in the series:

> *Al Wheeler:* long partly undressed girl, plain background and elongated two word title....
>
> *Mavis Seidlitz:* feature Mavis in a situation on the cover each time; she's a cross between Marilyn Monroe and Judy Holliday. Possibly give her a detailed atmosphere background and a longer title....
>
> *Danny Boyd:* women could wear the maximum [Wheeler minimum] ie high fashion in gowns, jewellery, matador pants—or any other garment from *Vogue* and *Harpers* that also looks sexy. Maximum can also be strapless and not curve concealing. (Horwitz 1958).

The different cover treatments visually replicate the 'types' of textual females. Al Wheeler's 'playmate pals' are his playthings and thus fun body display is important; he also worked in a sunny Californian environment and thus swimsuits were appropriate wear. Danny Boyd is a New York private eye who requires more sophisticated women in more fashionable attire. On the other hand, Mavis is a private investigator and is given a busy background because she is a working woman. Mavis's clothes are sexy yet realistic. By the 1960s the trend was moving away from sensational covers, which is shown in the McGinnis covers; his style mimics a high fashion style. His women are thinner and less voluptuous; the emphasis is on the clothing, not the bodies.

A cover is more than the illustration. Cover design blends fonts, colors, text size, and layout in an effort to produce a visual semiotics. While the covers declare a male protagonist/author, the 'heroes' are dwarfed to a fully fleshed female (*Hi Fi Fadeout*), relegated to the background (*The Hard Racket*) or absent (*Duchess Double-X*). Semantically powerful words—'stripper', 'tramp', 'blonde', 'redhead', 'baby', 'cutie', 'dame', and 'sweetheart'—are repeated in titles to offer potential insight into the narrative. Sometimes, however, the covers were misleading. Because of strict deadlines, artists illustrated from titles rather from the written text; for instance, *Hard Racket* is not about the 'hard' life of prostitution but about the 'racket', the Mafia. No doubt many readers were disappointed when the women on the cover rarely provided the fictional thrills they promised.

Conclusion

Fashion is identity. Complex cultural and personal issues inform the costuming of the cover girl. Her outfits are not fashion statements but are signifiers—of her power, her station, and her narrative function, and these are transmitted by the creator, probably unconsciously, to the onlooker. The cover girls of the 1950s crime novels are not merely idealized representations of females. They also offer visual resistance and images of power and control. In fact, analysis of the females and their garments tells us today many things about the 1950s culture. They speak of the fears of women in public spaces—they are visual reminders of the changing roles of women. Women who had worked in munitions factories had to return to their homes; but the career girl, the *chanteuse*, and the nightclub *habitué* are visual hangovers that embody the new culture of capable women. Their depictions can be threatening or sexually alluring—they change over time and across genres.

Covers are intrinsically tied not to art but to semantics; and further analysis of the titles, font, size, and other marketing issues will present a fuller understanding of a book's paratext and the book industry as a whole. Furthermore, the covers are markers of a type of publication—and locate that publication in a complicated and ever-changing industry. And while the concentration of this chapter has been the crime pulp fiction of the 1950s, other genres sport covers with equal semiotic potential. The wrangler gear of the western female, the see-through space suits of the intergalactic woman, and the demure dresses of the romance heroine all impart messages. Because the pulp covers of this time retain an unshakeable hold on popular visual imagination sixty years after their original appearances, the seductive females smolder at us today from T-shirts, postcards, mousepads, card holders, and fridge magnets, reminding us of a bygone era, but they still remain powerful purveyors of meaning. Their most important fashion accessory is their appearance—the clothes and accessories that tell us what type of woman they are.

As Jessica Rabbit crooned, 'I'm not bad—I'm just drawn that way.'

References

Bruzzi, S. (1997), *Undressing Cinema: Clothing and Identity in the Movies*, London: Routledge.

Butler, J. (2004), *Undoing Gender*, London and New York: Routledge.

Cowley, Malcolm (1954), *The Literary Situation*, New York: Viking.

Genette, Gérard (1997), *Paratexts: Thresholds of Interpretation*, Cambridge: Cambridge University Press.

Goffman, Erving (1979) *Gender Advertisements*, Cambridge, MA: Harvard University Press.

Harris, Kristina (1992), 'Inside Christian Dior's New Look', http://www.vintageconnection. net/NewLook.htm. Accessed 10 October 2012.

Horwitz, Stanley (1958), Letter to Victor Weybright, 24 November, New American Library Archive 1943–1962, MSS 070, Series 2, Box 15, Folder 217, Fales Library and Special Collections, New York University Libraries, New York.

Johnson-Woods, Toni (2008), 'The Promiscuous Carter Brown', *Journal of the Association for the Study of Australian Literature*, Special Issue on: The Colonial Present: Australian Writing in the 21st Century (ed. Gillian Whitlock and Victoria Kuttainen), pp. 163–83.

McDowell, Colin (2002), 'Twin Sets', The Fashion Website, October, http://www.colinmcdowell.com/fashion/twin-sets/t-set.html. Accessed 10 October 2012.

Matthews, Nicole and Moody, Nickianne (2007), *Judging a Book by Its Cover: Fans, Publishers, Designers, and the Marketing of Fiction*, Aldershot: Ashgate.

Osmond, Suzanne (2011), '"Her Infinite Variety": Representations of Shakespeare's *Cleopatra* in Fashion, Film and Theatre', *Film, Fashion & Consumption*, 1.1, pp 55–79.

Who Framed Roger Rabbit?, directed by Robert Zemeckis, Walt Disney Pictures, 1988.

Notes

1 Originally, 'pulp fiction' referred to all-fiction magazines printed on cheap, wood-pulp paper (for example, *Black Mask*). Over the years, 'pulp' has become shorthand for mass-produced fiction that is formulaic rather than literary. Australian pulps were slim (usually fewer than one hundred pages), stapled publications about 18–20 cm tall; they are more accurately called 'digests'.

2 Varga changed his name from Vargas.

3 I use the phrase 'cover girls' because it has become linguistic shorthand for the women on the cover of magazines, books, etc.; however, none of the females depicted are girls but are women.

4 The Merriam-Webster dictionary defines 'cheesecake' as 'a photographic display of shapely and scantily clothed female figures' (http://www.merriam-webster.com/dictionary/cheesecake). Surprisingly few of these women are posed in a supine position and thus are rarely subordinate to the male.

5 'Carter Brown' was really Alan G. Yates. For more information on Yates and Signet, see Johnson-Woods (2008).

Chapter 6

Territories of Knowledge and Nostalgia in Modern Fashion Designer Life Writing

Ilya Parkins

As Caroline Evans notes in a discussion of French designer Jean Patou's American mannequins, in fashion, '[t]he look of standardization and an industrial aesthetic was commonly perceived to be an American one' (Evans 2008: 250). Evans's article traces 'tensions in early-twentieth-century modernity: between creativity and business, between France and America, and between elite consumption and mass production' (261). It builds on the work of Nancy Troy, who shows in her 2003 book, *Couture Culture*, how early-twentieth-century designers promoted concepts of authenticity in an anxious battle to suppress the inbuilt logic of copying and standardization that defined fashion, and that mining the perceived opposition between France and the United States (or 'America', as the United States was most commonly called) was an important strategy in that battle. Here, I work from the important insights of Troy and Evans to foreground the strained relationship between France and America in the discourses of fashion houses. But I begin from the autobiographical articulations of designers themselves, because they open up new dimensions—an epistemological one, and an intimate, psychic one—that allow us to think about how the designer is implicated in the maintenance of a discourse of national differences—and further, what the designer might tell us about the role of fashion in modernity.

The autobiographical work of fashion designers has enjoyed very little sustained critical attention in its own right. Probably because of its obviously commercial underpinnings, it has not been taken seriously as documentation of designers' subjectivity. To look for designers' subjectivity, though, misses the larger point about designer memoirs and autobiographies: that, particularly in the modern era, the era of fashion's massification, of its increasingly visible cultural presence, these texts are crucial indices of designers' attempts to craft a public persona—and to secure a lasting cultural legacy. No matter whether they are ghostwritten or penned by the designers themselves, no matter how carefully strategized and potentially 'inauthentic' their expressions of sentiment might be, they stand as documents of the peculiar condition of fashion designer celebrity—and in this way, I argue, they speak to larger questions about the place taken by fashion and the designer in the cultural landscape of early-twentieth-century modernity.

Indeed, when we read the designer autobiography as a document of celebrity self-fashioning, its relevance to the question of the modern—to both cultural modernism and industrial modernity—becomes clear. Most early-twentieth-century designers were engaged on some level with the logic of the new; the critical and commercial success of fashion was associated with a drive toward novelty that aligned it both with the drive of cultural *avant gardistes* toward innovation in idea and artistic form, and with the increasing technological sophistication of industrial production, which itself signified a very different kind of newness. As a line of fashion theorists stretching from Walter Benjamin through Ulrich Lehmann and Caroline Evans has shown, fashion's attachment to novelty is consistently compromised from within, or haunted, by the past, which reappears constantly in its cycles and is often referenced explicitly in couture. Fashion, in this account, has been shown to be a constellation of past and present, to use the terms of Walter Benjamin (Benjamin 1999; see also Lehmann 2000; Evans 2003; Vinken 2005). Of course, this was not explicitly acknowledged in the early twentieth century. In this period, designers' careers were built upon these two poles—aesthetic and industrial—of modernity; success depended on their ability to convincingly establish themselves as modern subjects, who held the sartorial keys to admitting others into the promise of the modern. If they were successful enough to publish memoirs and other autobiographical writings, then these careers were also, of necessity, exercises in the production and management of a public persona. The career of a popular early-twentieth-century fashion designer, then, was defined by at least two things: a cultivation of novelty, and a convincing and coherent spectacle of that novelty to consumers.

The designer memoir was a pillar in the establishment of a coherently modern identity, a foundation of this 'branding' effort. Even when published at the end of the design career, autobiographical writing did the work of establishing what critic Aaron Jaffe calls a 'modernist imprimatur'. In *Modernism and the Culture of Celebrity*, Jaffe explains this concept: 'By the word "imprimatur," I mean...that the modernist literary object bears the stamp of its producer prominently. At once as a distinctive mark and a sanctioning impression, the imprimatur, as I define it, turns the author into a formal artifact, fusing it to the text as a reified signature of value' (Jaffe 2005: 20). I argue that fashion designer autobiographies functioned as Jaffe suggests the modernist imprimatur did: they enabled the accrual of value to the designers—even in retrospect—on the basis of perceptions of their individuality, which in turn derived from a sense of their modern iconoclasm. Though Jaffe has developed the concept to speak to the particularities of literary modernism, it is worth noting that it has a special relevance for the fashion designer, who literally cultivated a distinct signature to signify the un-reproducibility of her or his sartorial artistry.

Now, it may well be that designer autobiographical work is invested in the creation of a coherent signature. But try as they might to base their couturier branding efforts on a consistent picture of a personality, the works reveal the ideological pressures brought to bear in their creation. Marked by tensions and contradictions—notably between an undercurrent of conservatism that would appear to fly in the face of the revolutionary sensibility the designers were concerned to articulate—the autobiographical works make apparent the labor of their production. Hence they also reveal something of the labor invested in the creation of designer identities. And, as I will suggest here, that labor—whether or not it is a 'genuine' reflection of the psychic states of designers—reveals something about the general cultural positioning of the couturier in modernity.

One of the layers of tension that becomes apparent in an examination of the formation of a modernist imprimatur in the autobiographical writing of Paul Poiret (active from the 1900s–1920s) and Elsa Schiaparelli (active from the late 1920s-1950s), is a persistent—and constantly threatened—opposition between what I would call two different modernities, distinguished by their geographic coordinates. The works seem to bear agitated witness to— but, crucially, they also help to produce—a conflict between two different manners of being modern, two *styles de vie* and aesthetic orientations which were respectively yoked to France, where the designers resided, and America. For example, in her 1954 memoir, *Shocking Life*, Schiaparelli describes her understanding of the acts of cultural translation necessary when she—long based in Paris, though Italian by birth—began an American lecture tour during World War II. She writes:

America had always been more than hospitable and friendly to me. She had made it possible for me to obtain a unique place in the world. France gave me the inspiration, America the sympathetic approval and the result. Here I was trying to tell America...that it was impossible to replace France in the realm of our particular creative work. There are impalpable reasons that have made France what she is...I pointed out that America, which had made terrific steps forward, employs methods built upon a vast and limitless scale of thought and production, whilst ours are those of a beautiful atelier of research and fantasy. (Schiaparelli [1954] 2007: 112–13)

Schiaparelli takes pains here to clarify her goodwill toward America. Even in expressing her sympathy for the country, though, she relies on a conceptual opposition between France and America. It is one that aligns France with an aesthetic modernism that has deep, even transhistorical roots, and the United States with an ethos of industrial modernization. This is an altogether predictable formulation, relying as it does on the dichotomization of aesthetics and the market which have been problematized over the last fifteen years. (See Jensen 1993; Dettmar and Watt 1996; Burns 1996; Turner 2003; and Jaffe 2005.)

Twenty years earlier, recounting his own fashion career in the first of three autobiographical works, *En habillant l'époque* (1930)—published in English as *King of Fashion* or *My First Fifty Years*—a fervently anti-American Paul Poiret described Americans thus:

An American has to see an article manufactured, completed, solid in front of him, so that he can copy it servilely. Their absolute lack of imagination prevents them from conceiving the unforeseen and the hypothetical. Like Saint Thomas, they only believe what they have seen. This must restrict them in science and in art, for it restricts their field of activity to the data of experience. (Poiret 1931: 275–76)

Here Poiret is dismissing Americans as empiricists, enslaved by sense data. What is remarkable about this passage is the invocation of epistemological categories to describe the opposition between France and America. In approaching the question in this way,

Poiret invites us to reconsider the dichotomous positioning of the two nations as a war between competing modern ways of knowing. This approach is fruitful, too, in analyzing Schiaparelli: recall her formulation, cited above, of Americans employing 'a vast and limitless scale of thought and production', whereas the French are invested in 'research and fantasy', and their aesthetic dominance has occurred for 'impalpable reasons' (112–13). The invocation of scale situates American methods of production spatially, whereas the alignment of French production with fantasy suggests an intriguingly unsituated and in that sense ethereal, ultimately unknowable, process. The delineation of a particularly French kind of unknowability in opposition to American empiricism thus becomes shorthand for the dichotomy of transcendent artistry and vulgar industry.

Two related things are notable about this spatial opposition. The first is that taken together, Poiret and Schiaparelli encourage a rereading of France and America as incompatible epistemes. Their life writing serves to delineate two different kinds of knowledge—the autobiographical act is, for these designers, implicated in the construction of themselves as particular kinds of (French) knowers, against the knower implied by the empiricism of the United States. The creation of the fashion designer's modernist signature involves the designation of the designer as a knowing subject. This designation is highly suggestive in conceiving of the role of both fashion and its designers in the early-twentieth-century cultural landscape. As a form that is at once fantastic and material, ephemerally inconstant and visually spectacular, fashion itself necessarily complicates the epistemic opposition between abstract and experientially verifiable knowledges. The designers' uneasy straddling of this divide indicates the fragility of the division between aesthetic abstraction and the materiality of the market in the rapidly democratizing twentieth-century fashion industry.

Bringing to bear an epistemic analysis on these texts reveals a second dimension of the fashion designer persona, one which might be said to exist as a counterweight to the generally frothy depictions of fashion designers in the mass media in this period. The texts underline a persistent melancholy in the two designers, one which might be said to wear away at the celebratory tone that each strikes. This melancholy is directly related to the epistemological split that characterizes the relationship of America and France; it emerges from what they deem the successful encroachment of an American, empiricist episteme upon their own French one. The apparent demise of their own episteme punctures the progressivist, future-oriented rhetoric that characterizes each work, as melancholy shades into nostalgia, a modality that develops a melancholy character as it confronts the sheer inaccessibility of the past, its irreconcilability with the present (Fritzsche 2001: 1592). An epistemological analysis of these texts, then, also allows us to understand melancholy not only as typifying the condition of the modern fashion designer, but also potentially sheds new light on the question of fashion's temporal structure as a perplexing crystallization of past and present.

Though Poiret and Schiaparelli are two very different designers, working in slightly different times, a comparative reading of their autobiographical works yields some important insights that allow us to begin to generalize about the condition of the fashion designer in modernity. In fact, it is precisely the divergent character of their life writing that makes a comparative examination so effective. The tone of their work differs substantially. Poiret's three autobiographical publications, *En habillant l'époque, Revenez-y* (1932), and *Art et phynance* (1934), might well be described as defensive rehabilitations of the designer's own name, coming as they did at the end of the final, troubled decade of Poiret's career and the failure of his business. Poiret's works are also conventional in their rhetoric and structure; they are chronological narratives that position the author and his aesthetic philosophy unambiguously at their center; they might be read as rhetorical pleas for a coherent identity. Schiaparelli's single autobiographical work, *Shocking Life*, though it is also a chronological narrative, does not offer the same kind of apparently straightforward framework. Rather, it is characterized by what Caroline Evans calls 'a tendency to make-believe....[I]t is...playful and puzzling, full of distancing devices that serve to highlight the contingent and precarious nature of identity' (Evans 2008: 23). On one level, then, Schiaparelli's work offers a strong contrast to Poiret's. Thus it is all the more remarkable that, from their divergent approaches, we find emerging an analogous set of epistemological and temporal concerns. It is for this reason, I contend, that the two texts can be used together to cautiously theorize about the state of the modern designer's public persona, and can also tell us something about the psychic stakes of fashion as a cultural industry.

To understand the way that territory and epistemology are intertwined in these texts, I will begin by more closely examining how knowledge is mapped onto place. One of the most striking features of Schiaparelli's autobiography is her constant alignment with ethereality; she notes that she 'continued to believe in miracles' (Schiaparelli [1954] 2007: 9) and characterizes herself as a 'mystic' who 'could not bend [herself] to the laws of religion' (20). Her 'belief was directly connected to the source of harmony and creation', but she 'could not bring [herself] to go through the channels of man' (20). Here she establishes her anti-materialist ethic, revealing a yearning to disavow the physical and conventional structures that constrain her. For a fashion designer—whose career was, of necessity, built on her mastery of materials—this constant invocation of the extra-material as foundational to her character is telling. One might argue that the clothing she designs actually bears out this tension between matter and immateriality, as her oeuvre is famously characterized by its surrealist play, its incorporation of principles of uncertainty which engage the viewer as a—profoundly uncertain—knower. Schiaparelli summarizes it bluntly near the end of the book by saying that she strongly believes in the unknown, and that at the end of her career she was in more profound contact with the beyond—indeed, this is what prompted her to retire. The beyond is the means by which she spatializes—or perhaps more accurately, *de*spatializes—the unknowable she so prizes. As her career draws to a close and she publishes this reflection on her life and work, she evinces a certain desperation to transcend the parameters of space and time.

Poiret's autobiographical writing repeatedly makes similar moves, invoking a kind of unlocatable non-place as the realm of the artistry within which he is so concerned to position himself, against commerce. For him, this is often figured as dream or imagination, which, he notes in *Art et phynance*, is—though 'unreal'—able because of its deterritorialized quality to engender the conventional space of reality. Here, he asks himself, which is more powerful, reality or dreams, and answers: 'I think that dream is more powerful, because it engenders reality' (Poiret 1934: 21). This accords a constitutive power to the immaterial, the un-situated, that effectively privileges non-place over conventional space. The tendency to privilege this category of Nowhere is threaded through all of his writing, often taking the form of a classic concern with an eternal beauty, which in turn works to align the aesthetic principle on which his work is founded with a cultural value that is deemed to transcend time and space.

What is curious about this invocation of Nowhere as a governing principle in both of these texts is the constant compromising of this spacelessness. Nowhere is by definition unlocatable, of course, yet the designers frequently bring Nowhere down to earth, as it were, by locating it in France. At the very least, France is, by virtue of being the antithesis of America, an important facilitator or enabler of the unsituated values that they so prize. In locating themselves in this non-spatial space that is obliquely and intermittently aligned with the aesthetic possibilities represented by France, Schiaparelli and Poiret are each able to distinguish themselves from the material topography of the United States, given shape in their work through descriptions of cities, lecture halls, stores, and factories—in effect, through representations of materiality of the nation. What is striking in each author's major work is the mundane nature of descriptions of America—street scenes, banal department stores, for instance—as opposed to descriptions of place in France, the latter of which are largely tied to the singular sites of the designers' ateliers, showrooms, and homes. The French spaces are privileged and themselves semi-transcendent because of their association with the designers as mediators of unknowability. The American sites, oriented in these accounts to crude and pedestrian spectacles of production or consumption, are, by contrast, fatally grounded, inexorably material. They are transparently knowable, whereas the kinds of knowing that might be facilitated by the incompletely described geography of France are uncertain, immaterial, and ultimately unstable.

What might give us pause in the work of both designers is a strange, intermittent attribution of spatial transcendence to America, which I noted above. This sometimes seems to compromise their insistence on the epistemic difference between themselves and Americans. Recall again that Schiaparelli describes the 'vast and limitless scale of thought and production' in America, contrasting it to the French 'atelier of research and fantasy' (Schiaparelli [1954] 2007: 112–13). Poiret also points to this vastness, aligning it with a certain monumentality: 'their conceptions are vaster and more monumental than ours' (Poiret 1931: 270). A kind of limitlessness comes into play here, but its attachment to the object-based world of industrial production differentiates it from the ultimate material transcendence of the French. Indeed, the figuration of vastness and transcendence is derived from the size of the American landscape—it is tied to space—and for that reason it does not represent a transcendent beyond. The beyond prized by Poiret and Schiaparelli has no such spatial correlates.

I would like to suggest that this contrastive motif effectively establishes both as practitioners of a kind of transcendent modernism, emergent from a free-floating, un-situated plane. It dematerializes the designers and the labor they are engaged in, as modern artist-industrialists. There is clearly something liberating in that kind of weightlessless, and it seems to become a refuge from modernity even as it is invoked in the name of modernist experiment. Fashion and its worlds seem sometimes in the modern period to speak obliquely to the yearning of various modernists for an escape valve from the pressures of modernity. In the case of Poiret and Schiaparelli, who bear the weight of the tension between art and commerce, that is an escape into liquidity that offers respite from the tension yet also helps to shore up their retroactive branding of themselves as particular kinds of subjects. The move to deterritorialize thus constructs them as subjects, constructs their houses as having an appropriately artistic and transcendental legacy, and offers them subjective dissolution as a balm for the overburdened, modern spirit.

In making this move away from space, Schiaparelli and Poiret are suggesting something about the content and value of knowledge, and the construction of the knower, in France. But more importantly, they are also pointing to a French knower specific to the fashion industry. The disavowal of spatiality is necessarily a disavowal of the process of production upon which their businesses rely. Their refusal to locate themselves and their form of knowledge—triangulated as it is with creativity and imagination—effects an erasure of the process of production that plainly recalls commodity fetishism. Commodity fetishism—involving, in the classic Marxian formulation, the obscuring or effacement of the process of commodity production, so that the commodity takes on a magical cast—is certainly a predictably invoked construct in any discussion of fashion. But here it becomes visible in a different way. What is notable is that what are being erased here are not necessarily the conditions of production of the object—in the case of the fashion industry, the clothing—but the conditions of production of (French) knowledge and French epistemic subjects themselves; in this case, the conditions of emergence of the designer, as designer becomes commodity. Julie Rak notes that, in mass-marketed life writing, though the work's success depends on the depiction of a coherent subject, 'the taking-on of narrative subjectivity in the text means that the writing subject of autobiography must become an object in order to package his or her identity for consumption' (Rak 2002: 155). In these autobiographical texts, the establishment of competing epistemes is a central ingredient in the development of a saleable public persona for the designers.

For, of course, one buys a commodity. If the subject of the autobiography is a commodity, it is this objectified subject that a consumer is purchasing. In their unlocated-ness, the designers as representatives of a French way of knowing offer to consumers the promise of access—through purchase—to a way of knowing and by extension a way of life. What is noteworthy about these texts is that they reveal an engagement in the retrospective branding and marketing of designers and their houses on multiple levels: especially since the fashion houses are no longer operative, what is being promoted through the construction of the designers as particular kinds of epistemic subjects is an epistemological standpoint (or non-standpoint, as it were). Modern fashion becomes visible as attempting to preserve, or perhaps germinate, a kind of knowledge whose existence appears to be threatened by the very conditions of industrial production that increasingly defined it. And, as the life writing shows us, its designers came to embody that tension. Their publications, so easily dismissible as mere mass-market drivel, seem to bear the traces of this encounter between competing epistemes, and this lends the works a melancholy quality that flies in the face of their purpose and the celebratory publicity efforts attached to them.

Recognizing the melancholic quality of the designers' self-representations calls us to attend to the kind of narrative that is told in these works about the designers' *changing* relationship to America as an episteme that is incompatible with their own. Both texts are characterized by an initial voicing of a certain hope in relation to America, which eventually gives way to disenchantment with American industry and empiricism. In her text, Schiaparelli evokes this very early on, suggesting that her first trip to America, a decade before she began designing clothing, called her violently to her senses from an optimistic mythologizing about American possibilities: 'America, the magic dream of the world, holds out expectations beyond what can humanly be fulfilled' (Schiaparelli [1954] 2007: 28). All of Schiaparelli's later descriptions of America are read through this initial expression of disappointment. With her descriptions of her time in exile there during World War II, the disappointment takes on a melancholy cast. She writes, for instance, that '[i] nexplicable undercurrents had been lapping round her like waves in the dark; subdued, monotonous waves that wear down' (Schiaparelli [1954] 2007: 145). The more time she spends in America over the course of her career, the more forcefully she locates herself as a different kind of knower from that apparently produced and privileged by the Americans. The implied transformation of the image of America from a site of magic and hope functions as a particular kind of nostalgic knowledge narrative, one that laments the loss of childish naiveté but also strategically opposes Schiaparelli to that naiveté.

Poiret makes a similar, if more explicit, move, but does so by nostalgically attributing such naiveté directly to the Americans. He argues that the only French person equipped to understand the American psyche is 'the elementary schoolboy' (Poiret 1931: 279), a naive empiricist who can navigate the overwhelming onslaught of sensory data that America represents through its crowds, its architecture, its hectic visual culture. This figure is invested with a kind of epistemic privilege that the French do not have; in a particularly noteworthy passage, Poiret writes this of the French: 'the form of our education does not always make it easy for us to understand the mass of this people. On the contrary, it handicaps us, and our impedimenta of knowledge, culture, and riches encumbers us as soon as we are on the boat' to the United States. (Poiret 1931: 179) Here, then, the empiricism of America is equated with a lack of education, or at least, of education in the liberal arts which are understood to constitute civilization.

Thus both Poiret and Schiaparelli respond to the category of naive or ignorant knowledge. Though their locations of this naiveté are divergent, their generally nostalgic gloss on the category of naive knowledge and its association with American empiricism also works to establish both as worldly and yet world-weary knowers. This apparent compliment about the promise of American knowledge becomes a comment on the sophistication of the designer and a denigration of the American sensibility.

Indeed, the figuration of unknowability and mystery as a kind of cross to be heroically borne by the French fashion designer in the face of the onslaught of American consumer culture is strong in these texts, and I would argue that it even functions as the central theme of both accounts. The portrayal of melancholic artistry in both texts is rooted in the sense of the designers as endangered epistemic subjects. And if we take this life writing as a study in the retroactive construction of a public persona, the building of a legacy—as the texts' publication at the end of each designer's career suggests that we must—then we must consider what it means that the designers are invested in an understanding of themselves as heroic yet sacrificial offerings in the relationship between competing modern epistemes, one of which, they know since they are writing retrospective accounts, will emerge victorious.

Each knows that America is the winner of the game they were engaged in. Poiret fought a war against the copy, the unlicensed reproduction, which was, in a sense, a French war with America. As Troy points out in *Couture Culture*, Poiret's later career was marked by his attempts to find a third way between American industry and French imagination (Troy 2003). His inability to regain his prewar glory in the 1920s is detailed in *Art et phynance*, a memoir entirely devoted to describing the dissolution of his enterprise and marked by an ill-concealed rage at the financiers who swindled him as he attempted to rebuild. Ultimately Poiret's house failed, even as he gave over his name to the apparently Americanized ready-to-wear lines that he had initially so disparaged. His failure seems to account for the bitter tone of his autobiographical *oeuvre*; the melancholy that overwhelms his attempts to rescue his legacy from its bastardization in the 1920s and early 1930s stems from the recognition that he was unable to stave off the forces of American empiricism.

For her part, Schiaparelli watched the changing of the fashion guard after World War II, the loss of Parisian supremacy to American manufacturing might. This she recounts in a melancholic tone. In the closing pages of *Shocking Life*, she describes her decision to retire in 1954:

> I knew then that in order to build more solidly one is sometimes obliged to destroy. That one should learn to understand the language of the people who do not know the difference between meat and flesh, and at the same time help to build a new elegance of manners and clothes, a new aristocracy, fit to co-ordinate with the crude rhythm of modern life. (Schiaparelli [1954] 2007: 207)

Schiaparelli's account differs from Poiret's in this respect; she is more circumspect, less bitter, about the necessity of finding a third way between the French and American epistemes and modes of production, perhaps because she never struggled the way that Poiret did in his enterprise, but rather chose to retire while she remained successful. This passage nevertheless evinces a recognition that she, too, has failed, if less spectacularly than Poiret.

She still chooses a guardedly optimistic tone—after all, she wants to 'build more solidly' the domains of fashion and style—but recognizes that her own, French episteme has, for the moment, been vanquished by the American way.

These autobiographies thus offer not only an account of competing epistemes, but of the dissolution of their own. In both texts, there is a slippage: America goes from being figured as a nation of oafish yet benign empiricists, to a threatening, even monstrous entity. In Schiaparelli's text, this is evident in her description of her exile in America during World War II. During that period, she says (referring to herself in the third person, as she does intermittently throughout the text, '[s]omething was wrong. A malignant force was working against Schiap, though where it came from she never knew. Just now, in this dismantled world, whatever Schiap did was either fought against or distorted by an invisible demon hand' (Schiaparelli [1954] 2007: 145). America comes to represent evil here (and it is interesting to note, as an aside, how in a sense unknowability is transfigured, shown this time in an American guise, but having taken on a demonic aspect that is very different from French unknowability). Poiret's representation of America's monstrosity is different; it shades into the embodied grotesque, for instance in its depictions of Americans as 'a Gargantua, with one hundred and twenty million mouths, all gaping upon the same continent' (Poiret 1931: 279). Such imagery obviously demands the reader's sympathy for the embattled designer, and even buttresses their self-portrayals in iconoclastic, heroic terms. The triumph of an American episteme that is monstrous in its scale and its mechanization presents itself as yet another opportunity to retroactively shore up the designers' particularly transcendent modernism and secure a legacy.

The narrative of encroachment, though, also establishes the designers as nostalgic subjects. In aligning America with industrial modernity, against a kind of transhistorical modernity—a modern time that nevertheless is marked by its deep roots in prior aesthetic and intellectual traditions—the authors both suggest that this past has been overtaken, lost. Nostalgia itself is a temporal conundrum, as Peter Fritzsche's theorization of the rise of nostalgia in the wake of the French Revolution makes clear; it is made possible by 'a broader reconfiguration of temporality' characterized by concepts of 'historical discontinuity and historical periodicity' that construct the past as inaccessible and other to the present moment (Fritzsche 2001: 1588). As Fritzsche explains,

> While nostalgia takes the past as its mournful subject, it holds it at arm's length. The virtues of the past are cherished and their passage is lamented, but there is no doubt that they are no longer retrievable. In other words, nostalgia constitutes itself by what it cannot possess and defines itself by its inability to approach its subject, a paradox that is the essence of nostalgia's melancholia. (1595)

Fritzsche's concept of modern nostalgic melancholy also establishes nostalgia's epistemological stakes: with the emergence of understandings of historical rupture and discontinuity, 'the past turned into a problem of knowledge and became a source of disquiet, a nagging, unmasterable presence of absence' (1588). Nostalgia foregrounds the subjective interpretation of the past. It asks how one might know that which was not present, but was 'inaccessible and bounded' (1592). even though it continued to live on in personal memory and in the very constitution of the self. Nostalgia is a reflection of the self's insertion, in modernity, into the historical epoch, so that history is personalized, takes on an intimate dimension. For Fritzsche, this unique temporal structure is at the root of the proliferation of memoir and autobiography in the modern period (1608).

Fritzsche's discussion of nostalgic melancholy identifies this unique temporal consciousness in the proliferation of narratives of loss and dispossession, which trace the subjective negotiations of large-scale historical events and traumas. Though he is treating the first half of the nineteenth century, his theorization of these stories of exile and dispossession as indicative of the internalization of a shifting historical consciousness in modernity provides an intriguing means by which to understand Poiret's and Schiaparelli's fashion autobiographies. Against the studied and intermittently joyful eccentricity of Schiaparelli's self-portrait, against the self-aggrandizing tone of Poiret's, these works can be read as accounts of loss and dispossession. And, considering their contexts—the world of modern fashion, premised and dependent as it was on the constant reinvention of the new—this sense of loss tells us something about the purpose of their life writing, and its relationship to the broader fashion industry.

In my introduction, I noted Aaron Jaffe's concept of the modernist imprimatur, from which emerges the modern literary celebrity as brand. Mobilizing the idea of the modernist imprimatur as a coherent signature or personal brand is useful for fashion studies, though certainly different from the way it functions in literary modernism. Literary modernism was a domain where the discussion of money and markets was overtly discouraged, whereas the fashion industry was powered by these things. At any rate, the notion of the imprimatur takes on an intriguing cast when the modernist in question is writing to *retrospectively* establish a coherent identity, to impose that signature on themselves at the *end* of their careers. What, to be blunt, is the point of establishing a coherent, brand-related identity if there is no material gain to be made from it—if, as with both of these designers, the businesses in question are shuttered? There is no question that at least part of the equation is material gain—and this holds especially true for Poiret, who faced serious financial problems in the post-career period in which he published these three autobiographies. That Schiaparelli published her work immediately after the closing of her house (and when she was not facing significant financial difficulties and that Poiret obsessively published not one, but three, autobiographies) suggests that something more than profit was at stake in the writing of what ultimately consolidated a modernist imprimatur. If Fritzsche's framework of nostalgia as a symptom of modern loss and dispossession holds true, then it becomes possible to read these works as testimonials to the loss represented by a globalizing culture, one characterized by multiple, seemingly incompatible, epistemes. In the face of that loss, their recounting of their careers takes on a very specific cast; these works can be read as efforts to fix and memorialize not just themselves, but an entire way of knowing. At the very end of her autobiography, Schiaparelli makes plain that, in retiring from the fashion industry, she had submitted to the logic of the new that defined fashion and its modernity; she must 'make an absolute change' (Schiaparelli [1954] 2007: 207). She gives a sense of what is at stake in this submission when she writes that, in retiring, 'I must not only free myself from the excess baggage of possessions and jealousy, but I must also tear myself away from the bondage of love and devotion. It meant tears and relief, it meant tightening my own heart without mercy; there must be no softness and no regrets' (207). Schiaparelli suggests that the capitulation is painful enough to require emotional fortitude. Poiret's major work, *King of Fashion*, ends on a similar note. He recounts the dissolution of his house in unusually cursory terms, after describing its ascendancy in rich detail: 'It was the end of everything. A few days later I was turned into a limited company. Everyone knows the rest of the story' (Poiret 1931: 330). Here his affected brevity also attests that the triumph of the American episteme—which is, in his mind, the cause of his demise—is too painful to dwell on. Both Poiret and Schiaparelli erect psychic defenses of a kind, then, against feelings of loss that originate from their sense that a way of knowing has been superseded, and with its demise, their very sense of self is threatened.

This question of the designers' sense of their own identities begins to reveal for us the import of this textual legacy of melancholy and loss. It underscores what is at stake in these autobiographies for those interested in the relationship of early-twentieth-century fashion to broader structures of modernity. The texts reveal the intimate point of intersection between Poiret's and Schiaparelli's understandings of multiple regimes of knowledge, and their ambiguous positioning of themselves as modern subjects of a very particular type—artist-industrialists. Poiret and Schiaparelli's efforts to memorialize themselves as epistemic subjects point to anxieties—about the relationship between art and commerce, between the original and the copy, the elite and the mass market—that are intrinsic to the development of the fashion industry in the early twentieth century. But I suggest it shows us something more about this anxiety, because the self-representational labor reveals its subjective, melancholic dimension. Though it is important to remember that these are mass-marketed memoirs, clearly written with the aim of securing a legacy for a fashion house as a brand, they seem to bear the traces of a melancholic dissatisfaction. I propose that this melancholy is a major condition of modernity for the French fashion designer. And, further, that it emerges from the contradiction they live between a transcendent modernism with transhistorical underpinnings, and an industrial modernity that threatens not simply to overshadow their perceived uniqueness, authenticity, and artistry, but to render them obsolete as subjects. I cannot help but be reminded of the archetypal battle between modernization and cultural modernism that has been shown in recent modernist studies criticism to be a false dichotomy, but that certainly remained ideologically compelling—it was a tension that was all too real to people like Poiret and Schiaparelli and their publics. These designers can, I think, be read as bearers of this tension between art and commerce. And it is fashion that puts them there, with its simultaneous promise of cultural distinction and ideological massification. In this sense, I think the fashion memoirs point us to the way the ideological stakes of fashion, as a general modality of the modern, might be internalized by designers. As Caroline Evans notes in another context, 'Fashion, with its affinity for transformation, can act out instability and loss' (Evans 2003: 6) as foundational narratives of the modern. Fashion materializes these modalities, but it in itself does not allow us access to them as subjectively experienced. But instability and loss are what we find in the life writing of Poiret and Schiaparelli and this raises the question of the psychic stakes of the operations of different epistemological paradigms—and their relationship to fashion.

The question of the emotional content and resonance of two different, apparently nationalized epistemes matters because it foregrounds the specificity of fashion. Obviously, fashion itself bears the contradiction between art and commerce. In their writing, the designers have subjectified that tense encounter. Whether or not this is 'authentic' angst is not the issue. The issue is that this is yet another way in which the representation and reality of fashion come to be bound up with a modern imaginary that is always on the precipice of devastation. Gilles Lipovetsky writes in *The Empire of Fashion* that fashion 'pacifies social conflict but deepens subjective and intersubjective conflict: allows more individual freedom but generates greater malaise in living' (Lipovetsky 1994: 241). It does so by deepening the divides between social actors, rupturing their connections to each other, exacerbating the divisions characteristic of modernity as experienced in the metropole. It is not merely wearers and consumers of fashion who experience its alienating qualities. These texts by designers show us that they, too—in their bearing of fashion's contradictions—are touched by the profound relationship between fashion and alienation. Lipovetsky and Caroline Evans have argued that fashion privileges or highlights the profundity of modern anomie. It also, I would add, because it is such a personal and embodied modality, points us to the *intimately* experienced dimensions of this anomie. Poiret's and Schiaparelli's texts point us to this psychic dimension, and its linkage for them to the question of two competing modernities—an empirical or industrial one, and an unknowable, creative one—might enrich our understanding of fashion-related melancholia for subjects in general.

Finally, what is intriguing about the melancholic dimensions of these texts is the way that they contribute to the ongoing theorization of modern fashion's constellations of past and present, which I noted above. Since Benjamin—indeed, arguably, since Baudelaire—the apparent conundrum of fashion's enfolding of past into present has been fruitful territory for theorists of fashion. By showing readers the way this temporal complexity was borne out, for modern designers, in nostalgia, the life writing makes plain the pervasiveness of this construction, and most importantly its *personal* meaning for subjects associated with fashion. In these texts, the apparently philosophical problem of temporality becomes a question of subjective knowledge, a lived experience of dissonance. Part of what is so helpful is the way they materialize and personalize the temporal reconfigurations of modernity, which so often read as abstract and impersonal. This is instructive for us in thinking about fashion, as fashion also functions as an intimate join between body and world, linking individual, embodied subjects to mass movements. As Ann Rosalind Jones and Peter Stallybrass put it in their book on figurations of clothing in the early modern period, '[c]lothing is a worn world: a world of social relations put upon the wearer's body' (Jones and Stallybrass 2000: 3). The autobiographical work of modern designers begins to color in for us the ways that such a 'worn world' is mediated and experienced by the subjects who provided the materials, in the modern period, for the wearing.

Note

This paper was previously published under the title 'Early Twentieth-Century Fashion Designer Life Writing', in *CLCWeb: Comparative Literature and Culture* 13, no. 1 (March 2011).

References

Benjamin, W. (1999), *The Arcades Project* (trans. H. Eiland and K. McLaughlin), Cambridge: Belknap Press.

Burns, S. (1996), *Inventing the Modern Artist: Art and Culture in Gilded Age America*, New Haven, CT: Yale University Press.

Dettmar, K. and Watt, S., eds (1996), *Marketing Modernism: Self-Promotion, Canonization, and Re-Reading*, Ann Arbor: University of Michigan Press.

Evans, C. (1999), 'Masks, Mirrors and Mannequins: Elsa Schiaparelli and the Decentered Subject', *Fashion Theory*, 3.1, pp. 3–32.

—— (2003), *Fashion at the Edge: Spectacle, Modernity, and Deathliness*, New Haven, CT: Yale University Press.

—— (2008), 'Jean Patou's American Mannequins: Early Fashion Shows and Modernism', *Modernism/Modernity*, 15.2, pp. 243–63.

Fritzsche, P. (2001), 'Specters of History: On Nostalgia, Exile, and Modernity', *The American Historical Review*, 106.5, pp. 1587–1618.

Jaffe, A. (2005), *Modernism and the Culture of Celebrity*, Cambridge: Cambridge University Press.

Jensen, R. (1993), *Marketing Modernism in Fin-de-Siècle Europe*, Princeton, NJ: Princeton University Press.

Jones, A.R. and Stallybrass, P. (2000), *Worn Worlds: Renaissance Clothing and the Materials of Memory*, Cambridge: Cambridge University Press.

Lehmann, U. (2000), *Tigersprung: Fashion in Modernity*, Cambridge, MA: MIT Press.

Lipovetsky, G. (1994), *The Empire of Fashion: Dressing Modern Democracy* (trans. C. Porter), Princeton, NJ: Princeton University Press.

Poiret, P. (1930), *En habillant l'époque*, Paris: Grasset.

—— (1931), *King of Fashion* (trans. S.H. Guest), Philadelphia and London: J.B. Lippincott.

—— (1932), *Revenez-y*, Paris: Gallimard.

—— (1934), *Art et phynance*, Paris: Lutetia.

Rak, J. (2002), 'Autobiography and Production: The Case of Conrad Black', *International Journal of Canadian Studies,* 25, pp. 149–68.

Schiaparelli, E. ([1954] 2007), *Shocking Life: The Autobiography of Elsa Schiaparelli*, London: V&A Publications.

Troy, N.J. (2003), *Couture Culture: A Study in Modern Art and Fashion*, Cambridge, MA: MIT Press.

Turner, C. (2003), *Marketing Modernism between the Two World Wars*, Amherst: University of Massachusetts Press.

Vinken, B. (2005), *Fashion Zeitgeist: Trends and Cycles in the Fashion System* (trans. Mark Hewson), Oxford: Berg.

Chapter 7

Looking for Mr. Benson: The Black Leather Motorcycle Jacket and Narratives of Masculinities

Marvin J. Taylor

'He had on heavy black boots, button-fly jeans, a washed-out Levi's shirt and an old, greasy, leather jacket' (Preston 1992: 7)

With this description of a leatherman's wardrobe, Jamie, the narrator of John Preston's novel *Mr. Benson*, describes Aristotle Benson, the man who will become his master. Preston's novel is one of the classics of gay male S/M erotica—a one-hander, if you will—but it is more. It is a gateway into the symbolism of black leather as perceived within the larger culture, and more specifically to the shifting meaning of the black leather motorcycle jacket. How does Jamie come to realize that the hypermasculine Mr. Benson and his black leather jacket are the epitome of Jamie's erotic imaginary? What is the appeal of the black leather jacket? How did it come into being and how does it function in popular culture?

The chapter is an archeological dig, of sorts, to find a Foucauldian genealogy of the black leather motorcycle jacket from its creation by Irving Schott in 1928 through its many symbolic shifts from biker culture to juvenile delinquents, gay S/M, and punk rock. The shifting signification of the black leather jacket and notions of masculinity in American culture contrast with commonly held views about S/M culture. By reading *Mr. Benson* against this genealogy and against culturally accepted ideas about S/M, I will use the novel to unpack the relationship between narrator and reader as power dynamic. What role does the hypermasculine tradition of queer culture play in our understanding of the black leather jacket and of narrative?

John Preston's novel *Mr. Benson* was serialized in *Drummer*, a gay S/M porn magazine in 1979 and 1980 (from issue 29 to 38). *Drummer*, which began publication in 1975, quickly became the most popular magazine for the gay leather, bondage, and S/M (BDSM) scene. Though the scene had existed since at least the 1940s, most BDSM publications had very small print runs and their distribution was limited to sex shops. *Drummer* changed all that by its relatively large-scale distribution to newsstands and other magazine shops. *Drummer* signified not only the expansion of the scene, but also gay men's increased interest in hypermasculine self-styling. It is no mistake that the Village People disco band appeared in 1977, two years after the first issue of *Drummer* and featured a leatherman among its members. Gerald Walker's novel, *Cruising* (1970), about a gay serial killer in New York City, became a film of the same name (dir. Friedkin) starring Al Pacino—much to the dismay of some gay rights activists—in 1980. Further, Preston's novel sparked a fashion moment when gay men began wearing T-shirts with the words 'Looking for Mr. Benson' printed across their chests, from which I take my title. Late seventies culture in the United States seemed obsessed with gay leathermen.

Where Does the BLJ (not unlike the LBD—Little Black Dress) Come From?

The history of the black leather jacket is tied directly to the U.S. military. Linda Gregory notes that the first motorcycles were used by U.S. troops during World War I (Gregory 2003). The jackets they wore were made of brown leather and had buttons, ribbed collars, and cuffs, and looked very similar to those worn by the early air pilots. The problem with these jackets was that they allowed in air and provided insufficient warmth for the wearer. Very importantly, for our story, Irving and Jack Schott, two Russian Jewish immigrants, opened a store at 96 East Broadway on New York's Lower East Side in 1913. The brothers originally made rubber raincoats sold by door-to-door peddlers. Always interested in army surplus, the brothers were awarded a contract for making jackets for the U.S. military during World War I, and their business expanded (Anon n.d.).

Irving Schott was fascinated by motorcycles.[1] He began producing jackets for bikers that were distributed by one of the earliest motorcycle promoters, the Beck Company. These early jackets were buttoned, like the ones made for the military. In 1928, Irving, a representative from Beck, and a representative from Talon, the major zipper manufacturer, met at a clothing conference. Inspired, Irving went back to his shop and designed the first-ever jacket that included a zipper. He called it 'Perfecto', after his favorite cigar, rather than Schott because he didn't think his Jewish name would sell the coat. This is the ur-coat from which all later motorcycle jackets would derive. The Schott factory moved several times within Manhattan, and ultimately to New Jersey, where it is still in operation and run by the family. They employ circa 80 workers who make every part of every coat by hand. (Their line includes many other jackets, though the Perfecto is the best seller, so much so that there is a waiting list for these jackets.) The coats were sold at various vendors, but, interestingly, the Army/Navy stores always represented one of the largest retailers. Perhaps it makes sense: The Schott company's motto has always been 'Function and protection'.

Who bought all of these jackets? Schott was not the only maker; by the 1960s, Harley-Davidson, Beck, and a host of other clothiers, including Sears and Montgomery Ward, sold motorcycle jackets. There were motorcycle enthusiasts, events, and organizations from the 1930s onward, but the explosion of motorcycle gangs is directly tied to the aftermath of World War II.

Motorcycles played a very important role in World War II, especially in Africa. The motorcycle troops there were filled with daredevils who became addicted to the thrill of cycling. When they returned stateside to their bourgeois existences, they couldn't shake the cycling buzz (Anon 2006). Motorcycle clubs sprang up, mostly in southern California, in the 1940s. They remained more or less an underground culture until 1947, on a July 4th weekend, when the Boozefighters gang of 4,000 bikers rode into Hollister, California, and disrupted the peace.[2] The event ended when California State Troopers were brought in to restore order. *Life* magazine published an article about the Hollister events with a photo by Barney Peterson that demonized all bikers. A new 'monster' was created for the American public (Anon 2009). A new style of masculinity was also created.

Despite protestations from the American Motorcyclist Association, which had sponsored rallies since the 1930s without their having turned into drunken brawls like at Hollister, the image of the motorcyclist had changed. From military defense to men's recreation, they were now demonized, dangerous, and sexy. The most important moment in this history of the black leather jacket was the release of *The Wild One* (Benedek, 1953) in 1953, with Marlon Brando as Johnny Strabler. *The Wild One* was loosely based on the Hollister riot, and some members of the gang were actually involved in the production. Irving and Jack Schott provided all the motorcycle jackets for the movie. Brando famously wore the new '"W-style" One Star', which became an instant best seller for Schott. Brando's mumbling, formidable loser, who even the sheriff's daughter calls a 'fake', created a new kind of persona for American men. The outsider, antihero was born. From juvenile delinquents to bikers to leathermen to punks, the darker, more dangerous, more volatile, hypermasculine male found a common model, swathed in a black leather motorcycle jacket. This jacket, which is literally 'another skin' that protects riders, became a metaphorical second skin that the vulnerable antihero wears for protection. From this point onward, the jacket began to take on different meanings in different cultural groups.

Martin Rubin, in 'Make Love Make War: Cultural Confusion and the Biker Film Cycle', notes,

> Curiously, despite its tremendous impact on pop-culture iconography, *The Wild One* did not inspire a significant series of biker movies [but] by giving the social problem film a morally ambivalent, antiheroic edge, it fed into the upcoming juvenile-delinquent cycle, initiated the following year with *Blackboard Jungle* (Brooks, 1955) and *Rebel without a Cause* (Ray, 1955). (Rubin 1994: 360)

Brando's character was so popular that it entered into the psyche of many American boys and men who cathected it onto the black leather jacket. The jackets were banned in high schools across the country in 1955, which only increased their power and allure (Anon n.d.). The 'punk' identity was born.

Tom of Finland, the Finnish artist, had been drawing homoerotic visions of men in uniforms since the 1940s. His entire style changed following his viewing of *The Wild One*. Bikers in black leather began to appear regularly in his works. Edward Lucie Smith sums up Brando's effect on Tom of Finland:

> The film *The Wild One* (1953), starring Marlon Brando, glamorized outlaw biker culture. Biker clothing, most particularly leather jackets like the one Brando wore in the film, were added to the long list of fetish items that Tom featured in his drawings. Brando himself

had an appeal that functioned at least as powerfully with men as it did with women. His sexuality on screen, and as it later transpired, in real life, was powerfully and seductively ambiguous. (Lucie-Smith 2009: 22)

In 1956, Tom of Finland had several images published in *Physique Pictorial*, a magazine that was part of the southern California body building subculture and that catered to gay men (Lucie-Smith 2009: 22). Tom's images of hypermasculine men in leather gave U.S. queers a new sense of self, one that was especially important in the context of the McCarthy purges of homosexuals. Lucie-Smith expresses Tom's importance not only to queers but to straight men too:

Tom altered the way gay men think about themselves. He also changed the way in which non-gay people thought about homosexuals. While some 'straight' men felt uncomfortable with, or perhaps even threatened by, the new homo-masculine template of behavior that Tom proposed, others, despite themselves, found it alluring, and, for the most part unconsciously, absorbed aspects of Tom's imagery into their own lifestyles. He changed not only the way they dressed, but affected physical aspects of their personalities, such as stance and gesture. (Lucie-Smith 2009: 21)

Tom of Finland's drawings helped create the image of the leatherman, an image that permeated certain gay subcultures and opened new possibilities for the gay male erotic imaginary; the master/slave leather culture was born (Lucie-Smith 2009: 25). But it was more than just role playing and dress that Tom's drawing implied. As Camille Paglia says: 'In masculinizing the gay persona, Tom broke, for good or ill, with the cultural legacy of the brilliant Oscar Wilde, who promoted and flamboyantly embodied the androgynous aesthete.' Further, and in an unusual move for Paglia, she notes: 'In Tom of Finland, in contrast, the bottom partner retains his monumentality and explosive charge. Surrender is not annihilation but exhilarating play' (Paglia 2009: 82). She begins to describe male/male sex in a way reminiscent of Eve Sedgwick's 'homo-style', something Paglia was known to rail against (Sedgwick 1990: 159). I believe that Tom of Finland went so far as to create a character in his work that is based on Brando, as this image shows in Figure 7:1.

In any event, Tom of Finland began to elaborate an identity type, with dress and physical attributes that gay and straight men alike began to inhabit. In the underground gay worlds of New York, Chicago, and San Francisco, the leather scene became its own world with specific codes, rituals, and fashions.[3] By 1972 the scene was entering into mainstream gay culture so much so that Larry Townsend was able to publish the first edition of *The Leatherman's Handbook*, which provided a guide for anyone interested in leather and the misnamed 'S/M' culture. The book was read widely by gay men, not just by those in the leather scene. Similarly, Edmund White and Charles Silverstein's *The Joy of Gay Sex* (1977) included a section on leather and S/M. Perhaps, most importantly, Peter Berlin, one of the era's most famous porn stars, was featured in a film called *Nights in Black Leather* (1972)

Figure 7:1. Tom of Finland (Finland, 1920–1991) Untitled, 1963, Graphite
on paper, ToFF #63.25, © 1963 Tom of Finland Foundation.

that popularized the scene even further. The black leather motorcycle jacket became a main
staple in gay men's attire whether they were part of the S/M scene or not (Anon 2011). It
took on an entirely new meaning during the height of AIDS activism, when black leather
motorcycle jackets—that perfect second skin—along with work boots, short hair, jeans,
and T-shirts epitomized the couture of member of ACT UP (AIDS Coalition to Unleash
Power).

Near the end of Tom of Finland's life, he met and was cared for by a punk named Viki,
and Tom began to draw images of punks having sex (Hanson 2009: 492). The relationship
of punk to the black leather motorcycle jacket and to gay culture is complicated. On the
one hand, Tommy Ramone, in the first issue of *Punk* magazine, jokes that 'it's fashion'
(Harron 1976: 9.) On the other hand, some punks were queer and some were homophobic.

Etymologically, the word 'punk' meant a female whore. Later it was used about those who consorted with whores, especially men who had sex with men (Anon 2012). This meaning continued in modern prison lingo. During the mid-twentieth century, it also began to be used as a term to describe certain kinds of juvenile delinquents and other miscreants.

Marlon Brando, once again, was considered the quintessential punk. In fact, the same inaugural issue of *Punk* magazine opens with the famous still from *The Wild One* and the feature article is 'Marlon Brando, the Original Punk' by Joe Koch (Figure 7:2).

Punk magazine did more than any other media to give downtown New York City's rough-edged rock bands the name 'punk', coined originally by one of its founders, Legs McNeill. Koch's article describes the punk sensibility to explain Brando's characteristics:

Brando was cool without having to be invulnerable. A whole generation feeling that perhaps it was riding the train without a ticket saw Brando's 'Wild One' being told (by the sheriff's daughter, no less) that he was a fake: yet still, she stands up for him in the end. He provided a new, vicarious life for a public starting to feel intimidated by the always competent film heroes of the thirties and forties. Vulnerability in a leather jacket. Brando prowled, not as a predator, but as a formidable victim. When he breaks down the door to get at Eva Marie Saint in 'Waterfront', not only are the audience's threadbare fantasies of male aggression appealed to, but also, their humanity is recognized: Brando is demanding forgiveness. (Koch 1976: 1)

Figure 7:2. Movie still from *The Wild One*. © Columbia Pictures, 1953.

For Koch and his compatriots, Brando stands as a new kind of American man. He is not exactly the hypermasculine creation of Tom of Finland, but he is not a company man. He is a rebel, not exactly without a cause but who is deeply suspicious of causes, untrusting of systems, angry but not immediately violent. His signature is the black leather jacket, which hides his vulnerability and provides him with a protective second skin. He has rejected authority, but also rejected the middle- and upper-class kids who became hippies because they could afford to reject authority. He is more urban, more working class. He takes on the black leather jacket as a protest and as protection. Legs McNeill, when asked about the jacket by Jon Savage, said:

> JS: Where did that black leather thing come back in?
> LM: The Ramones.
> JS: So where did The Ramones get that black leather stuff from? James Dean?
> LM: Yeah, Brando. *The Wild One.* I walked out the next day after seeing The Ramones and bought my first leather jacket. They wore brown leather bomber jackets with fur and we thought that was gay, you didn't see any at [the Greenwich Village music club] CBGB's. If you had a black leather jacket, the streets parted in front of you. (Savage 2010: 122)

McNeill cites the Ramones as the originators of the leather jacket in the punk scene, but thinks their brown leather and fur are 'gay'. His punk is not going to show any alliance with glam. McNeill wants punk to stand for the masculinity without any femininity, which he conflates with gayness. He is harkening back to the juvenile delinquents, the outsider bikers. Yet along with the image of Brando, who he so much admires, comes the hypermasculinity and with it, male/male desire. Perhaps without quite knowing it, he chose 'punk' as the perfect word for this new identity because it is historically related to male/male sex and to an identity where the power dynamic is not just top down, but also bottom up. The influence of *The Wild One* created three paths: the juvenile delinquent, the biker outlaw, and the gay leatherman. Here they come together again in punk rock, and Irving Schott's black leather jacket returns to the Lower East Side, whence it came, only with a completely different set of meanings.

Just what do those meanings have to do with narrative and with Preston's novel? Jamie, the first-person narrator, tells his story in flashbacks from a point five years before, when he was transformed from a gay 'clone' or, as Mr. Benson calls him, a 'disco doll' (Preston 1992: 34), into the perfect slave. The novel has the feeling of a work composed over time: the early chapters read more like they were written for a porn magazine but, after a few chapters, the story begins to take shape. In fact, Preston wrote the first installment as a short story. It was so popular that the editors of *Drummer* asked him to expand it into a serialized novel ('Teddy Pig' 2005). Jamie is a small-town Midwesterner who moves to New York looking for a place where he fits in. In the opening scene he is a bit of a prancer, showing off his average good looks and fantastic butt in clothes from Bloomingdale's at a bar in Christopher Street that is a thinly disguised version of Boots and Saddles. Across the bar he sees a leatherman who captivates his imagination. Their meeting stirs something in Jamie that he cannot quite express. He is drawn to this man's hypermasculinity, his boots, leather jacket, dark shirt. For his part, Mr. Benson is cool and calculated. He does not like Jamie's shirt and underwear, so he demands that Jamie go into the bathroom and remove them. At first playing along, Jamie does so. Mr. Benson returns Jamie's black leather jacket, handcuffs him, and takes him to his lower Fifth Avenue penthouse apartment where Jamie spends a night of S/M sex that begins to alter his mind completely. Mr. Benson is a top[4] and a complete master. There is no simple role-playing in his relationships. Jamie begins to understand this when he thinks,

> I was deciding Mr. Benson was the man I wanted to love. If class and money and age were going to separate us, I would use my sexuality and a willingness to be powerless to overcome them. I would be a slave in order to love this man. (Preston 1992: 32).

The next third of the novel traces Jamie's introduction into the world of S/M sex, albeit a version that is more intense and masochistic than anything that happens in real life.[5] For instance, Jamie is a stay-at-home slave without a job, who can, at a moment's notice, perform even the most extreme sexual acts for Mr. Benson. We have entered the realm of romance, that is, a love story with fantasy elements.

To be accurate, we have, in fact, entered into the world of the popular romance novel, for *Mr. Benson* embodies all of the attributes of that genre. In her groundbreaking book, *A Natural History of the Romance Novel*, Paula Regis defines eight essential narrative elements that are common to the romance novel: (1) Society Defined; (2) The Meeting; (3) The Barrier; (4) The Attraction; (5) The Declaration; (6) Point of Ritual Death; (7) The Recognition; and (8) The Betrothal (Regis 2003: 30–38.) These elements need not appear in this exact order, but they all tend to appear in the romance novel. We have already seen the 'Society Defined' in Mr. Benson's descriptions of the average gay clone. It is elaborated by Jamie as he begins to see that his love for Mr. Benson will remove him from that society and propel him into another realm, that of Mr. Benson. 'The Meeting' is a highly eroticized scene at the bar and involves the importance of the black leather jacket as a signifier of the men's interest in each other. 'The Attraction' is abundantly clear throughout the novel. 'The Declaration' occurs when Jamie decides he'll use his powerlessness to love Mr. Benson. This is a crucial point for most romance novels. The narrator, almost always a woman, finds some way to 'tame' the 'alpha male' character she loves. Early feminist writers rejected the romance novel because, as Regis states, this narrative stance: 'extinguishes its own heroine, confining her within a story that ignores the full range of her concerns and abilities…and denies her independent goal-oriented action outside of love and marriage. [It] binds readers in their marriages or encourages them to get married: it equates marriage with success and glorifies sexual difference' (Regis 2003: 10).[6] Preston attempts something very different in this novel. While it is tempting to see Jamie merely as a 'feminine' narrator, that view is too facile. To do so would be to gender S/M relationships as imitative of heterosexuality. They are not. Jamie's gendered self is masculine, as we see when he dons full leather and goes out on the town at Mr. Benson's instructions. He is aggressive about his status as a bottom. (It is worth pointing out the similarity between the two men in the Tom of Finland illustration [Figure 7:1]). While the man on the right is a depiction of a Brando-like leatherman and presumably the top, the other man is just as masculine and formidable. The only intimation that he is a bottom is the position of his left leg and the socks folded over his boots, indicating that he is the one who will 'bend over'. (Jamie, as a bottom, is similar.) Without Jamie's really knowing why, Mr. Benson gives him a complete, custom-tailored suit of black leather and a wad of cash and tells him to leave and rent a hotel room for a few days. Distraught that he is being kicked out, Jamie goes to a bar and picks up a sadistic top who brutally beats him. Jamie learns the difference between true sadists, who do not care at all about their partners, and masters and slaves, where there is a carefully negotiated agreement as to limits between the two partners. As Mr. Benson says to Jamie when they first meet, 'Boy, don't ever tell me you can take more unless you mean it, understand?'(Preston 1992: 13). Mr. Benson is teaching Jamie a very important point about S/M culture: the 'safe word'. S/M sex depends upon the complete trust of the partners. They have a word that is used to stop the scene if it is going too far emotionally, physically, or morally for the bottom. This 'safe word' must be obeyed and all activity must change when it is invoked. Despite common expectations for S/M sex, the bottom is really in control of the activity. That is, the conflation of sadism and masochism in the commonly used term 'S/M' is a misnomer. Sadists do not care about their victims. The top in a true 'S/M' scene is, in fact, a part of a masochistic narrative, harkening back to the first use of the trope in Leopold von Sacher-Masoch's 1870 novel *Venus im Pelz* (*Venus in Furs*).

Perhaps the most complicated element of a romance novel is the 'Point of Ritual Death'. The ritual death takes place 'when the union between the hero and heroine, the hoped-for resolution, seem absolutely impossible, when it seems that the barrier will remain, more substantial than ever' (Regis 2003: 35). For Jamie, the ritual death comes when he thinks Mr. Benson has thrown him out for another man, Rick—not just any man, but a model whose face appears in advertisements all over the city. (In one of the book's many ironic passages, the new bottom is described as looking just like a popular *Gentlemen's Quarterly* model from the late 1970s, Ric Edwards, and even shares his first name.) Jamie feels that he has been abandoned, so he goes to the Mineshaft, New York City's most notorious leather bar, and climbs into the sling. He is fucked by several men:

Naked, shorn of hair, without anything more that what I had to offer: a body. I was no longer even in need. There was no need. Mr. Bensons find you when you don't expect them. That's a part of who they are, I thought. Mr. Benson wouldn't come to the Mineshaft looking for a slave; he'd find one on the street or in a Christopher Street bar—goddam it—in a magazine ad, just like the new slave Mr. Benson had found. And what was going to happen to that guy? I wondered. What would happen to him? He might be the face that means 'cigarettes' to half of America, it would make any difference. After what I had been through, I knew that even he would end up in a place like this, looking for any symbol that would help him try to take away the pain. (Preston 1992: 154)

In this instance the pain is not physical; it is the emotional death Jamie feels at being without Mr. Benson. Jamie is so in love with Mr. Benson that he feels he cannot go on without him. It turns out that Mr. Benson sent Jamie away because several young men have been disappearing from bars and clubs downtown and he wanted to protect Jamie.

Jamie experiences 'the Recognition' when Rick tells the story of how Mr. Benson was trying to protect him from getting caught up in the kidnapping ring. As in any good romance novel, Mr. Benson comes to the rescue just in time. The Arab slave traders are arrested and Jamie is rescued by Mr. Benson. All that remains is 'the Betrothal'. When they get back to Mr. Benson's penthouse, Mr. Benson says:

'Jamie,' he addressed me now.
'There's no ritual for a master and a slave that we alone know about. I mean, no way to tie the bond that a straight couple might have in a marriage. But I've decided to create one just for you.' (Preston 1992: 205)

He pierces Jamie's nipple with a gold bar that has a diamond on the end. Jamie's narrative comes to an end, like all good romances, with marriage to the man he loves.

But the novel is not over. Mr. Benson writes an 'Epilogue' in which he criticizes Jamie, saying: 'Bottoms are so typical. They inject everything with so much symbolism and so much jargon' (Preston 1992: 207). He attempts to rewrite their love story and to gain agency over the narrative, even going to far as to make a plea for tops, whom he believes are 'misunderstood' (Preston, 1992: 215). Mr. Benson's final transformation occurs in the last paragraph of the novel: 'More than that, once he trusted me, I knew I had a set of obligations to be the man he needed. I only have to be the man I want to be with a trick. Once I took on Jamie, I had to do more than that. I guess you could say I was challenged as much by him as he was by me' (Preston 1992: 219). Mr. Benson's narrative, however, lacks the same agency as Jamie's. It occupies a scant 13 pages out of 219 in the Bad Boy Books edition. Who has control of this narrative? It would seem obvious that it is Jamie. Jamie is the keeper of the words. He, like all writers, 'inject[s] everything with symbolism'. He understands a moment early in the novel when he has just entered Mr. Benson's penthouse: 'He took off his leather jacket and tossed it over mine on the couch' (Preston 1992: 15). There it was. The symbol of what both Jamie and Mr. Benson were searching for: to be two men who loved one another and took care of one another. Those second skins that protect motorcyclists stand in for the protections and obligations Jamie and Mr. Benson provide each other, man to man.

John Preston was staking out new identities for gay men in creating Jamie and Mr. Benson. He is borrowing experiences from the leather underworld that grew out of biker and beach bodybuilding culture in California after World War II. Jamie and

Mr. Benson are fictionalized versions of Tom of Finland's characters. Jamie is, in fact, 'the bottom partner [who] retains his monumentality and explosive charge. Surrender is not annihilation but exhilarating play' (Paglia 2009: 82). By using the tropes of the modern romance novel, Preston is able to explore different kinds of narrative and physical power that do not rely on the masculine/feminine gendering of narrative. In fact, within romance novel studies, the early feminist arguments about the role of the woman in the romance novels have been debunked, too. The transformative effects of the novels show gender to be a much more complicated set of social conventions and not just a simple masculine/feminine binary. *Mr. Benson*, the novel, as early as 1979, asks us to understand different kinds of masculinities— several years before Eve Sedgwick's groundbreaking work on gender and narrative.

A confusing mess of significations hangs on the black leather motorcycle jacket. From its roots in military uniforms to the protection of motorcyclists to the rebellious Wild One, to leathermen to punks, the black leather jacket signals a kind of American masculinity that provides, paradoxically, a mode for the hypermasculine and, thus, a model for masculine/masculine sex that is different from masculine/feminine sex. Jamie's attraction to Mr. Benson is the attraction of man to man outside of the traditionally acknowledged masculine/feminine construct of identity. One wonders what Irving Schott would think of the changes that have come about because of his passion for motorcycles and his desire to make something that offered both 'function and protection'.

References

Anon (n.d.), 'History of Schott N.Y.C.: The Classic American Success Story', Schott N.Y.C. website, http://www.schottnyc.com/about.cfm. Accessed 10 October 2012.

——— (2006), 'Motorcycle Club', Wikipedia, http://en.wikipedia.org/wiki/Motorcycle_club. Accessed 16 January 2012.

———(2007), 'Hollister Riot' Wikipedia, http://en.wikipedia.org/wiki/Hollister_riot. Accessed 16 January 2012.

———(2009), 'Boozefighters', Wikipedia, http://en.wikipedia.org/wiki/Boozefighters. Accessed 16 January 2012.

———(2011), 'Leather Subculture', Wikipedia, http://en.wikipedia.org/wiki/Leather_subculture. Accessed 16 January 2012.

——— (2012), 'Punk', Merriam-Webster Online Dictionary, http://www.merriam-webster. com/dictionary/punk. Accessed 16 January 2012.

Gregory, L. (2003), 'War Bikes: Motorcycles Have Played an Enduring Role in American Military Operations since the Army Enlisted Its First Two-Wheeled Cycle before WWI', *Soldiers Magazine*, August, http://findarticles.com/p/articles/mi_m0OXU/is_8_58/ai_ 106981877/. Accessed 16 January 2012.

Hanson, D. (2009), *Tom of Finland. XXL*, Cologne: Taschen.

Harron, M. (1976), 'The Ramones: Rock n' Roll—The Real Thing', *Punk*, 1.1, pp. 8–9

Koch, J. (1976), 'Marlon Brando: The Original Punk', *Punk*, 1.1, p. 1.

Lucie-Smith, E. (2009), 'Tom of Finland', in D. Hanson, *Tom of Finland: XXL*, Cologne: Taschen, p. 22.

Paglia, C. (2009), 'Sex Quest', in D. Hanson, *Tom of Finland: XXL*, Cologne: Taschen, p. 82

Preston, J. (1992), *Mr. Benson*, New York: Bad Boy Books.

Regis, P. (2003), *A Natural History of the Romance Novel*, Philadelphia: University of Pennsylvania Press.

Rubin, M. (1994). '"Make Love Make War": Cultural Confusion and the Biker Film Cycle', *Film History*, 6.3, pp. 355–381.

Savage, J. (2010), *The England's Dreaming Tapes: The Essential Complete Companion to England's Dreaming: The Seminal History of Punk*, New York: Faber and Faber. Advanced reader's copy.

Sedgwick, E. (1990), *The Epistemology of the Closet*, Berkeley: University of California Press.

Spring, J. (2010), *Secret Historian: The Life and Times of Samuel Steward, Professor, Tattoo Artist, and Sexual Renegade*, New York: Farrar, Straus, and Giroux.

'Teddy Pig' (2005), 'Leather Book Review: John Preston—Mr. Benson', Leather Flog blog, http://www.leatherflog.com/2005/11/leather-book-review-john-preston-mr.html. Accessed 10 October 2012.

Notes

1 Interview with Don King, a long-time staff member of Schott NYC, the family-owned business that still operates, now in Elizabeth, New Jersey. The author would like to thank Jennifer Goldster, Jason Schott, Don King, and the other members of the Schott family for their interest in this project and their generous giving of time to be interviewed and allowing access to the Schott archives and historic coat collection.

2 What actually happened in Hollister is still the source of debate. See the following: Anon (2012), 'Hollister riot', Wikipedia, http://en.wikipedia.org/wiki/Hollister_riot; Mark E. Gardiner (n.d.), 'The Real "Wild Ones": The 1947 Hollister Motorcycle Riot', Salinas Ramblers Motorcycle Club website, http://www.salinasramblersmc.org/history/Classic_Bike_Article.htm; and http://www.flboozefighter.com/bfmchistory.html.

3 It is interesting to note the development of the Chicago leather scene and how Chuck Renslow has influenced it (Spring 2010: 274).

4 The terms 'top' and 'bottom' refer to the dominant and submissive partners in anal intercourse.

5 For a fuller description of how *Mr. Benson* depicts a fantasy S/M world, see this review: 'Teddy Pig' (2009), 'John Preston: Mr. Benson (1979)', The Naughty Bits website, http://www.teddypig.com/2009/11/john-preston-mr-benson/.

6 It is interesting to note how often the language of bondage is used in the popular romance novel.

Chapter 8

Fashion Photography, Phallocentrism, and Feminist Critique

Louise Wallenberg

The photograph in black and white depicts a woman and a man. She is next to naked, dressed only in a bra and a tong, and she lays spread over the hover of a car. Her head is turned away from the onlooker and she seems immobile. Around her neck is a man's silk tie. She has been strangled, but looks nothing like a real victim of strangulation: she has no blue marks, her facial skin looks perfect, and there is no sign of battle. The man, dressed in an immaculate suit, stands behind her, holding the other end of the tie. He looks straight into the camera, as if saying, 'See, I killed her.'

Description of an ad for the male bespoke brand Duncan Quinn (Fall 2010)

There are excellent reasons for this refusal of the woman to look, not the least of which is that she is often asked to bear witness to her own powerlessness in the face of rape, mutilation, and murder.

Linda Williams, 'When the Woman Looks' ([1984] 1996)

The opening of this article, a description of a recent ad for Duncan Quinn, is used to visualize the sexism and misogyny inherent in many representations emanating from the fashion industry. Oddly, it is not until one describes them with words, and in that way visually and verbally deconstruct them, that one starts to see them for what they are; so indifferent, so blind, has one become to the aesthetics of fashion imagery that one no longer reacts to representations of dominance and sexual violence. This is, of course, highly problematic. The quotation following the description is used to further visualize this misogyny and the indifference toward it: film scholar Linda Williams's thirty-year-old critique—the article was originally published in 1984—is used as a reminder not only of how sexual violence toward women is the basis of popular cinema (and most of popular culture), but that its audience—i.e., its spectators and consumers—ought not refuse to look, to become indifferent, but rather, to start looking. Serving a male chauvinist and clearly misogynist discourse within which women are continuously being sexually objectified and dehumanized, fashion (as well as other) representations need to be questioned, discussed, and critiqued. Instead of looking the other way, avoiding discomfort, nausea, anger, one has to start to look, and through the act of really looking, to see the representations for what they really are.

This article emerges out of a rather extensive teaching experience in both film and fashion studies within higher education. As a film scholar teaching film theory, the image has for long been central to any analysis carried out in the classroom, and as a fashion scholar teaching representations of fashion, I have found that the fashion image has continued to occupy center stage. I have taught interpretations and ways of reading images by engaging in questions regarding representation and by using feminist studies, black studies, white studies, and queer studies as theoretical frameworks. However, some scholars, while critiquing the representations and the sexist messages that these images convey, have placed little emphasis on considering any possible 'reality', that is, the actual situation in which the images for intellectual analysis have been created, formed, and shaped.

This focus on the image and what it represents has also informed my own writing. Having written about feminist and queer film theory for over a decade, in particular representations of women and queers within specific genres of films, or even specific films, I have never tried to engage with the actual situation on the film set. Formed by film studies as a discipline, and in particular, by feminist film theory, my own research has been in line with a longstanding engagement with film as *text*.

Within fashion studies, an emerging field that grasps both the humanities and the social sciences, approaches informed by ethnographical research and methods are not only welcome, but also required. Although an investigative focus on the image and what it represents is needed, for this inquiry to really mean something, there is a need to also look at the 'reality' behind the images, that is, what the images are snapshots of in terms of working conditions and working relations for the agents within the business. Maybe by leaning toward organization or management studies, and by using a more ethnographically formed approach, there is a possibility of going beyond the very image.

Organization studies have shown an increasing interest in the booming organizations of the 'new' entertainment economy, yet organizational researchers still tend to focus their attention on organizations in mainstream sectors such as banking, information technology, and automobile manufacturing—and not on fashion (or film). On its part, film studies has tended to ignore the film industry's production processes altogether, focusing instead on film as art form or film as representation. (This said, there is an evolving field within the field of film studies called 'production studies', but to my knowledge this is an un-gendered field). On the whole, little attention has therefore been given to the actual film set and to the development of hierarchical interpersonal relations between different kinds of employees (actors, actresses, director(s), producer(s), stage hands, costume designer(s), etc.). Although feminist film theory has been highly occupied with Woman on film, very little research has been carried out, as pointed out above, in regards to women on the film set. Sadism and misogyny inform popular film production, and many feminist scholars have correctly argued that the cinematic image and narration is one of sadism, and that this representation is always in favor of Man, never of Woman, nor of women (Mulvey 1975; de Lauretis 1984). However, the field needs to welcome a scholarship that strives to lay bare the sadism and misogyny inherent in film production, criticizing a film theory which for decades has refused to look at the gendered reality of employees in the film industry. The intricate relations between film as representation and the working conditions of film production could be studied drawing on previous research on women (and men) in organizations (e.g., Acker 1992; Acker 1989; Calás and Smircich 1992; Calás and Smircich 1996; and Calás 2008).

For example, it is common knowledge that film actresses have been mistreated and violated on the film set; famous examples are Debbie Reynolds in *How the West Was Won* (Henry Hathaway, 1962), Tippi Hedren in *The Birds* (Alfred Hitchcock, 1963), and Susan George in *Straw Dogs* (Sam Peckinpah, 1971). Yet film studies and management studies alike have—so far—shown next to no interest in this. When engaging with biographical notes and interviews by the actresses in the above mentioned films, actresses who have dared to come forward to tell their story of domination and exploitation, it becomes clear that these films not only represent sexual violence and other forms of violence—but that the film sets in which these films were made also did violence to the women (Williams 1995; Spoto 1999; Kermode 2003; Barker 2006; Simkin 2011).

An Image Is an Image Is an Image

Representations are not just representations (Dyer 1993)—they come from somewhere and refer to and visualize real acts. Acts that are carried out on the screen, then, are not just fantasies; in order for them to be represented, they have to be presented and carried out, and hence, violence—sexual or other—toward women characters *on* film is also carried out toward women *in* film. And this is made possible by the gendered organizational relations of the film industry. The context can be studied by consulting biographical sources and interviews, by examining heated debates in various film journals and magazines, and by analyzing specific scenes. This means studying situational practices and their gendered relations and structures. Film not only as representation, as pure fiction, but as a situational practice in time and space, involving many people and unequal relationships between the people engaged in the filmmaking. Through the examination of biographical sources and interviews, it becomes apparent that voyeurism, sadism, and misogyny—since the early 1970s considered as the main ingredients of mainstream cinema by fore mostly feminist film scholars and historians—are also inscribed in the acts and relations of filmmaking.[1] In these documents, filmmaking is often recalled in a very negative manner as an experience that is clearly exploitive and degrading (see, e.g., Williams 1995; Kermode 2003; Simkin 2011). In some cases, the experience was forced upon the actresses by what they felt was the entire film team, mostly consisting of men, and hence, and, in some cases, clearly against their will.[2]

This imbalance and this open exploitation are, of course, made possible by the gendered organizational relations of the film industry, which is indeed a male-dominated industry. Most directors as narrators, *metteurs-en-scène*, and as the so-called 'voices of God' (see Nichols 1991) are—as we know—male; and further, male actors often play the main characters, often with some degree of both sadism and misogyny; and woman actors often play objectified and secondary characters, not seldom occupying a masochist position. Even in films with an active female protagonist, she is often objectified and put in degrading positions—for the viewers' pleasure. The film text, then, follows strict rules of female punishment: she is to be punished, physically and mentally, for wanting to be an active subject. Often this punishment is also of a sexual nature: hence, rape, and the threat of rape. Stevie Simkin is clear about the sexualized and unequal relations structuring the film industry when describing *Straw Dogs* (Sam Peckinpah, 1971) as a prime example of how male centered the industry is:

> The rape scene in *Straw Dogs* exists within a tightly controlled male environment: written by men, enforced on a reluctant young actress isolated and in fear of Peckinpah's capacity for humiliating and intimidating his actors…in a Hollywood that (still) demands that its stars meet certain standards of conventional beauty, and that they obediently parade it for their audiences, the rape scene of Amy on screen, and the ordeal Susan George endured behind the scenes, is one of the clearest illustrations of the dominant, persistent, controlling male hand over the industry. (Simkin 2011: 15)

As pointed out above, one would have expected that feminist film theory, which for more than forty years has held a central and most significant position within film studies, should have engaged with this unequal relation. It has, for sure, been relentless in its strive to uncover the misogyny of cinematic representation, yet, it has not really dared to examine the actual situation of real women on the film set: it has not dared to extricate itself from the tangle of the often highly theoretical discussions and analysis of film, which is an analysis that only considers women as signifiers, symbols, or theoretical concepts within the narrative structure of film. But the sadist, misogynist, and voyeuristic treatment of women characters, convincingly argued by Marjorie Rosen (1973), Molly Haskell ([1974] 1987), Laura Mulvey (1975), and Teresa de Lauretis (1984), is not only there on the screen: it is also staged, and carried out, as the film is being shot. The film set, then, is a space where violence toward women is carried out—under the prerequisite of making movies, and, at times, art.

Throughout film history, male and female actors alike have been injured on the set: male actors have fallen off their horses, breaking an arm or a leg, or they have missed a jump in action and broken their neck—but most often in action scenes in which they have been active subjects. Female actors, on the other hand, have been injured in different ways—and these ways have often been indeed sadistic and almost always *sexualized* and sexist. Violence, whether sexual or not, is carried out toward women on screen and on the set, positions women as passive, as subordinated, and as helpless. And yes, there is reason to believe that this not only applies to the film context: but to all contexts in which women appear as—is indistinguishable from—*Image* (Doane 1982) and men as controller of the object and of the gaze, and in which the narrative structure and the visualization of gender is highly sexualized, as well as dependent on the idea of sexual difference as natural and desirable.

Woman—Still—as Image

The ad shows a white naked woman spread out over a velvet cushion on her back, her knees bent and spreading her legs. The background is velvety black and together with the sharp light it makes her white skin painfully white. She wears golden slippers with high heels and a thick gold necklace, her face is carefully made up and her red curly hair is perfectly placed on the cushion. She is touching her breasts, her head thrown back, and her eyes closed. She seems immobile—yet her facial expression gives away pleasure. She looks like a living dead: bit by a vampire, killed by an overdose, or ready for sex.

Description of an ad for the perfume Opium from Yves Saint Laurent (late 1990s)

And so, by the help of the above described famous ad for the perfume Opium, the view is now switched to another field that produces representations that are characterized by, and come out of, an unequal gender structure. This field is, just like cinema, fueled by the obsession with Image(s) and with phallocentric sexuality.

And just like with the film industry and its representations, this is a field not really dealt with from a critical standpoint. Feminist theory has not really bothered with the fashion industry and with fashion photography from a standpoint that uncovers the fictionalization of the fashion image. In 2005, Sheila Jeffreys writes that 'It has become unpopular since the 1980s,...to point out that fashion reflects and serves to maintain female subordination' (Jeffreys 2005: 87). Well, fashion not only reflects and maintain this subordination: it also orchestrates it as well as thrives on it, making it not only 'sexy', but also *comme-il-faut*. Academics in the field of fashion studies—teaching fashion and researching fashion—ought to dare become more critical, if not political, with the risk of becoming unpopular as Jeffreys states. The business and the phenomenon studied is one thriving on and producing a blatant gender inequality, and this is something that academics must take into consideration. For sure, there are many more aspects of the fashion industry that academics ought to engage in and critically study: the unequal working hierarchies; the exploitation of workers in the garment industry; child labor, and the overall unequal relation between Western world and the non-Western world in terms of production and the use of natural resources. Yet, for this piece, it is the critique of unequal gender relations and the sexist and at times sadistic representation of women that in fashion is being fictionalized into Image that is being brought up to the forefront.

The discussion of the power of images has been crucial to most representation theory coming out of a cultural studies perspective, and this angle has opened up the at times overly theoretical standpoint within feminist film theory. And yet, the connection between an actual situation and its representation, has not been focused upon. Images are representations of a constructed reality, yes. Even documentary images are to a certain extent staged and constructed, as has been argued by film scholars Bill Nichols (1991) and Michael Renov (1993) and fiction always contains non-fictive elements, as has been argued by Vivian Sobshack (1984; 2004). Images present and re-present the 'real', but can never fully represent it. Yet, what is seen in images, what is represented, are representations of something that at the time of the shot was very real, real for the people involved. The event is staged, and we may assume that roles are played: but they are played out, and the setting, at least within the mainstream, is often one depending on a certain power imbalance with sexual connotations and/or expressions presented as desirable. This imbalance could be called heteronormativity—a power structure upholding heterosexuality as norm while relying on the notion of *sexual difference* as natural and necessary. An example of this is a Tom Ford spectacles advertisement from 2010 (shot by Terry Richardson), which shows a completely naked woman in high heels ironing a pair of men's pants and next to her, reading a paper, stands a man dressed in shirt, bow tie and jacket, boxer shorts, and high socks. While the picture can be read as ironic in terms of a possible critique of heteronormativity, it is still overtly sexualized and heterosexist. No matter the possible irony and critique, the woman, in her nakedness, is still available (if only to the gaze), and she is still serving (the male). He is still covered, only the lower part of his thighs showing, and he is engaged in an activity for his own pleasure, reading the papers, while waiting for her to serve him his ironed trousers.

Academics within the fields dealing with visual culture in various forms—film, fashion, photography, and art—are trained to read images, to interpret them, and ask about their meanings—and more than often to try to *counter-read* them to open up for valid and critical and theoretical interpretations. So well-trained are we, that even when encountering an image that we may find highly offensive, we try to re-read it so as to find some other meaning, and that other meaning is often colored with irony and satire. The most offensive image, in our eyes, can become a critique of what it is representing. Irony and satire function as a shield, and as proof of an intellectual capacity of re-reading. And this shield, our best students are expected to develop and carry as well.

Academic analysis, while astute and correct, is in fact a *distancing* from the image: and this distance works as a protection against seeing the images for what they are—and the unequal gender relations that they portray. In this way, the Duncan advertisement, described above, can be read as a ironic visual quotation of some innocent yet gaudy S&M representation of classic horror cinema, of exclusive underwear advertisement (like the French brand Aubade or the Italian brand La Perla), or of nineteenth-century Western art. When relating it to other images, demonstrating that representations are always re-presentations of earlier representations, they become harmless—and often, humorous and witty. We tell ourselves that it is all about play, and we applaud ourselves when we manage to discover their (possible) references. And, again, we fool ourselves of seeing them only as constructed images and not as the outcome of real situations.

Yet, these images are 'a relentless parade of insults' (Dyer 1993: 1). Further, they are part of a misogynist discourse that constantly points out how dead women are good women, and how women's objectified and victimized position is desirable and accepted. The academy needs to welcome back some anger and some real engagement when discussing images— and the situations and relations that they represent, and which through their constant reiteration make seem normal. A few filmmakers have already provided the larger audience and the academy with film texts that could serve to initiate debates in the classroom about the unequal relations that structure the fashion industry, and in particular the modeling aspects of it.

Jean Kilbourne's documentary series *Killing Us Softly* (1979–2010) is hands on when it comes to how fashion images and advertisement convey female subordination as desirable and natural. The more-than-a-decade-old documentary about the industry made by journalist Donal MacIntyre, as part of his series *MacIntyre Undercover* (BBC One, 1999–2003), is highly useful: MacIntyre went undercover posing as a fashion photographer, inveigling his way into the fashion agency Elite Models Management in Milan to uncover how girls as young as 13 and 14 years were not only being sexually abused but also provided with drugs. The documentary had such an impact in outing what was going on that two of the company's key men—Gerald Marie, president of Elite Europe, and Xavier Moreau, president of Elite Model Look, choose to resign. Gerald Marie, a man then in his 50s, had to resign—or else run the risk getting kicked off the board; in the documentary, he is filmed telling MacIntyre about his plans to seduce the finalists in the Elite Model Look contest (most of whom are 15 or 16 years old) and offering a model money for having sex with him. Model Carré Otis has helped reinforce the image of him as a sexual predator: in her biography *Beauty, Disrupted* (2010) she tells of how he continuously raped her at age 17, when he was her agent and she was starting out as a model for Elite Paris (Otis 2011). Yet, Marie is—again—head of Elite Paris: his misconduct is obviously not a problem for the agency. MacIntyre is not the only journalist that has tried to uncover the seediness of the fashion business; Michael Gross outs the industry's long history of blatant sexism and sexual exploitation of young women in his 1995 book *Model: The Ugly Business of Beautiful Women*. Through interviews with models, he uncovers the seedy side of the business involving drugs, abuse, and sexual exploitation of adolescent women. Another more contemporary example would be the documentaries *Picture Me* (Ole Schnell and Sarah Ziff, 2009) and *Girl Model* from 2011, in which filmmakers Ashley Sabin and David Redmon uncover how Siberian girls, coming from poor backgrounds and some as young as 13, are headhunted by cynic girl hunters and lured to Japan to make money as models, only to end up isolated and caged, and poorly paid. In this last example, the desire for youth—that is, pre-adolescence—as stipulated by the fashion industry is laid out painstakingly clear.

These examples are excellent entrances into debates within the academia about the fashion industry—and can work as springboards for a more critical and investigative research. Academia can make a difference, and there is no reason to believe that we as academics can not contribute to a more critical stance toward an industry that exploits underaged girls (and, of course, many of its garment workers all around the world). Fuelled by these visual documents and the testimonies that have recently been given by individuals who have been exploited in one way or another, and by turning to some plain old feminist scholarship (e.g., texts written by Marxist, radical, anti-porn, essentialist-with-a-twist scholars like Catherine MacKinnon, Heidi Hartmann, Carole Sheffield, Sandra Lee Bartky, Luce Irigaray, and

Annie Leclerc), one can start to discuss and analyze the unequal relational structures of the industry together with colleagues and students. These early feminist theories of the 1970s and 1980s should not be criticized for being passé: in fact, their discourse analysis and their social critique of how patriarchy constructs and create imbalance between the genders are highly applicable to the fashion industry and to fashion photography.

Fashion Photography

> The color photograph depicts three women. Two women are positioned in the front, both of them lying on their back in the sand in somewhat awkward positions, lifeless, as if dumped there. They wear high-heeled shoes, skin colored pantyhose and short skirts. Their upper bodies and faces are covered under new paper magazines. In the back the third woman is positioned in a phone booth, making a call. Her face shows agitation and desperation.
>
> Description of a photo by Guy Bourdin for the French shoe brand Charles Jourdan

> The masculine can partly look at itself, speculate about itself, represent itself and describe itself for what it is, whilst the feminine can try to speak to itself through a new language, but cannot describe itself from outside or in formal terms, except by identifying itself with the masculine, thus by losing itself.
>
> Luce Irigaray, *This Sex Which Is Not One* (1977)

High-end fashion photography—often-ascribed with artistic and *avant-garde* qualities—can get away with almost anything: even with representations that are unquestionably and utterly sexist, misogynist, homophobic, and racist. French photographer Guy Bourdin, to give just one example of a photographer who produces high-end fashion photography, has for long been applauded for the dreamy, cinematographic, *avant-garde*, and artistic qualities of his work, yet his images clearly frolic in and embellish sexual violence against women, not seldom flirting with pedophilia.

The dominant view on representations emanating from the high end of the fashion industry, images and ads produced by famous and recognized photographers, promote postmodern readings that put irony and satire at the center. To bring any actual political implications to light and to emphasize the discrimination that these images advocate and idealize, whether in a popular or in an academic setting, often leads to accusations of a (new) moral panic. (I am fully aware that I may end up being criticized for trying to incite a new moral panic, but this is a risk I am willing to take.)

A contemporary example of images that pass as fashion and as art although they obviously are indisputably pornographic and sexist, are the fashion photographs of American photographer Terry Richardson: his images have been questioned and critiqued by some, like the Swedish Näringslivets Etiska Råd mot Könsdiskriminerande Reklam (ERK) (Council of Business Ethics against Sexist Advertising) or feminist scholar Sheila Jeffreys (2005), yet he has over the years continued to hold a special status as a gaudy and groundbreaking photographer, and his work continues to be labeled artistic and edgy.[3] It was not, however, until spring 2010 that he was seriously critiqued, not so much for his sexist images, but for his misconduct and sexual exploitation of his young models. To these allegations he has reacted by stressing a professional and respectable attitude toward the people in front of the camera. The accusations against him nurtured a debate not only about Richardson, but also about the fashion industry, yet most journalists, academics, fashionistas, and bloggers have prevaricated, not wanting to discredit him totally and not wanting to discredit the industry either. Richardson responds to critics in his blog 'Terry Richardson's Diary',

> I just want to take a moment to say I'm really hurt by the recent and false allegations of insensitivity and misconduct. I feel fortunate to work with so many extraordinary people each and every day. I've always been considerate and respectful of the people I photograph and I view what I do as a real collaboration between myself and the people in front of the camera. To everyone who has embraced and supported me and my work, I am so grateful. Thank you, it means a lot. (Richardson 2010)

In fact, Richardson's work is an interesting example of how sexism and misogyny, when carried out in an almost undetectable way, becomes accepted and even desirable: examination of his *oeuvre* demonstrates that his images have become more sexist, misogynist, and pornographic. In his early shots (see, for example, his early spreads for *Harper's Bazaar US* in the late 1990s), frontal nudity was not as rampant as in his later work: and the explicit allusion to, or even representation of, sexual acts (fellatio, cunnilingus, vaginal and anal penetration) is something that has become prevalent only in the last decade. Step by step, his photographs have become more provocative—well, insulting, really—testing the boundaries of what will be accepted or not. Starting as a mere copycat of existing fashion aesthetics in the early 1990s, his images adopted an explicit and pornographic turn when he started to work for the Italian fashion brand Sisley. Sisley allowed him to create images that were clearly over the top, and in doing so he extended his own boundaries—a fact he acknowledges:

> Sisley was a great job for a long time because they were really just letting me be me, doing whatever the hell I wanted to do. It was all about sex pictures. I've always been able to walk that fine line, to balance myself, to do fashion and also do my naughty pictures. Why do I get away with it? I'm a genius. With a capital J. (Richardson and Hanson 2008)

Explicitly showing off what can only be understood as a sex addiction, his photographs of the last decade—together with the testimonies of a few models on how they have been treated on the set (see, e.g., Sauers 2010)—have suddenly left a sour taste in the reader's mouth. Whereas phallocentrism (i.e., the emphasis on a male point-of-view)—together with phallogocentrism has always been a strong guideline for mainstream cinema as well as for fashion photography, in Richardson's photos this centrism becomes all too apparent and literal. In the 2000s he has taken his 'pornomania' even further, and seems to have had the back-up needed from people in the business (from fashion magazine editors and designers—to models, even), and it all now seems to center around his dick.[4] And the dick, *his* dick, has now become a stand-in for his camera, whereas the camera earlier probably was a stand-in for his dick (Richardson and Hanson 2008).

The images he has produced over the years, in fact hold very few artistic qualities: they are images for fashion brands—Sisley and more upscale brands such as Gucci and Miu Miu—and most of them portray young women often in awkward situations, referencing bestiality and rape. Their clothes are ripped and show a lot of skin with an emphasis on thighs, breasts, and crotch as in many of his shots for Sisley and his shots for Tom Ford (nude women next to dressed men). In more recent photographs, those referred to as 'Terry's snapshots', the connection to a specific brand is missing—and the models appear in the nude, often with Richardson placing himself next to them, as if saying: 'Look, I made them undress.' Yet, his photos are read as fashion, due to his legacy as a well-known fashion photographer and due to the fact that the models either are fashion models or look like fashion models. Some of the infamous snapshots of the day, published in magazines such as *Purple Magazine* and/or on his own website, are pictures of fashion models, hence the link to fashion is still clear. However he also has snapshots depicting himself engaging in oral, vaginal (and anal?) sex with young women—often 'decapitated' with their faces out of frame, or even covered in black bags (see Richardson and Hanson 2008; Navo 2010). The focus in these photographs is penetration of a (female) body, hence these shots are nothing more than simple pornography. As a sex-fixated photographer, and one who assumedly has said, early on in his career: 'It's not who you know, it's who you blow', he here excludes the fashion element, and the model is positioned as just another fuck-able female body (Onstad 2011). Some pictures even exclude the model *in toto*: focusing on himself—that, is, his dick. Richardson demonstrates his obsession with his own penis (phallocentrism and narcissism in one) and his power as an established photographer by turning his shooting sequences into porn shoots, and getting away with it. In one photo that has been published on the Internet, Richardson sits at his desk, talking on the phone, his fly open, and a woman on her knees between his legs (apparently his 'assistant') giving him fellatio from in under his desk (see Yotka 2010). One shot, one image, one representation. One might wonder what led up to this situation—and more importantly, how did it end? The sexual exploitation is inscribed in this picture: the picture is all about the exploitation. And it is confirmed in the many shots where a grinning Richardson looks directly at the viewer giving them a thumbs up implying 'see I did it again'. Without any testimonies as to what actually happened before and after the click, it is difficult to pinpoint the exploitation—all we have is a still. It is—still—an image.

And so, when model Jamie Peck chose to speak up in 2010, she was applauded by many as she helped start a debate about not only Richardson's exploitation of young women, but also, about the fashion industry. In Peck's testimony, she spoke openly about what happened in his studio when she, aged 19, was doing a shoot for *Purple Magazine*. She recalled:

I told him I had my period so I wanted to keep my underwear on, and he asked me to take my tampon out for him to play with. 'I love tampons!' he said, in that psychotically upbeat way that temporarily convinces so many girls that what's fun for Uncle Terry is fun for them. (I can just imagine him chirping, 'Why don't you wear these fairy wings while I fuck you in the ass? Wouldn't that be like, so fun?' to some attenuated girl fresh off the boat from Eastern Europe. Either the man's totally delusional, or he gets off on the fact that many of these things are not, in fact, very much fun for the girls.) I politely declined his offer to make tea out of my bloody cunt plug. It was then that he decided to just get naked. Before I could say 'whoa, whoa, whoa!' dude was wearing only his tattoos and waggling the biggest dick I'd ever seen dangerously close to my unclothed person (granted, I hadn't seen very many yet). 'Why don't you take some pictures of me?' he asked. Um, sure. I'm not sure how he maneuvered me over to the couch, but at some point he strongly suggested I touch his terrifying penis. This is where I zoom out on the situation. I can remember doing this stuff, but even at the time, it was sort of like watching someone else do it, someone who couldn't possibly be me because I would never touch a creepy photographer's penis. The only explanation I can come up with is that he was so darn friendly and happy about it all, and his assistants were so stoked on it as well, that I didn't want to be the killjoy in the room. My new fake friends would've been bummed if I'd said no. I must have said something about finals, because he told me, 'if you make me come, you get an A.' So I did! Pretty fast, I might add. All over my left hand. His assistant handed me a towel. (Peck 2010)

This long quote illustrates how sexual coercion often works: it is not until after it has happened that the coerced realizes what was done to her/him, often with feelings of disgust and anguish following. In a work situation—in this specific case, a model turning up for a shoot, obviously admiring the photographer who might be able to help her in her career—in which nudity is expected, and in which the outcome is the production of sexy pictures, there is a fine line between the representation and real acts leading up to the representation. We also need to take into account that the pressure on a young model to be 'up for it' (i.e., not to be a prude or a child) is at stake here. Peck describes how she 'didn't want to be the killjoy in the room' and how she thought her 'new fake friends would've been bummed' if she had said no.

A few days before Peck had posted her story on the internet site *The Gloss*, famous model Rie Rasmussen had publically accused Richardson of sexually harassing young girls.[5] Rasmussen, of course, had not that much to lose from speaking up: she was in her early 30s, well-respected as a model, actress, and film director. For younger women just starting their modeling career, much more is at stake: Richardson has had immense power within the industry, and he has had long-standing relationships with influential magazines like *Vogue* and *Harper's Bazaar*, and commercial clients like the aforementioned Gucci and Sisley. They have all supported him—despite knowing of his sexual exploitation of young models. And so, Terry Richardson continues to get jobs with the most famous. The same unwillingness to act and to put a stop to this kind of exploitation of young girls is to be found in the relation to the photos produced for the brand American Apparel. There were a few critical voices regarding the brand's use of young girls posing in the nude for free a couple of years ago, and the strategy of the company has been to take this exploitation even further (see Chernikoff 2011)—which seems to have worked to their benefit since the critique has silenced.

The fashion industry, of course, has for a long time been a predatory and exploitive one, just like other entertainment industries (the film industry, the music industry, television, and pornography). It has been fueled by alcohol, drugs, money, and sex. Further, it is an industry which relies on sexual imagery and allure, no doubt. Sex—or the erotic—has been used to sell fashion, just like sex has been used to sell film and music. Within these industries, the photographed female body operates as an object of exchange—she is a commodity, she has exchange value as well as use value (Irigaray 1977). This does not mean that we have to accept this as the status quo: female commodification and subordination through sexual exploitation and outspread misogyny should not be accepted, not if we want to live in an equal society, not if we want life to be livable, not only bearable, for everyone (Butler 2004).

Conclusion

Fashion photography, just like the cinematic institution, is *about* woman, but it is not for her. This may seem contradictory since most fashion photography is targeted toward women as consumers and since women do constitute the majority of consumers of both fashion magazines and women's fashion. Yet, it is not for women: it is part of, as well as an expression of, a phallocentric and patriarchal culture in which male phallo(go) centrism is the dominant, a culture in which the idea of an unequal sexual difference as necessary and desirable is law. And phallo(go)centrism, without a doubt, goes hand in hand with capitalism, mass culture, and mass consumption. Within this culture, everything that can ensure pleasure and power to the male gaze is for sale. Within both fashion and film industry, young women's bodies are for sale: they have, as mentioned above, both an exchange value and a use value—as long as they are desirable to this gaze, that is (Irigaray 1977).

Without explicitly connecting capitalism with phallogocentrism critical theory would already in the 1930s (e.g., Benjamin 1936; Adorno and Horkheimer [1944] 1972; and Bloch, [1936–47] 1986), theorize culture industries—of which cinema was one—in terms of representations of capitalist society and/or as escapist entertainment (with its offering of dreams as a double movement between capitalist dominance and a possibility of a political potential). In the late 1960s and the early 70s, much due to feminist theory, the patriarchal dominance and its phallo(go)centrism in culture and society came under the magnifying glass. In critical film theory, psychoanalytical, semiotic, Marxist, and feminist theories helped broaden the horizon: a certain focus on the visual pleasures that cinema offered its spectator was cultivated, and these pleasures were understood to be predominantly male.

Once the female spectator convincingly was 'discovered' (Mulvey 1975), she was understood as being negated in terms of active subjecthood since cinema—as a technical and narrative apparatus—offered only male positions within, and in relation to, the screen and the narrative. Hence, an active female spectator positioning herself as subject could only be read in terms of transvestism (Mulvey 1975; Doane 1982). Relying closely on a feminist and psychoanalytical frame work, theorists during the 1970s and 1980s would ascribe to mainstream cinema voyeurism as guiding principle and a narrative structure built on sadism (Mulvey 1975; de Lauretis 1984)—with the male represented as sadist in his physical conquest of the female in order to be included in the homosocial sphere (a.k.a. 'the Symbolic order' and the Law of the father). The female was still represented as masochist in her domestication, imprisonment, or—in the worst scenario—in her own rape, mutilation, or murder (Williams [1984] 1996). Because of the introduction of queer theory in the early 1990s, much has moved forward within critical (feminist) film theory, opening up for a more flexible reading of film, its representations, and its (female) spectator. Mulvey, Williams and others would re-consider and revise their early (psychoanalytically) influenced take on cinema—and offer re-readings of their own seminal texts—in order to open up for a more possible feminine subject position both within the film text and within the audience (Mulvey 1975; Williams 2001). However, the dominant representation of women as sexual victims, of dead and violated women as good women, has remained. And very similar sexist and misogynist representations have only increased in number in high-end fashion photography.

Film and fashion, as two highly popular and commercial representations and narratives, speak of unequal sexual difference as desirable, even when trying to 'upset' this difference via a certain queering of gender. Fashion and film are, to speak with Teresa de Lauretis, 'gender technologies' (de Lauretis 1987). Further, as gender technologies they both rely on representing sexuality, gender, and death—and this by nurturing an idea of sexual difference within which women are positioned as sexual victims in an all phallocentric universe. Not only do these kinds of images present women as sexual Image, they also serve to feed what American feminist Carol Sheffield has called 'sexual terrorism', a terrorism that women live with and come to accept from a young age since it is part of a profound (and, in most societies, accepted) social control of women (Sheffield 1989). In black and white, or in color, the representations of sexual terrorism as 'natural' are there for us to consume: presented in glossy magazines, on billboards, presented with an immaculate aesthetics, and surrounded by goods we desire, and always in abundance.

Is it the abundance, the aesthetics, and the naturalization—if not normalization—that comes with it that help fashion and its high-end photography escape any thorough feminist critique within academia? Whereas sexist, racist, homophobic, and misogynist representations in both mainstream and artistic film have for long been the targets for serious critique, the fashion industry seems to be holding an impenetrable position. Sexism and misogyny, together with homophobia and racism, are inscribed in the images that fashion produces, but difficult to get at since fashion, and the fashionable, get in their way.

Why is it that feminists have had so little to say about fashion photography (and the fashion industry) and its exploitive and sexist core? And why do fashion images slip through into the acceptable, the tolerable—into what is expected? This has hardly to do with feminists traditionally not being interested in fashion. Rather, it might have to do with that fact that it is hard to critique what one possibly also enjoys. Yet, contradictory sentiments and conflicting understandings of a phenomenon have not hindered feminist critique before, rather the opposite. The contradiction—the love/hate relationship and the feeling of being both on the inside and the outside—is what feminist thought since its second wave has thrived on (e.g., Mulvey 1975; de Lauretis 1984; Flitterman-Lewis 1996).

And so, it is important to bring critical thinking and some feminist anger (back) into the classroom as well as into research and for academics to address contemporary sexist fashion photography and the unequal gendered structures on which fashion relies. Academics can make a difference: our work—our teaching, our research, our contributions to the public debate—is not without value, rather the opposite, and maybe this work can contribute to a more equal situation within the industry, as well as a change within fashion photography and the sexist images it produces.

Representation and fiction have a meaning, and they portray events that have been staged, yet also events that have taken place. Further, they have power in the way that they shape people's understanding of others and themselves, and when a certain image gets shown and published in the media over and over again, one comes to believe in that image. I will give Richard Dyer, whose work on representation still has an enormous importance, the last word since he skillfully manages to pinpoint what really is at stake here:

> How a group is represented, presented over again in cultural forms, how an image of a member of a group is taken as representative of that group, how that group is represented in the sense of spoken for and on behalf of (whether they represent, speak for themselves or not), these all have to do with how members of groups see themselves and others like themselves, how they see their place in society, their right to the rights a society claims to ensure it citizens. (Dyer 1993: 1)

References

Acker, J. (1989), *Doing Comparable Worth: Gender, Class and Pay Equity*, Philadelphia: Temple University Press.

——— (1992), 'Gendering Organizational Theory', in A.J. Mills and P. Tancred, eds, *Gendering Organizational Analysis*, London: Sage, pp. 248–60.

Adorno, T.W. and Horkheimer, M. ([1944] 1972), *Dialectic of Enlightenment*, New York: Herder and Herder (Original: *Dialektik der Aufklärung*).

Barker, M. (2006), 'Loving and Hating *Straw Dogs*: The Meaning of Audience Responses to a Controversial Film—Part 2: Rethinking *Straw Dogs* as a Film', *Particip@tions*, 3.1, http://www.participations.org/volume%203/issue%201/3_01_barker.htm. Accessed 10 October 2012.

Benjamin, W. (1936), Das Kunstwerk im Zeitalter seiner technichen Reproduzierbarkeit, Zeitschrift fur Sozialforschung 5 1

Bloch, E. ([1938–47] 1986), *The Principle of Hope* (trans. Neville Plaice, Stephen Plaice, and Paul Knight), Cambridge, MA: MIT Press.

Butler, J. (2004), *Undoing Gender*, London and New York: Routledge.

Calás, M. (2008), 'The Wedge or the Door Step?', *Gender, Work and Organization*, 15.3, pp. 298–302.

Calás, M. and Smircich, L. (1992), 'Re-writing Gender into Organizational Theorizing: Directions from Feminist Perspectives', in M. Reed and M. Hughes, eds, *Rethinking Organization: New Directions in Organization Theory and Analysis*, London: Sage, pp. 218–59.

—— (1996), 'From "The Woman's" Point of View: Feminist Approaches to Organization Studies', in S. Clegg, C. Hardy, and W. Nord, eds, *Handbook of Organization Studies*, London: Sage, pp. 218–57.

Chernikoff, L. (2011), 'American Apparel's Most Provocative Ads from 1995 to the Present: An Evolution', *Fashionista*, 21 January, http://fashionista.com/2011/01/american-apparels-most-provocative-ads-from-1995-to-the-present-an-evolution/. Accessed 10 October 2012.

De Lauretis, T. (1984), *Alice Doesn't: Feminism, Semiotics, Cinema*, Bloomington: Indiana University Press.

—— (1987), *Technologies of Gender: Essays on Theory, Film and Fiction*, Bloomington: Indiana University Press.

Doane, M.A. (1982), 'Film and the Masquerade: Theorising the Female Spectator', *Screen*, 23.3–4, pp. 74–87.

Dyer, R. (1993), *The Matter of Images: Essays on Representation*, London: Routledge.

Flitterman-Lewis, S. (1996), *To Desire Differently: Feminism and the French Cinema*, New York: Columbia University Press.

Göthlund, A. (2003), 'Makt och blickar i Sisleys modebilder', *Konsthistorisk tidskrift/Journal of Art History*, 7.3, pp. 206–16.

Haskell, M. ([1974] 1987), *From Reverence to Rape: The Treatment of Women in the Movies*, 2nd ed., Chicago: University of Chicago Press.

Irigaray, L. (1977), *Ce sexe qui n'en est pas un*, Paris: Les Éditions de Minuit.

Jeffreys, S. (2005), *Beauty and Misogyny: Harmful Cultural Practices in the West*, New York: Routledge.

Kermode, M. (2003), 'A Wild Bunch in Cornwall', *The Observer*, 3 August, http://www.guardian.co.uk/film/2003/aug/03/features.review. Accessed 10 October 2012.

Mulvey, L. (1975), 'Narrative Cinema and Visual Pleasure', *Screen*, 16.3, pp. 6–18.

Navo (2010), 'The Meat Market: "Uncle" Terry Richardson', Half Devil & Half Child: The Other Point of View in Fashion, 23 March, http://lopenavostudios.wordpress.com/2010/03/23/the-meat-market-uncle-terry-richardson-by-navo. Accessed 10 October 2012.

Mulvey, L. (1989), Visual and Other Pleasures: Collected Writings, London: Palgrave Macmillan.

Nichols, B. (1991), *Representing Reality: Issues and Concepts in Documentary*, Bloomington: Indiana University Press.

Onstad, K. (2011), 'When Will Fashion Wise Up to Creepy Terry Richardson?', *Globe and Mail*, 13 March, http://www.theglobeandmail.com/life/relationships/news-and-views/katrina-onstad/when-will-fashion-wise-up-to-creepy-terry-richardson/article1935752. Accessed 10 October 2012.

Otis C. (2011), Beauty, Dirupted: A Memoir, New York: It Books.

Peck, J. (2010), 'Terry Richardson Is Really Creepy: One Model's Story', *The Gloss*, 16 March, http://thegloss.com/fashion/terry-richardson-is-really-creepy-one-models-story/. Accessed 10 October 2012.

Renov, M. (1993), *Theorizing Documentary*, London: Routledge.

Richardson, T. and Hanson, D. (2008), *Terryworld*, Hong Kong: Taschen Books.

Richardson, T. (2010) blog post, Terry Richardson's Diary, 10 March, http://www.terrysdiary.com/post/461129664/i-just-want-to-take-a-moment-to-say-im-really. Accessed 10 October 2012.

Rosen, M. (1973), *Popcorn Venus: Women, Movies and the American Dream*, New York: Coward, McCann & Goeghegan.

Sauers, J. (2010), 'Meet Terry Richardson, The World's Most F—ked Up Fashion Photographer', *Jezebel*, 16 March, http://jezebel.com/5494634/meet-terry-richardson-the-worlds-most-fked-up-fashion-photographer%20+%20http://%20http://jezebel.com/5495699/exclusive-more-models-come-forward-with-allegations-against-fashion-photographer. Accessed 10 October 2012.

Sheffield, C. (1989), 'Sexual Terrorism', in J. Freeman, ed., *Women: A Feminist Perspective*, Palo Alto, CA: Mayfield, pp. 3–19.

Simkin, S. (2011), *Straw Dogs*, Basingstoke: Palgrave MacMillan.

Spoto, D. (1999), *The Dark Side of Genius: The Life of Alfred Hitchcock*, New York: Da Capo Press.

Sobschak, V. (1984), 'Inscribing Ethical Space: Ten Propositions on Death, Representation, and Documentary', *Quarterly Review of Film Studies*, 9.4, pp. 283–300.

—— (2004), *Carnal Thoughts: Embodiment and Moving Image Culture*, Los Angeles: University of California Press.

Williams, L. ([1984] 1996), 'When the Woman Looks', in B.K. Grant, ed., *The Dread of Difference: Gender and the Horror Film*, Austin: University of Texas Press, pp. 15–34.

—— (2001), 'When Women Look: A Sequel', *Senses of Cinema*, 15.61, http://sensesofcinema.com/2001/15/horror_women/. Accessed 10 October 2012.

Williams, L.R. (1995), 'Women Can Only Misbehave: Peckinpah, *Straw Dogs*, Feminism and Violence', *Sight & Sound*, 5.2, pp. 26–27.

Yotka, S. (2010), 'Sex in Fashion: It's about Honesty', *Fashionista*, 17 June, http://fashionista.com/2010/06/sex-in-fashion-its-about-honesty/. Accessed 10 October 2012.

Notes

1 Two classic examples of sadism and voyeuristic pleasure carried out toward actresses on screen and on the film set are Alfred Hitchcock's *The Birds* (1963) and Sam Peckinpah's *Straw Dogs* (1971). In *The Birds*, Tippi Hedren, playing the active and energetic lead, had a mental breakdown after days of filming the scene in which she was enclosed in a small space and attacked by birds. The breakdown was triggered when her eyelid was cut by a bird's beak—after days of having had birds thrown at her by men wearing protective masks and gloves. Susan George, in *Straw Dogs*, was practically forced to partake in an explicit rape scene, a scene which had not been in the script she had agreed—and signed—to film (see Williams 1995; Spoto 1999; Kermode 2003; Simkin 2011).

2 Susan George was, as mentioned above, forced to shoot a rape scene against her will (see, e.g., Williams 1995; Simkin 2011). In an interview, Debbie Reynolds recalls how she almost lost her life while filming *How the West Was Won* (1961) as she was forced to do a drowning scene against her will. Director Hathaway argued that it was crucial that she do the scene herself, although her role could have been carried out by a stuntwoman or even a dummy, and she finally gave in. In the finished film it is impossible to see whether it really is Reynolds or someone else being violently drowned in a heavy-flowing stream.

3 Between 1999 and 2003, Sisley was condemned no less than five times by ERK for its sexist and discriminating ads in Sweden. See Göthlund (2003).

4 'Phallogocentrism' (or, originally and more narrowly, 'logocentrism') is a neologism coined by Jacques Derrida that refers to the perceived tendency in Western thought to locate the center of any text or discourse within the *logos* (a Greek word meaning word, reason, or spirit) and the *phallus* (a representation of the male genitalia).

5 Rasmussen said: 'He takes girls who are young, manipulates them to take their clothes off and takes pictures of them they will be ashamed of. They are too afraid to say no because their agency booked them on the job and are too young to stand up for themselves.' See Anon, 'Model Snaps at Fashion Fotog', *New York Post*, 11 March, http://www.nypost.com/p/pagesix/model_snaps_at_fashion_fotog_P489aSOevwAo35ikoKsRKI#ixzz0zCSjpFPr.

Chapter 9

'He Can't Love Me if I'm Ugly': The Recurring Theme of Popular Beauty in the Television Soap Opera *Days of Our Lives*

Andrew Reilly and Nancy A. Rudd

requently, a facial scar plays a part in an on-going storyline on daytime soap operas. Many characters have experienced a facial scar and responded in numerous ways, from experiencing shame and guilt, to seeking revenge or going insane. This paper examines how facial scarring affects characters who appear on daytime soap operas. Three storylines from the television show *Days of Our Lives* are presented, and their potential impact on viewers' body image and perception of beauty are discussed from the perspectives of cultivation theory and objectification theory. We posit that viewers may internalize the storyline and use these projected standards of beauty as portrayed on the show to appraise their own appearances in relation to their feelings of worthiness to be loved.

Soap Operas

Daytime serialized television became known as 'soap operas' because they were designed to sell household items, such as soap, and used a melodramatic forum similar to opera that would showcase characters' (often excessive) angst and dilemmas. They promoted manufacturers' products by either incorporating them into the daily activities of the characters or by sponsoring a segment or an entire episode.

Listeners or viewers (soap operas originated on radio in the 1930s and transitioned to television in the 1940s) are drawn into the private lives of characters with whom they identify and with whom they develop parasocial relationships that can last for decades. Parasocial relationships with television characters are not reciprocal, but they do parallel real social interactions (Horton and Wohl 1956). Viewers may care deeply about the welfare of the characters (Hinsey 2011). For example, Erica Kane has been a primary character on *All My Children* since its debut in 1970 and viewers who have followed her for many years feel a strong attachment to her character.

Unlike most other entertainment forms, soap operas have the enviable attribute of longevity. Five times a week, fifty-two weeks a year (except for holidays), daytime soap operas offer viewers ritual sagas that tell stories over long periods of time using characters who viewers find sympathetic and with whom they can identify. The repeated exposure simulates experiences one might have with a work colleague, a close friend, a family member, or a constant companion. Viewers may come to think of these characters as friends, family members, love interests, or enemies.

The American actress and writer Irna Phillips (1901–1973) was the originator of many of the first American soap operas and the driving force behind making them a viable source of entertainment and product promotion. Her creations, which began in the 1930s, became some of the most legendary and successful of television series, including *Guiding Light*, which was televised for seventy-two years, *As the World Turns*, with a fifty-four year run, and *Another World*, which was televised for thirty-five years. In a 1944 speech Phillips said that soap operas not only entertain, but also that they educate the audience on 'how to cope with reality' (Seiter 1989). Early storylines from her shows dealt with generational and marital conflicts, such as mothers dealing with rebellious teenage children and husbands who 'step out' on their wives. Over time, what constitutes reality has been stretched from Phillips's original vision to more fantastic tales, such as demon-possession and multiple personalities, but soap operas nonetheless illustrate how people react in life-like circumstances, be they commonplace or extraordinary. In 1965, Phillips and two of her protégés, Ted and Betty Corday, launched a new soap opera using Phillips's family-centered format and used a portion of a Bible verse as its title: *Days of Our Lives*. As of this writing, it is the second-longest running American soap opera currently still in production (after *General Hospital*).

At the height of their popularity in the United States, daytime soap operas culled millions of viewers. Thirty million people tuned into watch the wedding of Luke and Laura on *General Hospital* in 1980 (Wolf 2006). *As the World Turns* was so popular in the 1970s that *The Carol Burnett Show*, a leading variety/sketch comedy television show of the time, ran a parody of it, *As the Stomach Turns*. During the 1969–1970 season, there were nineteen daytime soap operas on American television. By mid-January 2012 there were four. Although ratings have declined in recent years, a significant number of viewers continue to tune in. The Nielsen Ratings for the week of 26–30 December 2011 indicate that the average soap opera viewership during that week was roughly 3.3 million viewers in the United States (Toups 2012).

Yet, soap operas continue to thrive in different venues and markets. Nighttime soaps such as *Dallas, Dynasty, Knots Landing,* and *Falcon Crest* were ratings winners in the 1980s and today popular American nighttime soaps such as *Pretty Little Liars* and *Revenge* continue the paradigm of continued, dramatic, serial storytelling. The American soap opera *The Bold and the Beautiful* is highly successful in Italy (Block 2009). In Britain, *Coronation Street*, which began airing 1960, is currently the world's longest-running soap opera still in production, and *EastEnders*, launched in 1985, has garnered many awards. Korean miniseries (which follow the soap opera format but have a planned conclusion) are broadcast throughout Asia and the United States. Telenovellas, Spanish-language mini-series versions of soap operas, are broadcast throughout South America, Mexico, and in areas of the United States with significant Spanish-language populations. In addition to television broadcasting, soap operas are forging new ground by broadcasting on the Internet, with shows such as *EastEnders: E20, Showboat, Imaginary Bitches,* and *Venice*. Thus, soap operas, in some form, can be found on six of the seven continents.

Soap Opera Research

Soap opera research has spanned decades with some of the earliest studies beginning in the 1940s and focusing on the audience or the content (Rubin 1985). Research on soap operas was abundant in the 1970s and 1980s, when daytime serials were particularly popular and dominated the daytime schedule on the three main American networks. The topics of research were plentiful.

Studies included: audience motivations for watching soap operas (Alexander 1985; Carveth and Alexander 1985; Herzog 1944; Lemish 1985; Rubin 1985; Rubin and Perse 1987); narrative structure (Gripsrud 1995); theme (Ward 2000; Warner and Henry 1948); ethnicity of characters (Jenrette et al. 1999); romantic relationships (Harrington and Bielby 1991); sexual behavior (Greenberg and D'Alessio 1985); alcohol use (Lowrey 1980); conversation style (Riegel 1996; Fine 1981); morality (Sutherland and Siniawsky 1982); crime (Estep and Macdonald 1985; Hodges et al. 1981); gender roles (Downing 1974; Geraghty 1990); older characters (Cassata et al. 1980); and the significance of soap operas to the development of broadcasting (Hobson 2003) and promoting products (Seiter 1989). A thorough examination of the research reveals no study on beauty and appearance. For this study we approach soap operas as artifacts to study to theorize the relationship between content and viewer.

He Can't Love Me if I'm Ugly

One of the primary storylines found in soap operas is that of the star-crossed couple who must overcome continual difficulties to be together. Couples rarely experience long periods of joy because, it can be assumed, writers and producers believe that a happy couple is a boring couple. In these subplots, many obstacles to the union are thrown into the paths of couples in order to extend the television longevity of (i.e., interest in) the couple, and therefore, to continue to entertain viewers. By consequence, a parasocial relationship develops between viewers and characters. In addition to amnesia, kidnappings, other marriages, paternity puzzles, murder charges, addiction, assault, doppelgangers, and presumed death, the introduction of facial scars is a notable plot device that creates drama between couples in soap operas.

Facial scars have long been a staple of the soap opera landscape. Numerous characters from different soap operas have suffered from facial scarring—sometimes it is written into the storyline as a legitimate character trait, and at other times it is presented as a ruse or deception. Typically, in order to create drama and expand the storyline to three months, six months, or longer, the scar cannot be repaired immediately or in many cases is deemed 'irreparable' (at least until the narrative has played out). The victims of facial scarring are usually female. On *All My Children,* Julia Santos, a young heroine, was scarred in a tornado, Erica Kane, the glamorous model-turned-business executive, was scarred in a car crash, and Brot Monroe, the mysterious newcomer, was scarred in the war in Iraq.[1] On *Another World,*

Felicia Gallant, the sensational novelist, was scarred when she fell through a skylight. On *As the World Turns*, Barbara Ryan, longtime bitch-heroine, was scarred in an explosion while Lily Walsh, the young heiress, was scarred twice, once by a knife-wielding psychopath and once in an explosion. On *Days of Our Lives*, Eve Donovan, the teenage prostitute, was scarred by a serial killer. On *General Hospital*, Anna Devane, the international spy, sported a scar following an explosion; the scar was later revealed to be fake. On *Loving*, matriarch Isabelle Alden's face was scarred when she used tainted moisturizer. On *One Life to Live*, Todd Manning, the town pariah, was scarred when a woman he was attacking hit him with a crowbar; later, after the character underwent full-facial plastic surgery (to accommodate the appearance of a new actor in the role), Todd was again scarred in the same location on his cheek. On *Passions*, Pretty Crane, the spoiled and selfish heiress, was scarred when her sister threw pool acid in her face; later it was revealed that the scar was fake. On *Santa Barbara*, social outcast Pamela Capwell was suffering from a debilitating disease that scarred her face. And on *The Young and the Restless*, Vanessa Prentiss, a jealous mother, was scarred in a fire, Brittany Hodges, the young ingénue who craved excitement, was scarred by an electrified stripper pole, town psychopath David Kimble's face was intentionally scarred by a plastic surgeon he was holding hostage, and crazy cat-lover Patty Williams was scarred in an explosion.

Three storylines from *Days of Our Lives* were selected for analysis as representative of the theme we identified as *He can't love me if I'm ugly*. *Days of Our Lives* is particularly popular with women aged 18–34, a key demographic according to *Soap Opera Digest* and Robert Seidman (2011). In addition, it is representative of a classic, popular, American soap opera. The significance of these storylines lies in the potential impact they have on viewers' perceptions of themselves and how they interact in romantic relationships. In these storylines, the female victim is in a budding or established romantic relationship prior to an experience or situation that results in facial scarring. The scarring triggers a change in the character's self-perception, and it results in a behavioral response relative to the relationship: the character believes she is now ugly, and she breaks up with her love interest to spare him from having to be with someone hideous. The storylines are summarized as follows: in the 1970s, the super-couple on *Days of Our Lives* was Julie Horton and Doug Williams (Figure 9:1). Popular interest in this fictional couple was very keen, and in January 1976 they became the first soap opera couple to appear on the cover of *Time* magazine. In 1979, Julie and Doug were married and later that year a gas stove exploded and severely scarred Julie's face. Julie thought Doug pitied her, and she ran away, intending to divorce him. Doug protested that he loved her no matter what she looked like, and claimed that he was not so shallow as to love her only for her beauty. But she proceeded with the divorce. When her face was later restored to its original appearance through plastic surgery, she wanted Doug back. But it was too late; he had moved on with someone else.

A similar storyline appeared in *Days of Our Lives* in the 1990s with the introduction of another prominent soap couple: Carrie Brady and Austin Reed. Carrie was a young teenager who had won a modeling competition and became 'the Face of the 90s'. Austin was a young

Figure 9:1. The characters of Julie and Doug, as played by Susan Seaforth Hayes and Bill Hayes, were a highly popular soap opera couple in the 1970s. They were the first soap opera couple to be featured on a cover of *Time*. *Time* Magazine is a registered trademark of Time Inc. and is used under license.

Figure 9:2. Nadia Bjorlin played Chloe Lane beginning in 1999. When the character was paired with Brady Black a car accident left her face severely scarred creating drama for the couple. Image courtesy of Legacy Media Relations.

athlete who was involved in underground boxing. When he refused to throw a fight, his enemies tried to throw acid in his face, but Carrie got in the way and it was she, rather than Austin, who was mutilated with facial scars. At the hospital, Austin presented her with an engagement ring, but her father's insistence that the engagement be ended, coupled with her facial scars, led her to terminate the relationship. Months later, her face was repaired and the couple reunited, albeit briefly.

The following decade, Chloe Lane (Figure 9:2) and Brady Black were a popular pairing on *Days of Our Lives*. Chloe was in a car accident and suffered scars to her face. This story was all the more poignant because the Chloe character was originally introduced as an orphan who—as a high school student—was ridiculed for her looks: she wore glasses and dressed all in black. Other students called her 'ghoul girl' until friends helped her transform into a beautiful woman (minus the glasses). So it may be understood as part of the character's psyche and past experience that when a car accident disfigured her face, Chloe chose to let everyone think she had died in the accident, as she anticipated that her facial scars would lead to renewed name-calling. When Brady found out that she was alive, he promised to love Chloe no matter what she looked like. A facial-reconstruction surgery was further complicated when Chloe's nemesis tainted the surgical instruments with a flesh-eating bacteria, which further scarred her face. Eventually, Chloe's face was restored through successful surgery, and she revealed her newly reconstructed face to Brady on their wedding day.

In each of these storylines, the scars are prominently featured on the character's face. Julie's and Carrie's scars are on their cheeks and they cover them with bandages. They still are beautifully coiffed, wear flawless makeup and have great figures. Chloe's scar, however, is on her cheek, nose and forehead and she covers her face with scarves. Her scar is truly harrowing. At the time her storyline aired, advances in theatrical makeup yielded scars that looked more realistic than before. In addition, *Days of Our Lives* had a reputation for going over the top with its storylines (e.g., Marlena was once possessed by the devil, Vivian had buried alive her nemesis, Carly, and later had the embryo of another nemesis, Kate, implanted in her, and Hope had an alternate personality, Princess Gina, who was an international jewel thief). Thus, it appears that in Chloe's storyline, the producers were going for shock value.

Significance

We look at the impact these storylines may have on viewers through cultivation theory, which is derived from the work of media scholars Gerbner et al. (2002) and objectification theory, which is proposed in the work of psychology scholars Frederickson and Roberts (1997). Gerber et al. argue that copious amounts of television viewing shapes viewers' perceptions of social reality, and that the relationship between society, television, and the viewer is circular: television shows reflect existing social attitudes, and viewing those attitudes on TV shows reinforces the attitudes. More television viewing results in more influence and the likelihood that what one sees on television is an accurate depiction of real life.

Research on soap operas has demonstrated a link between soap opera viewing and perceptions of reality. Carveth and Alexander (1985) found that people who watch soap operas for enjoyment, rather than to identify with a character or to explore reality, are the most susceptible to perceiving television as reality. Other researchers, including Buerkel-Rothfuss and Mayes (1981), Perse (1986), and Potter and Chang (1990), have found connections between soap opera viewing and incorrect perceptions of actual, real-world demographics (e.g., percentage of doctors who are female; percentage of marriages that end in divorce; higher estimates of crime; violent death; affairs; mental illness; and illegitimate children), all of which are common occurrences on soap operas. Interestingly, Haferkamp (1999) found that dedicated soap opera viewing was related to a belief in dysfunctional relationships, that is, that relationships are going to be problematic, no matter what. The research of Miller (2005) examined the connection between soap opera viewing and expectations of relationships. She interviewed college-age viewers of *Days of Our Lives* and found that participants in her sample expected *real* romantic relationships to mirror *reel* relationships. However, Alexander (1985) studied adolescents' perceptions of reality and soap opera viewing, and found no support that soap opera viewing was related to the belief that relationships were fragile.

Frederickson and Roberts postulate on objectification theory suggests that people may internalize objectifying comments or 'gazes' from others, and may learn to think of themselves and evaluate themselves from a third-person perspective that is appearance-oriented. A person's body may become the primary defining aspect of his or her identity; one's worth may therefore be evaluated by oneself or others by virtue of how closely one's appearance matches the cultural ideal of attractiveness (Frederickson and Roberts 1997; Hill 2001). Self-objectification may result in psychological consequences, such as shame and anxiety about appearance. Indeed, Frederickson and Roberts (1997) suggest that women who self-objectify may feel shame if their appearance does not meet prescribed standards of beauty. Given that viewers of soap operas may have had their notions of beauty and social relationships cultivated by their viewing habits and the norms expressed in the storylines, it is reasonable to consider that female viewers may be hypercritical of their own appearances.

Objectification may be communicated through three avenues, according to Frederickson and Roberts. These include: (1) interpersonal contact, (2) media depictions of interpersonal contact, and (3) media depictions that emphasize certain body parts. Women are objectified in Western culture more than men, and this is carried out through verbal commentary, sexually objectifying gazes from others, and sexual discrimination or assault (Kozee 2005). If one's natural response to objectifying experience is to continually monitor the body, then we can see how the outcome might be constant anxiety about one's attractiveness and/or engaging in behaviors to try to improve the social treatment anticipated from others (Cash, Gillen, and Burns 1977; McKinley and Hyde 1996). A number of researchers have found links between constant body monitoring (body surveillance) and feelings of shame about the body in female college students (Tylka and Hill 2004), in female dancers compared to non-dancers (Tiggemann and Slater 2001), in adolescents (Slater and Tiggemann 2002), in women across the life span (Greenleaf 2005), and in both women and men (Tiggemann and Kuring 2004).

Research also tells us that people may feel somewhat disconnected from their physical selves when they adopt the perspective of the 'other' (Frederickson and Roberts 1997), and may try to change their appearance or the situation causing them anxiety. They may engage in disordered eating behavior (Pike 1995; Tylka and Hill 2004), cosmetic surgery (Kaw 1993), extreme weight training (Nowell and Ricciardelli 2008), and other appearance-altering behaviors.

The three storylines from *Days of Our Lives* imply that beauty is the foundation of romance and romantic relationships. Julie, Carrie, and Chloe all rejected their partners' interest because they felt their scars were anathema to true love, that the scars have made them a burden. The argument proposed in cultivation theory suggests that soap operas reflect current standards of female beauty, and that viewing soap operas reinforces this standard. Thus, these storylines have the potential to impact upon viewers' perceptions of beauty, and they suggest that one must be physically flawless to find true love. Objectification theory suggests that the beauty standards projected in the soap operas are internalized by viewers. This is particularly disturbing when we consider that soap operas are primarily marketed to women, especially to women aged 18 to 34, and that many viewers begin watching soap operas in their early teens.

Cultivation theory and objectification theory suggest that popular soap operas may cultivate viewers' beliefs that facial scars make one unworthy of love, may lead to strong feelings of social comparison among viewers, and, through objectification, may influence viewers' beliefs so that they come to feel that they are unworthy of affection if they have facial scars. Thus, common storylines in daytime soap operas may contribute to negative feelings about the self and to appearance dissatisfaction. It is commonplace that adults have some facial scars as a result of normal circumstances such as acne, chicken pox, cat scratches, etc., while others may have more serious scars from burns or surgery. We know that it is human nature to compare oneself to others on any number of criteria, including physical appearance, and to gauge how one is 'doing' in relation to others. Studies show that social comparison influences body satisfaction, and that comparing oneself to unrealistic standards of beauty causes negative self-appraisals. Research conducted by Strahan et al. (2006) revealed that self-appraisals were more negative among women when the cultural norms of beauty they referenced were salient. We contend that the *he can't love me if I'm ugly* storylines, and therefore the norms of beauty represented in soap operas, are seen as largely salient by soap opera viewers.

Typical targets for comparison that are identified in research on social comparison include celebrities, athletes, peers, family, and the media (e.g., Rudd and Carter 2006; Rudd and Lennon 1999; Harrison and Cantor 1997). Thus, if soap opera characters are seen as being salient targets for comparison, and if the storyline for those characters identify facial scars as sufficient reason to exit a love relationship, then it is reasonable to assume that viewers will be hypercritical of their own scars and of other physical characteristics that differ from the ideal, and more likely to question their worthiness to be in a love relationship.

Conclusion

A striking feature of the *he can't love me if I'm ugly* theme is that the male characters are not the ones with the problem. Doug, Austin, and Brady were all supportive of their respective wives/girlfriends. In fact, Doug was particularly incensed that Julie thought he was so shallow as to love her only for her beauty. Hence, the female characters are not only stigmatized as physically disfigured, but are also portrayed as vain, shallow, and of no worth beyond their looks. What may be worse, is that the female characters demonstrate self-objectification, believing themselves to be so flawed that they are not worthy of the attention or affection of others.

The commercial purpose of the soap opera is to advertise merchandise to a target audience in an entertaining way. It is the aim of the writers and producers to develop characters, situations, and storylines that appeal to the audience in order to create compelling tales. Romance and finding one's soul mate is the foundation of all daytime soap operas and obstacles are necessary for the characters to overcome in order to 'prove' their love to each other. We question why the female characters should be portrayed as feeling unworthy of being loved. A more socially responsible tale involving facial scarring, for example, could show the couple overcoming the social and psychological challenges of the scars and would have the female character find value in herself beyond her looks.

Given the prominence of the storyline of facial scarring in soap operas, we recommend that further research be conducted to examine how facial scarring and other less-than-perfect appearances are treated on other shows and how viewers respond to these characterizations. Such research would further elucidate the parasocial relationships that viewers may establish with the characters in soap operas, and would help scholars better understand the mechanisms through which identification with the characters affects feelings of acceptance of viewers' own physical appearances.

References

Alexander, A. (1985), 'Adolescents' Soap Opera Viewing and Relational Perceptions', *Journal of Broadcasting and Electronic Media*, 29.3, pp. 295–308.

Block, D. (2009), 'City in Italy Bestows Honorary Citizenship on *The Bold and the Beautiful's* Jennifer Gareis', Daytime Dial, http://daytimedial.blogspot.com/2009/05/gareis-big-bold-and-beautiful-in-italy.html. Accessed 10 October 2012.

Buerkel-Rothfuss, N.L. and Mayes, S. (1981), 'Soap Opera Viewing: The Cultivation Effect', *Journal of Communication*, 31, pp. 108–15.

Carveth, R. and Alexander, A. (1985), 'Soap Opera Viewing Motivations and the Cultivation Process', *Journal of Broadcasting and Electronic Media*, 29.3, pp. 259–73.

Cash, T., Gillen, B. and Burns, D. (1977), 'Sexism and Beautyism in Personnel Consultant Decision Making', *Journal of Applied Psychology*, 62.3, pp. 301–10.

Cassata, M.B., Anderson, P.A. and Skill, T.D. (1980), 'The Older Adult in Daytime Serial Drama', *Journal of Communication*, 30.1, pp. 48–49.

Downing, M. (1974), 'Heroine of the Daytime Serial', *Journal of Communication*, 24.2, pp. 130–37.

Estep, R. and Macdonald, P.T. (1985), 'Crime in the Afternoon: Murder and Robbery on Soap Operas', *Journal of Broadcasting and Electronic Media*, 29.3, pp. 323–31.

Fine, M.G. (1981), 'Soap Opera Conversations: The Talk That binds', *Journal of Communication*, 31.3, pp. 97–107.

Frederickson, B.L. and Roberts, T.A. (1997), 'Objectification Theory: Toward Understanding Women's Lived Experiences and Mental Health Risks', *Psychology of Women Quarterly*, 21.2, pp. 173–206.

Geraghty, C. (1990), *Women and Soap Opera*, Cambridge: Polity.

Gerbner, G., Morgan, M., Gross, L., Signorielli, N. and Shanahan, J. (2002), 'Growing Up with Television: Cultivation Processes', in J. Bryant and D. Zillmann, eds, *Media Effects: Advances in Theory and Research*, 2nd ed., Hillsdale, NJ: Lawrence Erlbaum.

Greenberg, B.S. and D'Alessio, D. (1985), 'Quantity and Quality of Sex in the Soaps', *Journal of Broadcasting and Electronic Media*, 29.3, pp. 309–21.

Greenleaf, C. (2005), 'Self-Objectification among Physically Active Women', *Sex Roles*, 52. 1–2, pp. 51–62.

Gripsrud, J. (1995), *The* Dynasty *Years: Hollywood Television and Critical Media Studies*, London: Routledge.

Haferkamp, C.J. (1999), 'Beliefs about Relationships in Relation to Television Viewing, Soap Opera Viewing, and Self-Monitoring', *Current Psychology*, 18.2, pp. 193–204.

Harrington, C.L. and Bielby, D.D. (1991), 'The Mythology of Modern Love: Representations of Romance in the 1980s', *Journal of Popular Culture*, 24.4, pp. 129–44.

Harrison, K. and Cantor, J. (1997), 'The Relationship between Media Consumption and Eating Disorders', *Journal of Communication*, 47.1, pp. 40–67.

Herzog, H. (1944), 'What Do We Really Know about Daytime Serial Listeners?', in P.F. Lazarfeld and F.N. Stanton, eds, *Radio Research, 1942–1943*, New York: Buell, Sloan & Pearce, pp. 3–33.

Hill, M.S. (2001), 'Examining Objectification Theory: Sexual Objectification's Link with Self-Objectification and Moderation by Sexual Orientation and Age in White Women', *Dissertation Abstracts International: Section B: The Sciences & Engineering*, 63 (7-B).

Hinsey, C. (2011), *Afternoon Delight: Why Soaps Still Matter*, Santa Monica, CA: 4th Street Media.

Hobson, D. (2003), *Soap Opera*, Cambridge: Polity.

Hodges, K.K., Brandt, D.A. and Kline, J. (1981), 'Competence, Guilt, and Victimization: Sex Differences in Attribution of Causality in Television Dramas', *Sex Roles*, 7, pp. 537–46.

Horton, D. and Wohl, R. (1956), 'Mass Communication and Para-Social Interaction: Observations on Intimacy at a Distance', *Psychiatry*, 19, pp. 215–29.

Jenrette, J., McIntosh, S. and Winterberger, S. (1999), '"Carlotta!": Changing Images of Hispanic-American Women in Daytime Soap Operas', *Journal of Popular Culture*, 33.2, pp. 37–48.

Kaw, E. (1993), 'Medicalization of Racial Features: Asian American Women and Cosmetic Surgery', *Medical Anthropology Quarterly*, 7.1, pp. 74–89.

Kozee, H. (2005), 'A Test of Objectification Theory with Lesbian and Heterosexual Women', MA thesis, Ohio State University, Columbus, OH.

Lemish, D. (1985), 'Soap Opera Viewing in College: A Naturalistic Inquiry', *Journal of Broadcasting and Electronic Media*, 29.3, pp. 275–93.

Lowrey, S.A. (1980), 'Soap and Dooze in the Afternoon: An Analysis of the Portrayal of alcohol Use in Daytime Serials', *Journal of Studies on Alcohol*, 41, pp. 829–38.

McKinley, N.M. and Hyde, J. (1996), 'Objectified Body Consciousness Scale', *Psychology of Women Quarterly*, 20.2, pp. 181–215.

Miller, E. (2005), personal communication. DeKalb, Illinois.

Nowell, C. and Ricciardelli, L. (2008), 'Appearance-Based Comments, Body Dissatisfaction and Drive for Muscularity in Males', *Body Image*, 5, pp. 337–45.

Perse, E.M. (1986), 'Soap Opera Viewing Patterns of College Students and Cultivation', *Journal of Broadcasting and Electronic Media*, 30.2, pp. 175–93.

Pike, K.M. (1995), 'Bulimic Symptomatology in High School Girls: Toward a Model Cumulative Risk', *Psychology of Women Quarterly*, 19, pp. 373–396.

Potter, W.J. and Chang, I.C. (1990), 'Television Exposure Measures and the cultivation Hypothesis', *Journal of Broadcasting and Electronic Media*, 34.3, pp. 313–33.

Riegel, H. (1996), 'Soap Operas and Gossip', *Journal of Popular Culture*, 29.9, pp. 201–9.

Rubin, A.M. (1985), 'Uses of Daytime Television Soap Operas by College Students', *Journal of Broadcasting and Electronic Media*, 29.1, pp. 241–58.

Rubin, A.M. and Perse, E.M. (1987), 'Audience Activity and Soap Opera Involvement: A Uses and Effects Investigation', *Human Communication Research*, 14.2, pp. 246–68.

Rudd, N.A. and Lennon, S.J. (1999), 'Social Power and Appearance Management among Women', in K.K.P. Johnson and S.J. Lennon, eds, *Appearance and Power*, New York: Berg, pp. 153–72.

Rudd, N.A. and Carter, J. (2006), 'Building Positive Body Image among Athletes: A Socially Responsible Approach', *Clothing & Textiles Research Journal*, 24.4, pp. 363–80.

Seidman, R. (2011), 'Soap Opera Ratings: "Days of Our Lives" Rebounds; "One Life to Live" Rises', TV by the Numbers, 4 August, http://tvbythenumbers.zap2it.com/2011/08/04/soap-opera-ratings-days-of-our-lives-rebounds-one-life-to-live-rises/99659/. Accessed 10 October 2012.

Seiter, E. (1989), 'To Teach and to Sell: Irna Phillips and Her Sponsors, 1930–1954', *Journal of Film and Video*, 41.1, pp. 21–35.

Slater, A. and Tiggemann, M. (2002,) 'A Test of Objectification Theory in Adolescent Girls', *Sex Roles*, 46, pp. 343–49.

Strahan, E., Wilson, A., Cressman, K. and Buote, V. (2006), 'Comparing to Perfection: How Cultural Norms for Appearance Affect Social Comparisons and Self-Image', *Body Image,* 3, pp. 211–27.

Sutherland, J.C. and Siniawsky, S.J. (1982), 'The Treatment and Resolution of Moral Violations on Soap Operas', *Journal of Communications,* 32.2, pp. 67–74.

Tiggemann, M. and Kuring, J. (2004), 'The Role of Body Objectification in Disordered Eating and Depressed Mood', *British Journal of Clinical Psychology,* 43.3, pp. 299–311.

Tiggemann, M. and Slater, A. (2001), 'A Test of Objectification Theory in Former Dancers and Non-Dancers', *Psychology of Women Quarterly,* 25.1, pp. 57–64.

Toups, X. (2012), 'Ratings: GH Hits New Low for Second Straight Week', 7 January, http://www.soapoperanetwork.com/ratings/ratings-gh-hits-new-low-for-second-straight-week. Accessed 10 October 2012.

Tylka, T.L. and Hill, M.S. (2004), 'Objectification Theory as It Relates to Disordered Eating among College Women', *Sex Roles,* 51.11–12, pp. 719–30.

Ward, S. (2000), 'Train and Nation: *CityExpress*—the Soap Opera', *Journal of Popular Culture,* 34.3, pp. 9–26.

Warner, W.L. and Henry, W.E. (1948), 'The Radio Day Time Serial: A Symbolic Analysis', *Genetic Psychology Monographs,* 37, pp. 7–69.

Wolf, B. (2006), 'Luke and Laura: Still the Ultimate TV Wedding', ABC News, 14 November, http://abcnews.go.com/Entertainment/WolfFiles/story?id=236498. Accessed 10 October 2012.

Note

1 The character's storyline mirrors the actor's real-life experience as a soldier in Iraq when his Humvee hit a landmine. The character's scars are the actual scars of the actor (J.R. Martinez).

Chapter 10

Redressing the Devil's Wardrobe: Representing and Re-Reading the Darker Side of Fashion in Chick Lit Novels

Anne Peirson-Smith

Some time soon, I hope, a twenty-first century Nancy Mitford will appear and write a genuinely funny and insightful book about fashion magazines and all the monstrous eccentrics who sail in them. But this? It's as tired as last season's combats, darling. (Cooke 2003)

This book changed my life…no I mean my wardrobe…you know it's not Jane Austen but I loved lots about it—the fashion, the bitch boss (who hasn't had one!) and the twisted fairytale ending with Cinders losing her prince and the job but gaining her integrity and freedom with lots of laughter and tears. It's just an easy read and an escape into a stylish world. (Jen, British, age 36)

Introduction

This chapter examines the intersecting and contested sites of fashion writing and the sub-genre of 'chick literature' in the quest to readdress the debate about the value of both sites with specific reference to the novel, *The Devil Wears Prada* (Weisberger 2003) (see Figure 10:1) and other selected texts. The vilification of female novels as pulp fiction and trashy, ephemeral fictional texts, founded on stereotypical form and content has a distinguished history in feminist critiques in the universe of the romance novel genre. Based on a close reading of this text and in-depth discussions with a sample of readers across a range of cultures, the chapter challenges these critiques. In doing so, it will suggest that despite the supposed superficial nature of their content and premise and their formulaic, consumer-centric focus, these fashion-framed novels or 'fashionista fiction' can also deal with real and serious issues relating to friendship, work, and lifestyle that resonate with the reader as active agent, often empowering them to make sense of their lived experiences. In a neo-feminist manner, reading these fictional texts can be a selective process defining a sense of the fashioned self in the narrative through the characters with a vicarious application to their own lives. Readers of fashion-focused novels, despite their dark press, are finding pleasure in the text and celebrating the joys of reading, shopping, career choice, female friendships, identity control, and escapist fantasies through real and imagined forms of dressing up.

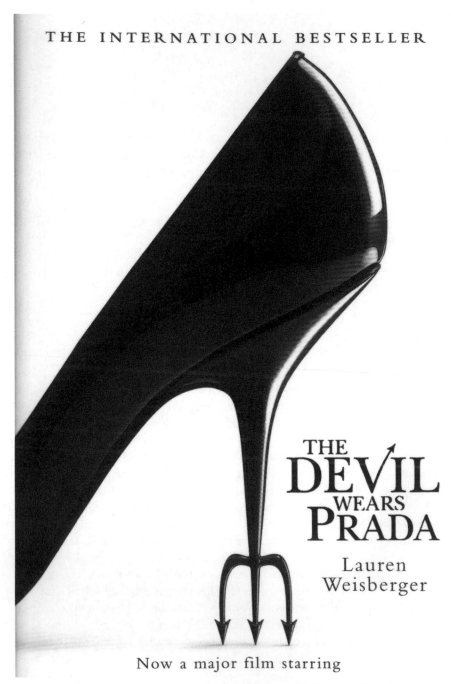

Figure 10:1. Book cover for *The Devil Wears Prada*, Weisberger, 2003. Photograph by author.

Firstly, the chapter will review the ways in which both fashion writing and the reading of this literary form, largely by a female readership, represent the subject of polarized debate in academic, literary, media, and reading circles. In this, fashion as a subject or pastime, in addition to fashion writing itself, have either been vilified as a shallow pleasure-seeking pursuit validating and reinforcing the capitalist system where 'fashionable dress and beautification of self are conventionally seen as expressions of subordination' (Wilson 1985: 13), or as a means of female empowerment for the new post-feminist woman. Secondly, it will examine claims as to how this specific literary genre has provided a new site of consumption. It operates as does any commercial brand by enabling the reader to discover truths about their particular lived experience while validating their membership of various fashion and lifestyle-based consumption communities. Thirdly, this position will be tested empirically by analyzing the responses of a selected group of readers specifically reading *The Devil Wears Prada* (*DWP*) as a means of exploring and validating the relationship between reader and consumption community. A multi-vocal reading of this often maligned genre will be provided by examining an encrusted text such as *The Devil Wears Prada* as the focus of this paper. This is a primary text coated with layers of satellite texts produced by cultural intermediaries such as critics, bloggers, and editors to promote or demote it, in addition to its reception by a particular interpretative community (Radway 1991). This reading will be informed empirically by engaging with representatives of a consumption community defined as a loosely connected readership group holding similar values and aspirations and consuming similar products. Incorporating these voices in the analysis can usefully uncover the wider experiential readings that they bring to bear on the text and their role in defining this specific consumption community.

Fashion's Bad Press

Critics from various ideological positions have denigrated both popular fiction and fashion writing; they are considered idle chatter written for mindless consumption. Despite Barthes acknowledgement of the professional discourse system underlining 'the written garment' of fashion journalism (Barthes 1983), fashion writing is generally considered as shallow. Typically, the fashion system and those who write about it are charged with 'furthering the superficial and spurious while undermining the substantial and genuine' (Davis 1992: 194). As Angela McRobbie notes of British fashion journalism:

> Fashion writing is informative or celebratory, it is never critical, only mildly ironical. Nowhere does it ever touch upon some of the most important dynamics of contemporary British fashion which hinge around fashion as a place of work and as a space of livelihoods. The editors and journalists rarely break ranks and produce more engaged and challenging writing on the subject. (McRobbie 1998: 173)

At the same time, fashion-based novels and films are often accused of shameless fashion brand product placement (Konig 2004). Equally, fashion editors and journalists are often accused of being public relations mouthpieces of the fashion brands that advertise in between the editorial sections of fashion magazines. This viewpoint is also acknowledged by fashion commentators, as Colin McDowell notes:

> Fashion writers, like any other commentators on artistic work, should be critics rather than popular cheerleaders. Loving frocks and the world of showbiz personalities are not enough. A fashion journalist needs to have the knowledge to differentiate between the good, the average and the bad—and to know why each one is what it is, just as a book critic can tell the difference between a Nobel winner and a Mills and Boon romance.... [Y]ou don't even need the fingers of one hand to count the number across the globe who do. (McDowell 2010)

Where fashion and pop fiction collide on the pages of fashion writing or fashion-framed novels, this coupling has also been accused of being essentially mind-numbingly trivial. The response to female-targeted popular fiction has been at best flippantly mocking and at worst openly hostile because society is 'seemingly suspicious of womanly things and concerns' (Konig 2004: 140). Also, perhaps because fashion is image driven and ephemeral (Breward 2003), it has rarely received critical attention by opinion formers in professional circles valuing the written word. This view is even voiced by the *DWP's* protagonist who considers that she may well be 'selling out' as a journalist by taking a job at *Runway*.

In truth, fashion is still largely gendered and marginalized by being 'relegated to the women's sections of broadsheet newspapers or celebrity gossip columns in daily newspapers who set aside whole pages and employ journalists to offer their opinions concerning the ideal size of female models or to present the latest in latex' (Barnard 1996: 1). Yet, fashion is seemingly of great interest to readers and viewers of print, broadcast, and online media; a Google search throws up thousands of pages of the written word devoted to the subject of fashion from articles to websites, blogs, and tweets. Equally, considerable time and energy are also devoted to writing and reading about fashion. In other words, it involves both an active producer and consumer as there appears to be an insatiable demand to discover more about fashion and to be immersed in its fictional world—as one of the respondents explained:

> Look, I'm a fashion junkie me. I can't get enough of reading about it in magazines, stories and films. Loved *DWP* and read all of the *Shopaholic* books and felt so sad when I'd done them all—yeah it's my obsession and my life. I have piles of fashion magazines and glossy books in my bedroom—I will never get rid of them—they are like friends and I get comfort from having them there and from dipping into that glamorous world whenever I like. (Sarah, British, age 41)

Chick Lit's Literary Origins

The origins of chick lit can be located in the broader sphere of popular or genre fiction (Cawelti 1976) and for some it represents a type of formula fiction in its predictable plots. Its lineage can be linked with the genre of the romance or Harlequin novels across the twentieth century residing in the 'for women, by women, about women' genre. Chick lit heroines are not exclusively tied up in a patriarchal world of traditional love and marriage; they contend with the broader concerns of womanhood: surviving professional and social challenges in urban settings. They perhaps share a closer contemporary connection with the 1980s 'sex and shopping'/'humping and hoarding' sagas of Judith Krantz and Jackie Collins whose dominant female characters power dressed, schemed, and slept their way to the top of corporate empires conspicuously flashing expensive designer bling as proof of success. Two decades later the protagonist is more fallible, 'employing a confessional style to appeal to readers who often identify with the heroines' battles with their bosses, boyfriends, and body image' (Ferriss and Young 2006b). The origins of the term 'chick lit' are contested. Used ironically by Cris Mazza (2006) in the title of a book on *avant-garde* women's writing (Mazza and DeShell 1995) and by James Wolcott referring to the trend for female newspaper columnists such as Candace Bushnell and Helen Fielding to peddle 'sheer girlishness' in journalism (Wolcott 1996: 54), the genre itself started to emerge in the mid-1990s. Suzanne Ferriss and Mallory Young (2006a) consider it to have been originally brought to life in Helen Fielding's *Bridget Jones's Diary* (1996), claiming that Bridget Jones's self-reflexive musings unleashed a literary sisterhood of hapless heroines in search of love, laughter, and career advancement. Others cite Melissa Bank's *The Girls' Guide to Hunting and Fishing (1999)*, as the first chick lit novel on the U.S. block (Vnuk 2005). Notwithstanding, these narratives feature a feisty protagonist who, despite appearing to have it all, is often wracked with insecurities and seeks solace in retail fashion therapy; for example, Becky Bloomwood's Olympian fashion consumption habits in the *Shopaholic* series (Kinsella 2000). The range of plotlines and the broadly defined demographic of the female lead character has evolved the genre into many subgenres—from 'widow lit' to 'ethnic chick lit'—and thus the genre has matured beyond a concern with the superficial.

In the relatively recent emergence of this genre and culture, the 'chickerati' have benefited financially and professionally by writing about the everywoman-type heroine. As with their Harlequin and 'sex 'n' shopping' sisters, these fictional females have been subjected to a chorus of disapproval from novelists, feminists, and commentators; opinions swing 'between its outright dismissal as trivial fiction and the unexamined embrace by fans who claim that it reflects the realities of life for contemporary single women' (Ferriss and Young 2006a). Feminist critics have bemoaned the blatant promotion of consumerist ideology and dependency on lifestyle images perpetuated by mass culture and the culture industries (McRobbie 2004; Ebert 2009). Suggestions that the reader is as hapless as her heroine are located in the bookstore and its marketing push. Hence, Maureen Dowd laments that the publishing industry is undermining the very canons of literature:

I was cruising through Borders…Suddenly I was swimming in pink. I turned frantically from display table to display table, but I couldn't find a novel without a pink cover. I was accosted by a sisterhood of cartoon women, sexy string beans in minis and stilettos, fashionably dashing about book covers with the requisite urban props—lattes, books, purses, shopping bags, guns and, most critically, a diamond ring.… I realized with growing alarm, chick lit was no longer a niche. It had staged a coup of the literature shelves. Hot babes had shimmied into the grizzled old boys' club, the land of Conrad, Faulkner and Maugham. The store was possessed with the devil spawn of *The Devil Wears Prada*. The blood-red high heel ending in a devil's pitchfork on the cover of the Lauren Weisberger best seller might as well be driving a stake through the heart of the classics. (Dowd 2007)

The fact that these texts generate such heated debate suggests that they are worthwhile objects of academic study as a socio-cultural phenomenon because of their supposed potential to undermine and disrupt the lived experience and social process.

While the fashion industry has become a potent social force, the chick lit genre has increased the cultural capital of fashion writing as it examines the tensions inherent in the female postmodern condition while exploring consumerism's role in female socialization. Consumers and readers are using texts and material artifacts in the search for daily meaning and an understanding of a gendered self. Fashion has become more democratized in its individual assertion of personal autonomy (Lipovetsky 1994). As Evans, echoing Giddens, observes, 'No longer derided as superficial, frivolous or deceitful, fashion essentially has an important role to play, not merely in adorning the body, but also in fashioning a modern, reflexive self' (2003: 6).

Reframed through the lens of these consumption communities and readers' aspirations to be part of fashion's glamorous modern universe with its 'concentration of designer brands, fab frocks, name models and celebrity guests all under the glare of publicity and feted with lavish hospitality—an irresistible cocktail of all that is desirable in contemporary commercial culture' (Buckley and Gundle 2000: 38), we should applaud the active readership for making this genre their own. These critiques of female readership habits are oversimplistic and patronizing. This is a readership with more eclectic reading habits than is often assumed by the critics. Essentially, these readers are often as self-aware and self-reflexive as their heroines of the contemporary issues they face.

Chick Lit Consumption Communities

Consciously or otherwise, fans exercise their subjective preferences constituting a distinct and recognizable social group bound together in their affective connection with a commodity brand. Albert Muniz and Thomas C. O'Guinn describe this social group as:

a specialized, non-geographically bound community…marked by a shared consciousness, rituals and traditions, and a sense of moral responsibility. Each of these qualities is, however, situated within a commercial and mass-mediated ethos, and has its own particular expression. Brand communities are participants in the brand's larger social construction and play a vital role in the brand's ultimate legacy. (Muniz and O'Guinn 2001: 413)

The chick lit community relate to the fictional events, characters, and consumption, as one book critic noted, 'It's fair to assume that nobody oblivious to names like Prada will be reading this story' (Maslin 2003). They are a heterogeneous demographic 20–50 years old, globally situated and cross-cultural group who consume literary genres from 'mum lit' to *Madame Bovary*. Characters have also been labeled as products of the fashion industry, advertising, and mass media in the sense that luxury purchases are regarded as the essential if not the sole element in the characters' identity quest. Hence, an examination of text and the reader's response to it should reveal if the author is attempting to tell readers what to think, or indeed what to think about.

The Reader Turns the Page

The site of the interpretative community as readership of the text is the focus of the next section. Their response to this text is analyzed in terms of why they were seduced or alienated by the text, what it meant in their lives, what pleasures they gained from it and its shortcomings. In-depth interviews were conducted with a sample of 25 females, ages ranging from 20–49, from India, Britain, Australia, the Philippines, China, France, Singapore, Hong Kong, Canada, and North America. Most had college degrees and considered themselves as part-time or full-time professionals. Ten of the respondents were members of book clubs or reading circles and regularly discussed books with their friends. From these interviews, four main themes emerged in terms of the textual satisfaction derived: detailed descriptions of aspirational retail items (fashion fix); behind-the-scenes examination of the fashion industry; fashion as individual empowerment; and fashion's transformative possibilities.

1. Fashion Fix: Consuming the Fashion-Centric Novel

The Devil Wears Prada (2003) narrates the sage of Andrea 'Andy' Sachs, a recent college graduate who acquires a job as an assistant to *Runway* magazine's editor-in-chief, Miranda Priestly (allegedly based on *Vogue* editor Anna Wintour). Central to the novel is the theme of fashion consumption. Most of the respondents in the group claimed that they delighted in reading fashion-centered books as they satisfied a desire to experience fashion brands vicariously. As Janet (Australian, age 39) explained:

> I really enjoyed this book because just like others I have read like the *Shopaholic* ones you can imagine what those high red leather Manolos would look like or that chic black Prada outfit and you become the person wearing them, not the girl in the book.

This vicarious substitution of real self for fictional persona also appears to fill the gap between aspiration and consuming reality as Dina (Indian, age 24) said:

> As a new grad, I just can't afford to buy any of these high-end fashion brand names—and of course I so would love to be able to do that. What self respecting 20-something doesn't? But I can satisfy, my fashion longing and get my fashion fix by reading these types of books like *DWP* that are loaded up with descriptions of my favorite fashion labels—my friends—Gucci, Dior, Prada, Celine, Marc Jacobs—you name it and it's way kinder on my credit card for sure!

So, despite the alleged shallow character development, readers project their fantasies into the narrative. The ability of these texts to fill an affective void was also the case when reading fashion magazine articles:

> I regard these novels about girls and their relationship with fashion as being the same as the fashion magazines that I read on a regular basis like *Cosmopolitan* or *Marie Clare* and *Elle* for fun in my downtime in contrast to the serious stuff I have to read for work. I also read these novels in the same way as magazines—fast and in my downtime like on the beach, the hairdressers, or on the bus to work. It helps to pass the time and make the most of my spare moments. And it's a real treat in the middle of all of the stress that we have to deal with in our busy lives. (Teresa, Hong Kong, age 35)

In terms of their relationship with fashion, chick lit and fashion magazines respondents did not appear enslaved by guilty consumption pleasures. Quite the opposite, they actively engage with it in the belief that it is not only their right, but also that it also has positive social benefits.

Reading a fashion-centered narrative also appears to provide a social bond. This is founded on the recognition of a familiar consumption landscape signposted with recognizable brands that both create a relatable world and a way of defining the taste and fashionability of the characters. These texts also appeal to a wider readership and demographic as they are shared not just between friendship ties but also kinship bonds as Katy (North American, age 28) observed:

> It's great to read books like this that cover fashion as you have to love fashion and know your labels—your Prada from Proenza Schouler—otherwise you just won't get it and it will mean nothing at all and it's not just about age group. My mom loved the book

too—she read my copy after me as she liked the look of that red shoe on the cover—and when we go shopping together we joke about the fact that she looks for outfits like Miranda Priestly and I go for an Andrea-type look—so we are a bit like the *DWP* team or that's how we joke about it anyways.

This also challenges the notion that these heroines represent a third wave of feminism or inhabit a post-feminist space enabling readers to reaffirm their position as a new generation in reaction to that represented by their mothers and the second wave feminists of a previous generation. In effect, a blurring of those terms renders them irrelevant as these novels are enjoyed across a broader, globally based demographic who are often multi-literate and widely read. So, this genre has a particular gratification for a range of needs within this consumption community.

2. Fashion's Revelation: Undressing the Fashion Industry

The book offered readers the opportunity to experience the glamorous illusionary world of fashion. This was typified by Greta (Spanish, age 37):

It was a revelation as I thoroughly enjoyed the knowledge that I gained from this novel about how a fashion bible such as *Vogue* is brought to life each month involving the cast of talent, lots of hard work, and how these fashion professionals cope with the unrelenting deadlines and the constant cycle of fashion changes, all driven and held on track by an unforgiving but visionary, tough-as-hell female boss. It made me really appreciate my fashion magazines in a new light and I read them now in more knowing way and don't throw them away anymore.

This impact of the narrative on lived experience was also experienced by Amanda (Australian, age 35) who claimed to have found professional inspiration in the book:

I found the high-octane world of fashion publishing portrayed in this book as energizing and heady. I'm a freelance news writer but this inspired me to pen a few fashion feature-based pieces for global magazines. Yet, ironically I moved in the opposite direction from Andrea and I benefitted from this book in a professional way as it reaffirmed what I'm doing and gave me creative ideas for my own professional work.

The realism of the exchanges between the overbearing boss and embattled assistant proved too much for one respondent with a fashion public relations background who confided:

The relationship between evil boss Miranda and hapless Andy was so well portrayed and opened up so many bad memories of my first PR job for a fashion brand that I actually couldn't read it to the end. I found myself breaking out in a cold sweat each time Andy's mobile phone rang as I recalled being owned by my first boss in the same way. (Mary, British, age 45)

Another respondent also confessed to feeling 'physical pain', having experienced a similar abusive situation with a client, and was keen to point out that she 'empathized with Andy's character yet didn't necessarily like her' (Janice, Canadian, age 36). She undoubtedly represents a conduit for critical debates that surround fashion's media presence; she is relatively ignorant about and totally uninterested in the world of fashion. She denigrates her job, despite the fact that co-workers constantly remind her 'this is a job that a million girls would kill for' (Weisberger 2003: 17). With aspirations to become a staff writer at *The New Yorker,* she dismisses *Runway.* As she muses at her pre-job interview, 'It was a fashion magazine for chrissake, one I wasn't even sure it contained any writing just lots of hungry looking models and glossy ads' (16). So while she 'likes clothes and bags and shoes as much as the next girl,…[she] didn't know anything about fashion and…didn't care' (56). Her lack of interest is sartorially signaled in her ill-matching and randomly assembled interview outfit, which consists of a 'cheap mismatched suit and very wrong shoes' (15). As a serious journalist she muses, '*They're not going to hire or reject me on the outfit alone,* I remember thinking. Clearly I was barely lucid' (13). Her 'Banana Republic heavy wardrobe' mirrors that of her close friend and boyfriend, and contrasts sharply with *Runway* staff, whom she describes as 'leggy, Twiggy types' whose 'gossip was punctuated only by the sound of their stilettos clacking on the floor…with such radiant blond hair…flawlessly made-up, turned out…bags and shoes I'd never seen on real people shouted, Prada! Armani! Versace!' (9-13). The hostile reviews of the book by fashion editors and critics often focused on the main character's unrealistic expectations about the job or in her inconsistencies of 'worshipping the very lifestyle that she supposedly eschews' (Cooke 2003). The contradictory stance of its protagonist in relation to the fashion world and all that it represents irritated many in the 'dropping names, labels and price tags while feigning disregard for these things' (Maslin 2003).

Andrea is not a typical fashion consumer and for much of the book operates as fashion's detractor, which perhaps alienates her from the typical readership. During interviews, most of the respondents loved to hate Miranda. In contrast, they expressed exasperation with Andy's contradictory response to fashion, and some confessed that they actually found the character more likable when she underwent the transformation from fashion clueless to fashion chic. Some considered this to reflect their own stance on fashion:

We all have a love-hate relationship with fashion very like Andrea in the book because we love the labels but can't afford them and love the look but hate the models that wear them on the catwalk. That's why this was a good story because fashion is not always a positive world and this is what I saw in the book and in her attitude to it. (Jenna, Chinese, age 25)

While Andrea appears initially to be bucking the trend of the formulaic protagonist in terms of her marked lack of interest in fashion, conspicuous consumption, and fashion journalism, she sells her soul to the fashion demon in her transformation to fashionista via the effective seduction by *Runway's* core ideology that fashion is the only reason to exist and has to convey the right message: 'wearing a Prada turtleneck instead of one from Urban Outfitters was going to help me survive…and avoid the frequent and vicious wardrobe humiliation from the *Runway* editorial team' (Weisberger 2003: 132). In time, she drools over the fashion freebies from the 'Closet' of unreturned items provided for the magazine's fashion shoots. In many ways, for Andrea the free designer clothes from *Runway's* Closet operate as a transformational talisman, providing her with a transitory happiness, new-found confidence, and contextualized social acceptance. But while the moral tale ends with Andrea rejecting her suffocating role, she keeps a few choice fashion items including 'the Diane Von Furstenberg wrap-dress…sexy D&G jeans and utterly classic, quilted chain handle purse' (389) as tokens of surviving *Runway*. Or perhaps they reflect her new fashion appreciation as a secret convert to conspicuous consumption which, after all, few can resist.

3. Fashion as Power: Empowerment Clothes and Body Maintenance

Just as 'fashion-tastical' descriptions run rampant throughout the text, they also serve as a defining marker of the individual characters. The sartorially impeccable diabolical boss, Miranda Priestly, is the embodiment of the fashion industry as cultural intermediary *par excellence*. Andrea admits that '[from her] snakeskin Gucci trench…belted jacket that cinched her already tiny waist and complemented the perfectly fitted pencil skirt,…[she] looked dynamite' (Weisberger 2003: 151).

Fashion items for Miranda are a 'performative prop' (see Goffman 1959) to signal her personality and control: her 'signature brown and white Gucci snakeskin trench coat [makes Miranda look] like a snake' (292). She dominates her staff and especially her assistant—daily she dumps on the assistant's desk a variety of designer coats 'as heavy as a wet down comforter' (113). This dynamic defines their ongoing contested interaction from what they wear to how their respective appearance is managed. Miranda appears to gain dominance in this relationship by getting Andrea to concede by dressing according to *Runway* expectations and in line with the high-style message that has to be conveyed by all of its employees as corporate dress code. Yet, the protagonist reverts to her original wardrobe of 'cheap mismatched suit and very wrong shoes' (15) on securing her next freelance writing job post-*Runway* untainted by the fripperies and frothy delusions of the fashion system. Arguably, the real romance in this text is played out between the two women with glamour as the visual signifier of power and success. Gaining a sense of empowerment through the presentation of sartorial self was also highlighted by respondents typified by Steph (North American, age 34):

This dragon lady boss and emasculated PA are so relatable for me. In fact, working for ten years in the global PR industry I found the book so real that I couldn't read it all at one go! But the truth is that as my career progressed and in order to survive impossible line managers and bombastic clients I did acquire a power wardrobe of high-end fashion labels that acted as visible armor against the slings and arrows of life in the mad media zone. In my sharply tailored black Armani suit with crisp white silk cotton mix blouse I meant business and often won it too in that outfit.

The role of fashion in the narrative operates not just as the setting for the protagonist to play out her workplace anxieties, but also operates as a key part of character development and projection and is essential to visually mapping out the plot. Even the extra romantic interest in the form of up-and-coming smooth-talking literati, Christian Collingsworth, is presented as an up-market version of her working-class boyfriend from his shiny, square-toed loafers that sported the irrefutable 'Gucci tassel' to the 'Diesel jeans…the perfect parts faded, long and wide enough at the bottom that they dragged a little behind the shiny loafers…a plain white t-shirt definitely an Armani, Hugo Boss…with a whole lot more Euro style and a whole lot less Abercrombie' (124).

Miranda and her professional potency are not just defined by the high-end label—she personifies the fashion system itself. Andrea admits, 'you can't get to the top of two major industries in New York City handing out candy all day long' (136). This point aligns with Pamela Church Gibson and Stella Bruzzi's critique of fashion in the television series *Sex and the City* as having a dual role comprising 'two parallel but mutually referential trajectories' (Bruzzi and Church Gibson 2004: 116). Fashion delineates and develops character through costume as in traditional novels and films, yet also in the meditational use of fashion and fashion brands to assume their own identity as a sign of their social importance. However, fashion does not detract from the narrative as it is woven into its seam given the central location of the plot in the head office of a premier fashion publication. Fashion as a narrative device also signifies the triumph of chic over geek and validates the whole ethos of the fashion world—that appearance is your most powerful calling card. Having sold her soul to fashion, Andrea switches from fashion virgin to the dark side of fashion 'glamazon' in Mephistophelian fashion. She endures fashion's bondage and grits her teeth through the humiliation of an unrelenting dress code; for example, when Miranda upbraids her about the shoes she is wearing. 'Ahn-dre-ah, they're unacceptable. My girls need to represent *Runway* magazine and those shoes are not the message I'm looking to convey. Find some decent footwear in the Closet' (Weisberger 2003: 271). For Gabby (North American, age 32), the footwear trope was critical to demarcating the fashionable from the unfashionable in the story:

It was all about the shoes. It was a bit like the old adage, 'You can tell a person from their shoes' as every key person on the book was described through what they wore on their feet and the main character was transformed as soon as she put on a way high pair of Jimmy Choos and squirmed when Miranda's beady eye landed on her Anne Taylor Loft bargain loafers. The shoes gave them power and cred as they do for us all.

Other respondents noted that while Miranda's wardrobe was critical in defining her persona and projecting her character, it also fulfilled the promise of the book's title. For one respondent this was the most fascinating part:

> Miranda was my reason to keep on reading because of her terrifying attitude and her complete self-obsession. And it was all about the way that she symbolized the hard and cruel world of fashion that has such a glamorous, glitzy exterior which is so at odds with the unforgiving machine that it really is on the inside. (Jane, Hong Kong, age 33)

For many respondents and critics, Miranda was the most authentic and memorable part of the text while representing the most entertaining character whose acerbic attitude and ever-changing appearance kept them turning the page:

> I looked forward to Miranda's next entrance on each page and a description of her outfit— the floor-length mink coat, the snakeskin Gucci trench, the beaded red Chanel evening gown, the white Hermes scarf. You knew that it would be a different get up each time and would reinforce the fact that she was the most powerful person in the office and in the fashion world itself. That's real and appropriate power dressing. (Karen, British, age 47)

4. Fashion's Happy Ever After: The Cinderella Motif and Social Masquerade

The transformation trope, Cinderella's makeover from ragged servant girl to ball-gowned princess, is a standard component of fairytales. It is also a device beloved of fashion makeover-style magazine articles intent on 'the construction of an image that matches cultural expectations' (Buckley and Gundle 2000: 42). The endless possibilities provided from the Cinderella motif and social masquerade appealed to most of the informants who regarded the ability to change their appearance as a given. As Cally (French, age 28) explained:

> We girls all love to dress up and wear different clothes for different situations to communicate different things about ourselves. And we do believe in fairy tales, but these are now on our terms as this book shows. We don't need to wait for the fairy godmother to dress us up because we do that ourselves with a little help from Mr. Jacobs and Ms. Prada. Then we are ready for whatever life throws at us and even if the ending isn't blissfully happy we look good and feel better about ourselves, which makes it easier to believe in the dream that you want to pursue. I like to read novels that take that approach with their heroine. That's a big vote of thanks to the fashion fairy!

Therefore, it appears that these novels operate as a style manifesto giving readers in a consumption community the permission to become their own fairy godmother. Of course, these novels are hymnals to conspicuous consumption and while they have been criticized on the basis of appealing to an insider group of those in the know about fashion brands, alongside being thinly disguised forms of product placement, they do appear to have successfully found their market niche and a willing consumption community. True to form, the hypnotic effect of the impossibly fashionable, fantastical environment at *Runway* wears off when Cinderella-like Andy quits, leaving the circus of Paris Fashion Week behind and exits a career in fashion forever.

Devil Worship: Conclusion

Respondents explained that the popularity of fashion-framed novels resided in their ability to provide relatable scenarios about friendship, workplace, and lifestyle that resonate with the reader as active agent, often empowering them to make sense of their lived experiences across cultures. Reading these fictional texts can be a selective process defining a sense of the fashioned self in the narrative, through the characters and vicarious application to their own lives. The same can be said of the role and content of texts emerging from the professional world of fashion journalism, which also provided the setting for *The Devil Wears Prada*.

Readers appear to find pleasure in the text and the joys of reading, shopping and money management, career choice, female friendships, identity control, and glamorous escapist fantasies through real and imagined dressing up in the pages of *Vogue* and chick lit novels where a girl can get her fashion fix, learn more about the fashion industry, and find power in the reaffirmation of self in the constantly changing presentation of self. As Imelda Whelehan observes:

> one of the most powerful features of chicklit as a genre is that it seeks that identification which doesn't simply come from empathy with the central female characters, but rather in understanding the world they inhabit, and actually accepting that women's lives are governed by quite different realities (2004: 8).

In many ways, fashion is an important part of that lived existence as it provides glamour, self-empowerment, recreation, topics for conversation, bonding, and common ground, while operating as a form of control over self in the form of body management and presentation of self, as the interview responses above illustrates.

In the pages of these novels a space is forged where fashion is a spectacle to be imagined and enjoyed. As the literary heroine fills her wardrobe and dresses for success in life and love, the fashion brands that she wears are the one thing that she can control temporarily, even if she buys them on credit. Consequently, the readership negotiates and makes sense of consumption as a form of resistance and self-empowerment in their right to consume chosen texts at will. As one respondent claimed:

I love the fact that we're still reading novels at all and if it takes novels like this to keep people reading—bring it on. And I share these books with my friends—so we spread the word…[I]t's an interesting topic to talk about—and why not? Life is too hard and serious—we need cheering up and it's great to celebrate overcoming life's challenges through these characters. (Cat, Hong Kong, age 31)

The golden days of the genre may however be numbered (Mesure 2009). Popular cultural forms reflect the zeitgeist and as the global economic recession prevails, a new genre— 'recessionista' lit—is offering a harsh wake-up call: '[T]hese cautionary tales show what happens when it goes wrong. They tell the stories of yummy mummies who have to cut up their credit cards and sell their Jimmy Choos on eBay' (Stocks 2009). It is the same girl, with the same anxieties, and even though different circumstances prevail, fashion and consumption will still be central to the plot in terms of making eco-chic and sustainability sexy. Andy would have been a poster child for this trend in her rejection of high fashion and devotion to down-style or shabby chic. Heralding the triumph of one genre over another misses the point, however—people still need to escape from their issues by stepping into someone else's Jimmy Choos. As one informant said, 'I read this stuff because I want to be someone else and live their lives when I feel like it and then I leave it all behind and get on with my life.' (Anna, Singapore, age 26)

By minimizing the importance of fashion, fashion writing and their notable consumption is to undermine and challenge the lifestyle choices of many in a patronizing way. It also ignores the larger social needs on display and at large here. As Betts suggests:

Surely there are much larger social forces at work in fashion, as in all subcultures, and the Mirandas of the world, as much as they seem like casualties of their own psychology, are also reflections of us—our ideas of style, our hunger for glamour, our age-old need for a consummate antagonist in a chic red suit. (Betts 2003)

By gazing into the mirror of fashion in fiction, readers are viewing a world of fashion writing that they desire and aspire toward as a means of dealing with their own dilemmas through their dreams. It is a world that exists largely because consumption communities have emerged to support it—in fact, they demand it while stocks still last.

So, in the words of Miranda Priestly—'That's all'.

References

Banks, M. (1999), *The Girls' Guide to Hunting and Fishing*, New York: Viking Books.

Barnard, M. (1996), *Fashion as Communication*, London: Routledge.

Barthes, R. (1983), *The Fashion System* (trans. Matthew Ward and Richard Howard), Berkeley: University of California Press.

Betts, K. (2003), 'Anna Dearest', *New York Times*, 13 April, http://www.nytimes.com/2003/04/13/books/anna-dearest.html. Accessed 15 July 2010.

—— (2007), 'Miuccia's Material World', *Time Magazine*, Style and Design Supplement, Spring, pp. 32–35.

Breward, C. (2003), *Fashion*, Oxford: Oxford University Press.

Bruzzi, S. and Church Gibson, P. (2004), 'Fashion is the Fifth Character: Fashion, Costume and Character in *Sex and the City*', in Kim Akass and Janet McCabe, eds, *Reading Sex and the City*, London: I.B. Taurus. pp. 115–29.

Buckley, R.C.V. and Gundle, S. (2000), 'Fashion and Glamour', in Nicola White and Ian Griffiths, eds, *The Fashion Business*, Oxford: Berg, pp. 37–54.

Bushnell, C. (1996), *Sex and the City*. New York: Grand Central Publishing.

Cawelti J.G. (1976), *Adventure, Mystery and Romance: Formula Stories as Art and Popular Culture*, Chicago: University of Chicago Press.

Cooke, R. (2003), 'Fashion Faux Pas', *The Observer*, 28 September, http://www.guardian.co.uk/books/2003/sep/28/fiction.features. Accessed 15 July 2010.

Cox Gurdon, M. (2011), 'Chick Lit and the Master/Slave Dialectic', in Naomi Schafer Riley and Christine Rosen, eds, *Acculturated*, West Conshocken, PA: Templeton Press, pp. 23–33.

Davis, F. (1992), *Fashion, Culture and Identity*. Chicago: University of Chicago Press.

Donahue, D. (2003), '*Devil Wears Prada* Feels Worn'. *USA Today*, 16 April, http://www.usatoday.com/life/books/reviews/2003-04-16-prada_x.htm. Accessed 24 August 2010.

Dowd, M. (2007), 'Heels over Hemingway', *New York Times*, February 10, http://www.nytimes.com/2007/02/10/opinion/10dowd.html. Accessed 10 October 2012.

Ebert, T.L. (2009), *The Task of Cultural Critique*. Urbana: University of Illinois Press.

Evans, C. (2003), *Fashion at the Edge*. New Haven, CT: Yale University Press.

Ferriss, S. and Young, M. (2006a), 'Chicks, Girls and Choice', *Junctures*, 6, pp. 87–97.

—— (2006b), *Chick Lit: The New Woman's Fiction*, London: Routledge.

Gill, R. and Herdieckerhoff, E. (2006), 'Rewriting the Romance: New Femininities in Chick Lit?', London: LSE Research Online. http://eprints.lse.ac.uk/2514. Accessed 10 October 2012.

Goffman, I. (1959), *The Presentation of Self in Everyday Life*. New York: Doubleday.

Goldblatt, M. (2003), 'The Devil & the Gray Lady: All about Vogue', *National Review*, 10 June 10, http://www.nationalreview.com/articles/207173/devil-gray-lady/mark-goldblatt. Accessed 15 August 2010.

Kinsella, S. (2000), *The Secret Dreamworld of a Shopaholic*, London: Black Swan Books.

Knowles, J. (2004), 'Editorial', *Diegesis: Journal of the Association for Research in Popular Fictions*, Special issue on Chicklit, ed. Jo Knowles, 8, Winter, p. 3.

Konig, A. (2004), '*Sex and the City*: A Fashion Editor's Dream?', in Kim Akass and Janet McCabe, eds, *Reading Sex and the City*, London: I.B. Taurus, pp. 130–43.

Lipovetsky, G. (1994), *The Empire of Fashion: Dressing Modern Democracy* (trans. Catherine Porter), Princeton, NJ: Princeton University Press.

Maslin, J. (2003), 'Elegant Magazine Avalanche of Dirt', *New York Times*, 14 April, http://www.nytimes.com/2003/04/14/books/books-of-the-times-elegant-magazine-avalanche-of-dirt.html. Accessed 10 June 2010.

Mazza, C. and DeShell, J. eds. (1995), *Chick-Lit: Postfeminist Fiction*, Florida: FC2, Florida State University Press.

Mazza, C. (2006), 'Who's Laughing Now? A Short History of Chick Lit and the Perversion of a Genre', in Suzanne Ferriss and Mallory Young, eds, *Chick Lit: The New Woman's Fiction*, New York: Routledge.

McDowell, C. (2010), 'What's Wrong with Fashion Journalism?', Colin McDowell's blog, 3 January, http://colin-mcdowell.blogspot.ie/2010/01/whats-wrong-with-fashion-journalism.html. Accessed 10 October 2012.

McRobbie, A. (1998), *British Fashion Design: Rag Trade or Image Industry?*, London: Routledge.

—— (2004), 'Postfeminism and Popular Culture'. *Feminist Media Studies*, 4.3, pp. 253–64.

Mesure, S. (2009), 'End of a Chapter: Chick Lit Takes on the Credit Crunch', *The Independent*, 30 August, http://www.independent.co.uk/arts-entertainment/books/news/end-of-a-chapter-chick-lit-takes-on-the-credit-crunch-1779378.html. Accessed 10 October 2012.

Muniz, A.M Jr. and O'Guinn, T.C. (2001), 'Brand Communities', *Journal of Consumer Research*, 27.4 March, pp. 412–432.

Radway, J. (1991), 'Interpretive Communities and Variable Literacies: The Functions of Romance Reading', in C. Mukerji and M. Schudson, eds, *Rethinking Popular Culture: Contemporary Perspectives on Cultural Studies*, Berkeley: University of California Press, pp. 465–86.

Stocks, J. (2009), 'Sex and Shopping: Chick Lit Makes Way for Recessionista Reads as Credit Crunch Leaves Its Mark on Bookshelves'. *Mail Online*, 1 September, http://www.dailymail.co.uk/femail/article-1210397/Sex-shopping-chick-lit-makes-way-recessionista-reads-credit-crunch-leaves-mark-book-shelves.html. Accessed 10 October 2012.

Vnuk, R. (2005), 'Collection Development "Chick Lit": Hip Lit for Hip Chicks', *Library Journal*, 15 July, http://www.libraryjournal.com/article/CA623004.html. Accessed 10 October 2012.

Weisberger, L. (2003), *The Devil Wears Prada*, London: Harper.

—— (2010), 'What's Going On / Bio', Lauren Weisberger home page, http://www.laurenweisberger.com/bio.php. Accessed 21 September 2010.

Whelehan, I. (2000), *Overloaded: Popular Culture and the Future of Feminism*, London: The Women's Press.

—— (2004), 'High Anxiety: Feminist Chicklit and Women in the Noughties', *Diegesis: Journal of the Association for Research in Popular Fictions*, Special issue on Chicklit, ed. Jo Knowles, 8, Winter, pp. 5–11.

—— (2005), *The Feminist Bestseller*, Hampshire: Palgrave Macmillan.

Wilson, E. (1985), *Adorned in Dreams: Fashion and Modernity*, London: Virago Press.

Wolcott, J. (1996), 'Hear Me Purr', *The New Yorker*, 20 May, pp. 54–55.

Chapter 11

Redeeming the Voices of Reform

Patricia A. Cunningham

M yths seem to persist in fashion despite efforts to dispel them. One such myth that has been difficult to eradicate is that nineteenth-century dress reform had no influence on fashion. This is one of many 'fictions' about fashion in popular culture. No doubt there are many explanations for why this particular myth persists. It could be a lack of understanding regarding the breadth of women's clothing reform, as the whole story rarely is told. The myth appears to be based upon the Turkish-style trousers promoted in the mid-nineteenth century by water cure physicians, feminists, and reformers that at the time were deemed too masculine. Yet efforts toward dress reform took place continuously well into the twentieth century, and included not simply trousers, but artistic dress and undergarments.

The move to reform women's clothing was not a cause promoted by a single large organization or political party. Instead, the movement emerged from the concerted efforts of individuals and small groups with diverse interests, but with similar goals regarding the need to improve women's dress. While some did not call themselves dress reformers, many people in the United States and Europe were involved in improving women's dress. They came from a wide range of backgrounds, including educators, artists, designers, retailers, health reformers, physicians, publishers, editors, writers, dancers, physical educators, sports enthusiasts, and members of arts organizations and women's clubs. Some were actively involved with the British Aesthetic and the Arts and Crafts movements. Not only was there great diversity among the reformers, but their efforts occurred over a span of roughly 75 to 80 years. Clearly dress reform was not a mere fad that lasted only a moment in time. To say that dress reform had no influence on fashion is simply not correct, for many of the reformers themselves were actively involved in the fashion industry as both professional designers and retailers. And, of course, the comfort, practicality, and aesthetics of women's fashions did improve over time.

However, since the myth persists, it is appropriate to examine the reform efforts made by those working within the fashion industry and the ways in which the public gained information about clothing reform. In my previous broad examination of dress reform in Europe and America, *Reforming Women's Fashion, 1850–1920: Politics, Health, and Art* (Cunningham 2003), I considered the women's rights activists and health reformers who promoted various forms of trousers (Bloomers), the sanitary reformers who promoted reform undergarments (subversive reform), and the aesthetic reformers who advocated artistic dress. I did not emphasize the point that reformers were working in the fashion industry, nor did I focus on how reform ideas were communicated by the industry. The question of influence was there but was not central to the goal of mapping the breadth of reform and the variety of garments suggested by the reformers.

This chapter thus serves as a reconsideration of the dress reform efforts of artists, designers, manufacturers, and retailers working in the fashion industry as well as the reformers who supported them in allied fields. Also reconsidered are the ways in which reform ideas were disseminated through public display (exhibitions, expositions, and store display), shops, dress studios, and lecture-demonstrations. These included such public events as the Healtheries Exhibition in London (1883), the Exhibition of the Artistic and Healthy Dress Union held in London in 1896 and the Exhibition of Reform Dress in Krefeld, Germany (1900), to name but a few.

The actual reform activity carried out by groups and individuals *within the fashion industry* counters the myth that reformers had no influence on fashion. Reformers working in fashion businesses were couturiers, custom dressmakers, retailers, magazine editors, illustrators, and manufacturers. A sampling of fashion practitioners reveals their diversity: the retailers Liberty & Co. in London and Wertheim's Department Store in Berlin; fashion magazines, such as *Wiener Mode;* couture designers Worth, Fortuny, Poiret, Vionnet, and Chanel in Paris; and custom designer Kate Manville in Chicago, among others. It is important to know exactly what these reformers desired to change, why they believed a change was needed, and, most important, how they communicated this desire. Communication was central to making a difference. There were many supporters who aided the communication efforts of those within the fashion industry.

What the Reformers Desired

In many respects dress reformers were asking that people alter their thinking, not just about clothing, but also about social rules and etiquette in order to accept new forms of dress that would provide comfort, ease, and mobility to women and improve their health. Women wanted clothing with greater ease of movement so they could take on greater public roles in society. For others, the ideas of good health and beauty went hand in hand. The reformers believed that the natural body was more beautiful than one distorted by various restrictive undergarments and the accompanying bulky outer garments supported by them. For many, reform was about aesthetics and the need to apply the principles of art to fashion. The reformers were remarkable people dedicated to the cause. They made their desires known to the public through writings, but more importantly through visual display and public lectures that allowed women and men to view, listen, and learn about dress reform. These learning opportunities took place at exhibitions and expositions, at dress studios and shops, and at lecture-demonstrations (Cunningham 2003; Wrisley 2006).

Art Exhibitions and Expositions

Many practitioners in art, design, and architecture and other fields supported dress reform. Their exhibitions were a means to communicate the need to the public. Paintings in art exhibitions offered spectators visual images of women that provided new ways of dressing. In the mid- to late nineteenth century, artists, especially the Pre-Raphaelites in London, provided images of aesthetic dress that was viewed as a means to reform women's clothing. Their works became known to the public through exhibitions in London at the Royal Academy, the Grosvenor Gallery, and the Hogarth Club. Thus clothing depicted in Pre-Raphaelite paintings served as models for women in the late 1870s and the 1880s who desired to dress in an aesthetic or artistic manner. These women adhered to the ideals of what Max Beerbohm termed the 'Cult of Beauty'. This 'Cult' had as its goal not merely reform in dress, but like the Pre-Raphaelites, a reformation in all of the fine and decorative arts (Newton 1974: 34).

The 'health exhibitions' held in London also were places to gain knowledge of dress reform. The Healtheries, as the health exhibitions came to be called, had as their purpose to illustrate the most advanced knowledge regarding sanitary practices, health, food, and dress. The Rational Dress Association presented an exhibition of reform dress in Prince's Hall, Piccadilly in May, 1883. The object of the exhibition, as stated by the association's honorary secretary, Mrs. E.M. King, was to 'teach a lesson—a lesson with illustrations—to those who make dresses, and to those who wear them' (Anon [1883] 1978: 2). The judges of the Rational Dress Association Exhibition were unanimous in awarding every one of the prizes to trousers. They agreed that these trousers best fulfilled the criteria for the perfect dress, mainly:

1. Freedom of movement; 2.Absence of pressure over any part of the body; 3. Not more weight than is necessary for warmth, and both weight and warmth evenly distributed; 4. Grace and beauty combined with comfort and convenience; 5. Not departing too conspicuously from the ordinary dress of the time. (Anon [1883] 1978: 16, 33–35)

Many of the exhibitors were well-known fashion companies. They came from Britain, the United States, Italy, France, and Switzerland. In their booths they displayed reform dresses for many occasions including tea gowns and many dresses to be worn with various types of trousers—the latter included outfits for sport, and dresses with trousers for walking, traveling, and the evening. The exhibitors used the term 'trousers' to refer to bifurcated garments, but they also labeled them as wide, full or narrow, such as full Turkish trousers, or narrow knickerbocker trousers. Sometimes they combined the styles.

The £50 first prize went to a custom dressmaker, Mrs. Brownjohn, for a 'dress with trousers' that was praised highly by the judges for meeting the five criteria of the association, and also for being made with great skill, avoiding clumsiness in the trousers, and fitting well without the aid of a corset. Brownjohn had a great many orders for this style. Of particular note was

'A Dress of the Future', which was a knickerbocker (trouser) costume 'with hardly any skirt and no draperies of any kind'. Mrs. King had the high fashion house of Worth design the 'Dress of the Future' for herself. The exhibition also included a number of mostly bifurcated garments for sports—mountain climbing, skating, cricket, boating, tricycling, lawn tennis, boating, bathing, riding, and calisthenics. These were meant to be practical and appropriate for their intended use (Anon [1883] 1978: 16, 33–35).

Art exhibitions in Germany and Austria also were sites where women could view reform styles. One of the earliest was in Krefeld, Germany. In April of 1900, Dr. Deneken, director of the Kaiser Wilhelm Museum in Krefeld, asked several well-known architects, artists, and designers to create reform clothing for an exhibition in the Town Hall to be held in conjunction with a Tailor's Exhibition. The Belgian artist Henry Van de Velde gave a talk and exhibited his own reform dresses. Other artists who exhibited were well-known architects and designers in Germany: Alfred Mohrbutter, Curt Hermann, Richard Riemerschmid, Bernard Pankok, Otto Krüger, Margarethe von Brauchitsch, and Paul Schultze-Naumburg.

However, not all visitors to the exhibition agreed with the choices suggested for reform, especially Maria van de Velde. In critiquing the Krefeld exhibition, Van de Velde mentioned two mistakes (1901: 44). First, she noted, the quality of construction was imperfect, but second, and even more neglectful, was that the artistic garments did not approach the idea of reform decisively enough in the cut and composition of the dresses. The central core idea, she argued, was to invent more logical, healthier, and beautiful clothing than fashion can manage. She commented further on the decisive gap between real innovators and those content with 'artistic interference only in the ornaments', placing her husband among the real innovators, of course (1901: 44).

Yet the exhibition was important for, as noted by Leonie von Wilckens (1980: 198–203), the success of the Krefeld exhibit generated similar events of artist-designed reform dress in other German cities as well—Leipzig, Dresden, Wiesbaden, Darmstadt, and Berlin. In 1901 a special division for artistic clothing also was set up in Dresden in conjunction with the Exhibition of Art and Industry. Reform styles likewise appeared in the exhibition center in Darmstadt in 1901. Peter Behrens, architect, designer, and founding member of the Munich Secession in 1892, and his wife, Lilli, designed artistic clothing for women. While there are few records of Lilli's designs, those of Peter Behrens are well documented (Figure 11:1). His ideas for reform dress were very severe with little ornamentation, an approach which contrasted sharply with the artistic styles of Van de Velde and Mohrbutter that included soft flowing lines and decorative applications.

The Berlin exhibit focused on two of the best-known supporters of women's reform dress in Germany, the artists Paul Schultze-Naumberg and Else Oppler-Legbaud, who was director of the Dress Reform Department in Wertheimer's department store in Berlin. Schultze-Naumberg lectured at the exhibition on the need to free women's bodies through the application of aesthetic ideas of dress reform, and stressed the goal of the exhibition which was to encourage fainthearted women to transform themselves (Cunningham 2003: 178–82).

Figure 11:1. Peter Behren's reform dress for his wife.
(Source: *Deutsch Kunst und Dekoration* [1909]).

Else Oppler-Legbaud organized an exhibition of artistic clothing at Wertheimer's store in 1904. For this exhibition, Anna Muthesius spoke on the progress made in artistic reform dress, noting improvement in construction, color, materials, and in the individual fit and suitability to the wearer. In writing about artistic dress, Muthesius used the phrase 'personal clothing' to define the style (1904: 441–43). For her, the concept of dressing to express individuality was imperative. She believed that the dress should conform to the needs of individuals and express the unique creativity of the artist.

London exhibitions that defined reform dress took place under the auspices of The Artistic and Healthy Dress Union, a group of artists, designers, and others who actively promoted dress reform. The Union group included Dr. Sophie Bryant, artists Henry Holiday and Walter Crane, and the retailer Arthur Lasenby Liberty. At their meetings, numerous members of the organization, including Liberty, spoke on such subjects as aesthetics in dress and the progress of taste in dress. One of the Union's most impressive public achievements was the presentation in May 1896 of a series of 'Living Pictures' illustrating dress in the past, present, and future. Among the tableaux were '*Aglaia* the Three Graces' with three women in gowns similar to classical Greek chitons, and an 'Evening Scene' arranged by Arthur Lasenby Liberty and Louise Jopling. The latter included eight women dressed in classical gowns and seven men in velvet suits with knee breeches and silk stockings. All were examples of artistic reform styles promoted by the group. In his memoirs, *Reminiscences of My Life*, Henry Holiday recalled that the hall was crowded and the tableaux were deemed a great success. (1914: 404–12).

A much larger event was the Columbian Exposition held in Chicago in 1893 where visitors could learn about both trousers and artistic reform dress. That dress reform became a prominent women's issue at this exposition was not by chance. In February 1891, at the first convention of the National Council of Women in Washington D.C., Frances E. Willard, a well-known educator, spoke on the subject of dress reform. At that meeting, the council established the Dress Committee and a framework for carrying out a crusade for rational dress at the exposition. The Dress Committee recommended three practical trouser styles to wear to the fair: the Syrian costume, the gymnasium suit, and the American costume. The Syrian has a 'divided skirt' (trousers), with the fullness of each leg gathered at the ankle (Russell 1893a: 76).

As Richard Weimann (1981: 531–34) has observed, most women who spoke on dress reform at the World's Fair wore one of the suggested styles. The well-known advocate for improving women's dress, Annie Jenness Miller, wore her own style, an American costume with an Eton jacket, short divided skirt, and gaiters. Others who wore reform dress included Professor Hayes of Wellesley College, who read a paper entitled 'Dress and Sociology'. Hayes wore a short blue serge dress with ten pockets, enough to satisfy Frances Willard, who advocated pockets on women's dresses. Mrs. B.O. Flower wore a Syrian dress, as did Emily A. Brine, M.D., of Boston, who stated that with 'physical culture, careful diet and correct dress the American woman may attain to consummate beauty, grace and strength'. Laura Lee, an artist from Boston, also wore the Syrian gown (Figure 11:2). She believed that women needed nothing 'so much as freedom in dress'. Miss H.J. Wescott, another Bostonian, noted that she was asked many times for the pattern of the dress she wore. Isis B. Martin, who regularly wore reform dress, observed that it was getting to be an old thing, that people stared less. With so many Boston women wearing it, the Syrian costume became known as 'Boston Rational Dress' (Weimann 1981: 533).

Artistic dress also was represented at the exposition. Henrietta Russell, Director of Physical Culture for the Columbian Exposition, and a leader in the movement for physical training designed by Delsarte, appeared on the Exposition program as an illustration of the modern idea of Greek drapery. Mrs. Steele, representing artistic dress was 'a quiet symphony in gray', a perfect example of aesthetics as studied by the Physical Culture and Correct Dress Society of Chicago (Russell 1893b: 312–16). Of particular interest was the dress exhibit provided

Figure 11:2. Laura Lee in the Syrian reform style
worn at the Columbian Exposition in 1893.
(Source: *Arena Magazine* [1893]).

by the Chicago club. For on mannequins having 'the proportions of Venus de Medici were shown a working dress and apron, a street suit, and reception gown and several evening dresses' (Russell 1893b: 312–16). All were intended to reveal the natural beauty of a woman's form when unbounded by a corset. According to the society, to fully engage in reform of dress, women must first learn to appreciate a beautiful form, thus they recommended that members study the classical statuary on display at the Art Institute of Chicago. They also suggested that members acquire a photograph of the Venus de Milo (Parker 1897: 23).

Reform within the Fashion Industry

Women could view and purchase artistic reform styles at a number of retail establishments. In London, the Liberty Company clearly embraced dress reform and established a dress department in 1884. The founder of the store, Arthur Lasenby Liberty, stated that its aim was to 'reestablish the craft of dressmaking upon some hygienic, intelligible, progressive basis'. The styles Liberty promoted were based on the clothing worn in ancient Greece and Rome and from styles worn in the Middle Ages. They made them in the soft drapable silks that Liberty had been importing and duplicating in its own workshops (Anon 1886: 3–6).

What became known as the 'Liberty style' was popular in England in the 1880s, but it may have been outside of England that Liberty's reform efforts were most influential in conveying to a broader public ideas regarding artistic dress reform (Anon 1893: 5). There were a number of ways that the Liberty style became known. First, the store published frequent catalogues beginning in the 1880s. But more important, perhaps, in the late 1880s Liberty began to sell its clothing and fabrics outside of England. The company set up shops and arranged to place what they called depots (small in-store 'boutiques') in specialty stores in New York, Boston, and Chicago, as well as in major cities in England, Scotland, and Ireland. A Liberty

A Liberty shop opened in Paris in November 1900 and remained open until 1932. The soft Liberty silk fabrics, so essential to draping the classically inspired styles, made quite an impression at the Paris Exhibitions of 1889 and 1900. In Europe, the name Liberty became so strongly associated with reform dress that reform gowns were referred to as being in the 'Liberty style'. For many years, well into the twentieth century, the Liberty Company continued to offer reform dresses as 'styles that would never go out of fashion' (Cunningham 2003: 133).

In Austria, Gustav Klimt believed in dress reform for women. In his portraits women are often clad in long, loose-flowing garments, which may have been of his own design. His very close friend in Vienna was the fashion designer Emilie Flöge. Thus, it is quite possible that Klimt collaborated with her in designing reform dresses for her fashion salon. Certainly, the modern reform dresses would have a shared aesthetic with the very modern interior of her salon, which had been designed in 1904 by the most *avant-garde* of designers in Vienna—Koloman Moser and Josef Hoffman. The Flöge gowns that appear in the art journal *Hohe Warte* (1905/1906) are similar to the very stark styles of the German dress reform artists, especially those of the architect Peter Behrens. Emilie Flöge often wore reform-style gowns herself. She posed for the photographer D'Ora wearing a loose, ruffled artistic gown (Kultermann 1978: 35–36). At this time, reform gowns also frequently appeared in the pages of *Wiener Mode*, the Vienna fashion magazine (Figure 11:3).

Dressmakers and custom designers in America also made up artistic reform dress to order. In *Dress and How to Improve It,* Frances Parker offered places in Chicago where gowns could be made. These included dressmakers

who can suit the individual, who has an eye for color, who will finish a dress well; one who can make a dress that is comfortable and at the same time will not depart so far from the conventional that the wearer will be the 'observed of all observers'. (1897: 125)

Annie Jenness Miller's suggestions in 1887 for places where women could acquire reform garments in Chicago included the Sanitary Publishing Co. on La Salle Street that sold the 'Bates waist' (a reform underbodice worn by Frances Willard), Mrs. Pike's on Madison Street, and Mrs. Cressman's. All were recognized as headquarters for dress reform. That these dressmakers believed in dress reform is made clear by their dress labels, one of which reads, 'Kate Manville, Dress Reform Artist, Chicago' (Anon 1887: 1).

Lectures on Reform

If not attending art exhibitions, the theater, world's fairs, or seeking out a dress reform shop, women in the United States also could attend lectures to learn about dress reform. The British message regarding reform, brought to Americans through publications and lectures, also was supported at home by many reformers, such as Annie Jenness Miller.

Figure 11:3. A summer dress in the reform style.
(Source: *Wiener Mode* 20 [1907]: 881).

Her major point was that women should look to the classical world for a standard of beauty. That is, women in the United States should strive to achieve the natural beauty of the Venus de Milo. They should cease wearing restrictive clothing that went against Nature, and they should apply the classical principles of art to their dress. This message was repeated often by Oscar Wilde as he traveled across America in 1882 as the front man for the British production of the operetta *Patience*. While in the United States, Wilde lectured widely on such subjects as 'Women's Dress' and 'Slaves of Fashion', in which he deplored the evils of corsetry. In another lecture, he advised women to make their dress hygienic by suspending the weight of the clothing from the shoulders and reducing the number of layers (Cunningham 2003: 135).

Public lectures were a popular means to provide a broader understanding of the need to free women from constrictive, uncomfortable, and unhealthy clothing. The lectures and other activities of Annie Jenness Miller, a publisher, editor, and designer, and her sister, Mabel Jenness, were quite instructive. In the 1880s and 1890s these two New Englanders tirelessly offered advice on beauty to women. They believed that the only way for women to attain true beauty was to apply artistic principles to their dress and to adopt the exercise system of Francois Delsarte. Annie Jenness Miller is perhaps best known as the editor of the publication *Dress,* an illustrated monthly magazine devoted to the practical and beautiful in women's and children's clothing, which was published in New York City between 1887 and 1898. *Dress* offered patterns for reform dresses that readers could purchase with little difficulty. The sisters were authors of books and pamphlets on beauty, rational dress, and physical culture. They were regular speakers on a lecture circuit offering advice and giving demonstrations regarding physical culture and correct dress to various women's organizations throughout the United States.

Annie Jenness Miller and Mabel Jenness spread the message that women could achieve greater freedom in dress and enhance their beauty by combining Delsartean physical culture, artistic dress, and rational (commonsense) undergarments. One of their goals in their lectures was to establish dress reform clubs, especially in the major cities where they spoke. The purpose of the dress clubs would be to serve as a mutual support group for women desiring to improve their health by adopting artistic dress.

During the winter of 1890–91 the sisters gave a series of lectures in New York, Boston, and other large cities. Subjects included: 'Healthful and Artistic Dress', 'The Cultivation of Individuality', 'Artistic Care of the Body', and 'Congruities and Art in Dress'. The first lecture, 'Healthful and Artistic Dress', was illustrated with certain physical movements showing the difference between the grace and elegance gained by Delsartean physical culture and the unartistic effects produced by 'fake dressing' and the compression of the 'essential organs' caused by corsets. They also showed eight artistic gowns designed for different occasions (Anon 1890: 244).

The ideas that the Jenness sisters promoted were not unique to them. Mabel Jenness had been well schooled in the Delsartean philosophy of physical culture at the Monroe Conservatory of Oratory in Boston. It is interesting to note that another author and lecturer on improving women's health in dress, Frances S. Parker, had also studied oratory in Boston and learned about Delsartean philosophy before she took her own first steps toward dress reform. And, perhaps the best known follower of Delsarte, Henrietta Russell (Meckel 1989: 68–70) had also studied with Monroe in Boston. Russell presented her system of physical culture and dress reform in a great number of lectures and demonstrations throughout the United States and Europe in the 1880s and 1890s. As noted previously, she had been in charge of the artistic dress exhibition at the Columbian Exposition in Chicago in 1893 (Parker 1897: 13).

The relationship between the Jenness sisters and the Monroe Conservatory (now Emerson College) continued into the 1890s. The December 1896 issue of the *Emerson College Magazine* offered a series of articles on the importance of attaining unity through physical culture. The articles reference both Annie Jenness Miller and Charles Wesley Emerson on the issue of dress. In 'A Plea for Rational Dress', Annie Blalock, teacher of 'Physical Culture and Oratory' at Emerson College, drew on the example of the Greeks, noting that 'it is to the statues of the Venus de Medici, and Venus de Milo, that we turn for proper education in regards to women's forms' (Pupils of the Senior Class 1896: 48–51). It was not unusual for educators to draw on classical statuary as a source for natural beauty. In the 1860s Vassar College set up a statue of the Venus de Milo to serve as inspiration during callisthenic classes.

Educating the public was a major goal of the dress reformers in both the United States and Europe. The potential for reaching the public through large exhibitions, expositions, lectures, and shops was unlimited. These events and places were successful in marketing reform ideology. It is clear that the practitioners of fashion, designers, and retailers aided the efforts toward reform in dress, and that they in turn were supported by others who shared their beliefs. In 1893, when it became obvious to Arthur Lasenby Liberty that his ideas for a revival of classical dress were being copied, he tried to set the record straight. As a committed reformer, he wanted to be given credit for introducing artistic reform dress. In Liberty Catalog no. 25, 1893, Liberty claims that his company invented artistic dress. The notice, titled 'How was the Empire Mode Reintroduced' states that the Liberty Company copied original classically inspired Empire-style gowns as worn during the Napoleonic era and sold them in their Paris shop 'prior to the fashion for the Empire mode being reintroduced from Paris into England'. Thus it is clear that Arthur Liberty did not want Paris to have credit for the initiative in stimulating an interesting, industrial, and artistic development, that was, as he stated, rightly the effort of the Liberty Company.

Arthur Liberty was correct in stating that his company set a precedent for designers to adopt artistic reform style, particularly in Britain and Europe. The artistic, comfortable, classical, and medieval revival styles had been readily available since 1884 in the Liberty store in London, as well as in various depots throughout the world and particularly in Paris since 1900. Artistic reform dress was seen in galleries in Austria, Germany, and the Netherlands, and sold in department stores in Germany during the first five years of the new century. By 1906 reform styles appeared on the fashion pages of the Viennese fashion magazine *Wiener Mode*, and in the *Queen*, a London publication. Of all the reform garments being produced, it appears that the artistic, classically inspired designs created by the Liberty Company were the most popular. Thus, it is not surprising to find the fashion designers Mariano Fortuny and Paul Poiret embracing the classical style a few years later. In the first decade of the twentieth century, ideas of simplicity were in the air, and the new lightweight silks that Liberty had made popular were readily available to serve this need. In the 1910s and 1920s the now much-celebrated and influential Paris couturiers, Madeleine Vionnet and Coco Chanel, also continued to push forward ideas of simplicity in dress as originally promoted by the artistic dress reformers. Simplicity in fashion became the rule in the 1920s, and practical trousers, such as beach pajamas, continued to find their place in sports and outdoor activities.

This study of the involvement in dress reform by practitioners of fashion makes it clear that dress reform in the late nineteenth and early twentieth century was not completely outside the realm of fashion. The fashion industry was, in fact, part of the solution to improving women's clothing and subsequently their beauty and health. And regarding the success of the dress reform campaign in the nineteenth century it would be beneficial to consider Walter Crane's observations written in 1894. In looking back on the progress of taste in dress, he observed, 'the aesthetic movement did indicate a general desire for greater beauty in ordinary life and gave us...charming materials and colours', which, in combination with genuine taste, produced 'beautiful and simple dresses' (1894: 8).

References

Anon (1887), 'Advertisement', *Dress, a Monthly Magazine*, 1, September, p. 189.

—— (1890), 'Announcement', *Jenness Miller Magazine*, 5, November, p. 244.

—— ([1883] 1978), *Exhibition of the Rational Dress Association...Catalogue of Exhibits and List of Exhibitors*, New York and London: Garland Press.

—— (1886), 'Liberty Developments in Form and Colour', *Liberty & Co. Ltd. Catalogue*, 9.

—— (1893), 'Evolution in Costume, Illustrated by Past Fashion Plates and Present Adaptations of the Empire and Early Victorian period', *Liberty & Co. Ltd. Catalogue*, 25 November, pp, 5, 8.

Crane, Walter (1894), 'Of the Progress of Taste in Dress...in Relation to Art Education', *Aglaia*, 3.

—— (1905), *Ideals in Art*, London: George Bell.

Cunningham, Patricia A. (1990), 'Annie Jenness Miller and Mabel Jenness: Promoters of Physical Culture and Correct Dress', *Dress*, 16, pp. 48–62.

—— (2003), *Reforming Women's Fashion, 1850–1920: Politics, Health, and Art*, Kent, OH: Kent State University Press.

Holiday, Henry (1914), *Henry Holiday: Reminiscences of My Life*, London: Heinemann.

Kultermann, Udo (1978), 'Gustav Klimt, Emilie Flöge und die modereform in Wien um 1900' ('Gustav Klimt, Emilie Flöge and Dress Reform in Vienna around 1900'), *Alte und Moderne Kunst*, 23, pp. 34–39.

Meckel, Richard A. (1989), 'Henrietta Russell: Delsartean Prophet of the Gilded Age', *Journal of American Culture*, 12, pp. 65–78.

Miller, Annie Jenness (1890), 'Editorial comment', *Dress, the Jenness Miller Magazine*, 5, September, pp.142–43.

—— (1887), 'What Others Are Doing for Improved Dress', *Dress, the Monthly Magazine*, 1, November, pp. 292–93.

Muthesius, Anna (1903), *Das Eigenkleid der Frau (The Proper Dress of Women)*, Krefield: Kramer & Baum.

—— (1904), 'Die ausstellung kunstlerischer frauenkleider in Waren-Haus Wertheim, Berlin' ('The Exhibition of Artistic Women's Costume at Wertheim's Store in Berlin'), *Deutsche Kunst und Dekoration*, 14, pp. 441–56.

Newton, Stella Mary (1974), *Health, Art and Reason: Dress Reformers of the Nineteenth Century*, London: John Murray.

Parker, Frances Stuart (1897), *Dress and How to Improve It*, Chicago: Chicago Legal News Company.

Pupils of the Senior Class (1894), 'Some Thought on Hygiene and Aesthetic Dress', *Emerson College Magazine*, 5, December, pp. 48–51.

Russell, Frances E. (1893a), 'Freedom in Dress for Women', *Arena*, 8, pp. 70–79.

—— (1893b), 'The Rational Dress Movement in the Columbian Year', *Arena*, 9, pp. 308–9.

Schultze-Naumberg, Paul (1903), 'Die austellung "die neue frauentracht" in Berlin' ('The Exhibition of "The New Women's Costume" in Berlin), *Dekorative Kunst*, 6, pp. 76–79.

Van de Velde, Henry (1902), 'Das neue kunst-prinzip in der moderner frauen-kleidung' ('New Art Principles in Modern Women's Clothing'), *Deutsche Kunst und Dekoration*, 10, pp. 362–86.

Van de Velde, Maria (1901), 'Sonderaustellung moderner daamen kostume' ('Special Exhibition of Modern Women's Clothing'), *Dekorative Kunst*, 7, p. 44.

Von Wilckens, Leonie (1980), 'Kunstlerkleid und reform kleid- textilkunst in Nürnberg' ('Artistic Clothing and Reform Dress-Textile Art in Nürnberg'), in Peter-Klaus Schuster, *Peter Behrens und Nürnberg: Geschmackswandel in Deutschland: Historismus, Jugendstil u.d. Anfänge d. Industrieform: Nationalmuseum Nürnberg, 20 September-9 November 1980*, München: Prestel, pp. 198–203.

Weimann, Jeanne M. (1981), *The Fair Women*, Chicago: Academy Press, pp. 531–34.

Wrisley, Melyssa (2006), '"Fashion I Despised": Charlotte Perkins Gilman and American Dress Reform, 1880–1920', *Dress*, 33, pp. 97–110.

Chapter 12

The Language of Luxury in Eighteenth-Century France

Paula von Wachenfeldt

Introduction

'People have declaimed against luxury for two thousand years, in verse and in prose, and people have always delighted in it' (Voltaire 2006: 200). This statement of Voltaire resumes the persisting debate on luxury ever since ancient times, from Aristotle[1] to the Romans[2] and up to our contemporary time. In the Old Testament, the many detailed dress descriptions witness fashion's meaning and use. Dress embodies God's will and becomes a means of distinction of the chosen people. In Exodus, God commands Moses to bring Aaron and his sons, separate them from other Isrealites in order to make them his priests. God chooses 'majestic' sacred clothes for Aaron: embroidered tunic, turban, and belt. The material and colors are meticulously described: from the size of the pocket to the type and placement of the many precious stones—ruby, topaz, sapphire, diamond, and amethyst—that should decorate the dress (Alliance Biblique Universelle 1983: Exodus 28).

Luxury is associated with power and appearance and this association reveals an historical tradition filled with symbolic, moral, and religious elements. Can all superfluous elements be considered as luxury? And what are the boundaries for unnecessary things? Luxury and necessity cannot be understood separately and must be considered in relation to each other and in relation to the system of cultural and social values where they exist (Perrot 1995: 18). In this system of signs and tastes, luxury is a desire for those who cannot attain it and an enjoyment for those who can. From this viewpoint, hierarchies, prestige, and inequalities become the target of social and moral debates.

Luxury does not exist unless it is conceived as an excess by society. It is an indicator of riches and has a low utility function. It is an indulgence 'that is thought desirable or pleasing by an individual' (Berry 1994: 40), representing the frivolity of the object. It is also a matter of relativity since 'one person's luxury can be another's necessity' (Berry 1994: 33) and even 'one generation's indulgence becomes the next generation's necessity' (Twitchell 2002: 43). This complexity places luxury in a specific social context where both aesthetic and ethics interact as a marker of prevailing tastes and moral codes. Every society creates its own luxury, and history has shown that it is always needed to please and reflect the status and power of those who can afford it. In feudal times, religious or chivalrous luxury was a mark of respect, glory, and fear. However, this communal sense of luxury has been replaced by the value of individual comfort of the luxury good. With an increasing economic flow, material culture spread to a larger group becoming a sign of the new wealth and prosperity. The middle class began its journey to comfort and pleasure, claiming the right of 'deserved wealth' in opposition to the 'inherited wealth' of the nobility. In the eighteenth century, debates about luxury revealed the arrival of an early modern consumer society concerned with politics, economy, and culture. This fact shows an interesting transition from the ancient world to the modern one.[3] Enlightenment culture, as Maxine Berg and Elizabeth Eger demonstrate, represents on one hand an adaptation to luxury 'as a positive social force' and on the other hand a fear of a 'social evil' and 'plebeian idleness' (2003: 2).

Considering its composite nature and its effects on politics and economy, it is not surprising that luxury as a topic has attracted considerable academic attention in a broad range of studies regarding brands, luxury fashion management, consumption of luxury goods, and luxury history. However, this chapter focuses on the ideological discourse[4] as it is debated by the two enlightenment philosophers: Voltaire and Rousseau. Voltaire's poem 'Le Mondain' ('The Wordling') (1736a/1901) and Rousseau's essay *Discours sur l'origine et les fondements de l'inégalité parmi les hommes* (*Discourse on the Origins of Inequality*) represent the new rhetoric that was used to defend or condemn material culture. From being a symbol of distinction and exclusion in the aristocratic era of classicism, material culture has come to speak for the new wealth and the commercial prosperity of the industrial and the middle classes. Discussions on luxury dominated the Enlightenment debates and covered areas such as moral philosophy, economics and politics. This issue was a natural result of the 'civilizing process'[5] (Elias 1982), the increased knowledge of foreign societies and the importation of goods like silk, cotton and porcelain. Eighteenth-century political and ideological debates developed a public opinion discourse where the salons played a major role. Visiting the

Figure 12:1. French Snuffbox with a colored engraving representing Voltaire, Rousseau and Franklin, 1790s. Above the figures is an inscription: '*Le flambeau de l'univers*' ('The Light of the World'). (Source: Hallwyll Museum, Stockholm; photographer: Samuel Uhrdin).

salons, cafés and attending exhibitions were important social activities that paved the way for critical observations and the emergence of political and aesthetic principles. Moreover, the literary salons became one of the most powerful social activities that affected many aspects of both French and foreign societies. Its culture contributed notably to the social development and the promoting of ideologies regarding human conditions and civilization. This chapter addresses ideological interests of eighteenth-century France and the contributing factors that continue to affect the debate on luxury.

While the arguments of contemporary popular culture on luxury are restricted to the frenetic consumption of lavish fashion objects and brands, the Enlightenment discourse was nourished by the value of human sensations, utility and comfort. The analysis of different rhetorical elements in Voltaire's poem and Rousseau's text reveal significant arguments that either supported the use of luxury or condemned it. This chapter illustrates how Voltaire's dialectic was based on physical impulses and needs while Rousseau's view was inspired by the natural and immediate impressions. Studying earlier polemics brings to light the rise of luxury discourse, offering a deeper understanding of the often simplified contemporary discussions. I will also draw a parallel to the structure of the salon in order to understand the required socio-cultural context of luxury.

The Union of the Subject and the Object

The luxury debate in France has its origin in some lessons that took place between 1700 and 1730. Pierre Bayle's *Réponses aux questions d'un provincial* (1704–1707); the reflections of the economists Boisguilbert, Cantillon, and Melon; and Bernard Mandeville's *Fable of the Bees* had a significant impact on the luxury debate. More than a hundred texts were published between 1736 and 1789 as a reaction to the debate (Roche 1998: 564, 567). Voltaire's contribution 'Le Mondain' shows his fervent engagement with the issue and his adherence to consumerism. The sources of the poem came from four different experiences in Voltaire's life: his own increasing richness, his visit to England and the prosperity of the commerce of the country, Mandeville's book *The Fable of the Bees*, and Melon's *Essai politique sur le commerce* (Morize 1909: 25–30). According to Roche, 'Mandeville's ideas had become well known in France through Melon, who passed them on to Montesquieu and Voltaire' (1998: 568–69).

Voltaire's poem 'Le Mondain' serves as manual to refined taste of every 'honest man'.[6] Beautiful architecture and ornaments (as in the passage below) give pleasure to the observer and become vital components of the well-being in Voltaire's view. This physical reaction is depicted through two senses in the original French text: the touch, represented by the softness and the ornaments and the sight embodied by art and luxury:

I love the pleasures of a court;	J'aime le luxe, et même la mollesse,
I love the arts of every sort;	Tous les plaisirs, les arts de toute espèce,

Magnificence, fine buildings, strikes me;	La propreté, le goût, les ornements:
In this, each man of sense is like me.	Tout honnête homme a de tels sentiments.
Voltaire (1901)	Voltaire (1736a)

When praising sumptuousness and comfort, Voltaire uses a sensual language that tempts the reader to value the good things in life. The taste of the wine and mousse, the touch and the sight of the silk and gold (in the French text) are all involved to create pleasures and delight:

Just at the time of Nature's birth,	Quand la nature était dans son enfance
Dark ignorance o'erspread the earth;	Nos bons aïeux vivaient dans l'ignorance
None then in wealth surpassed the rest,…	Ne connaissant ni le *tien* ni le *mien*….
Eve, first formed by the hand divine,	D'un bon vin frais ou la mousse ou la sève
Never so much as tasted wine.	Ne gratta point le triste gosier d'Ève;
Do you our ancestors admire,	La soie et l'or ne brillaient point chez eux,
	Admirez-vous pour cela nos aïeux ?
Because they wore no rich attire?	Il leur manquait l'industrie et l'aisance:
Ease was like wealth to them unknown,	Est-ce vertu? c'était pure ignorance.
Was't virtue? ignorance alone.	Voltaire (1736a)
Voltaire (1901)	

While nature suggests a barbarian way of living with ignorance, dirt, and discomfort, the industrial revolution teaches the flavor of good wines and mousse. Voltaire's poetry captures the heart of a social and political bourgeois ideal, praising in reality aristocratic consumption habits. Wealth, he maintains, promotes consumption and industrial development and creates working opportunities for the poor. It is undeniable that this perspective maintains rank and social differences since the poor must work and produce the luxury consumption of the rich. However, it can be argued that the consumption of the rich improves the social conditions of the poor; Voltaire criticizes a history that considers frugality a virtue. Luxury consumption benefits society since it generates social progress. Mandeville, source of inspiration for Voltaire, expresses the same idea of the necessity of luxury whose virtual power is fundamental to the public welfare: 'Fraud, Luxury, and Pride must live Whilst we the Benefits receive. Hunger's a dreadful Plague, no doubt, Yet who digests or thrives without? Do we not owe the Growth of Wine To the dry shabby crooked Vine?' (1970: 76).

In Voltaire good taste and material ease are indicators of a deep human desire that needs to be satisfied. Based on physical sensations and impressions, his arguments become hence recognizable to the reader. In 'Sur l'usage de la vie' where Voltaire meets the criticism against 'Le Mondain', he asserts that 'he sang the enjoyments of pure and permitted pleasures' and that his aim was to teach the art of being happy (Voltaire 1736b). [7] It is the worldwide human experience in Voltaire's images that are convincing reasons of the importance of luxury for the individual and for society. In the passage below it is the hearing (when the master approaches in the French version) and the smell (perfumes in both versions) that complete the use of the five senses in the poem:

Would you know in this cursed age,	Or maintenant voulez-vous, mes amis,
Against which zealots so much rage,	Savoir un peu, dans nos jours tant maudits,
To what men blessed with taste attend,	Soit à Paris, soit dans Londre, ou dans
In cities, how their time they spend?	Rome,
The arts that charm the human mind	Quel est le train des jours d'un honnête
	homme?
At all his house a welcome find;	Entrez chez lui: la foule des beaux-arts,
In building it, the architect	Enfants du gout, se montre à vos regards,
No grace passed over with neglect.	De mille mains l'éclatante industrie
To adorn the rooms, at once combine	De ces dehors orna la symétrie.
Poussin, Correggio the divine,	L'heureux pinceau, le superbe dessin
Their works on every panel placed	Du doux Courrège et du savant Poussin
Are in rich golden frames incased....	Sont encadrés dans l'or d'une bordure…
The Gobelin tapestry, whose dye	Des gobelins l'aiguille et la teinture
Can with the painter's pencil vie,	Dans ces tapis surpassent la peinture….
With gayest coloring appear	De ce salon je vois par la fenêtre,
As ornaments on every pier.	Dans des jardins, des myrtes en berceaux;
From the superb salon are seen	Je vois jaillir les bondissantes eaux.
Gardens with Cyprean myrtle green.	Mais du logis j'entends sortir le maître:
I see the sporting waters rise	…
By jets d'eau almost to the skies.	
…	Il court au bain: les parfums les plus doux
At Bath, his polished skin inhales	Rendent sa peau plus fraîche et plus polie.
Perfumes, sweet as Arabian gales.	Voltaire (1736a)
Voltaire (1901)	

Art, tapestry, and beautiful gardens are not social necessities and could therefore be considered luxuries in that they are superfluous objects. However, Voltaire presents them as vital elements in life since they incite happiness and joy. He further underlines the value of physical sensations so as to defend luxury production and consumption. This depicted lifestyle has an aristocratic character and though Voltaire was bourgeois by birth he became wealthy in time. It is remarkable how the social habits of the nobility were soon adopted by the prosperous middle class. As wealth spread to the lower classes, the imitation of aristocratic consumption habits increased and eventually masked social distance. In his studies about the Enlightenment, Roche states that

[P]eople at all levels of society were spending more on clothing and undergarments: in 1700 the average noble spent 1,800 livres on clothing; by 1789 the figure had risen to

6,000—an increase of 233 percent. For workers, expenditures on clothing rose from 42 to 115 livres, or 215 percent.... [H]abits of dress became more similar across classes: wardrobes contained the same types of clothing, although differences in quantity and quality ensured that the hierarchy was preserved.... Lower clothing costs made it possible to acquire new clothes more frequently. (1998: 558–59)

Voltaire's poem constitutes a new discourse promoting the urgent necessity of consumer goods for modern society. Enlightenment culture introduced a new attitude to commodities by establishing a relationship between material and intellectual culture. In Voltaire this relationship is very close, as it describes his own subjective experience. Also, this value of individualism shows a dissociation from Christian values where the idea of community—symbolized by the church—was central.[8] Previously, the luxury debate had a religious dimension where a rigorous Christian attitude condemned luxury and social pleasures, seen as symbolic of artificiality and alienation from a Christianized nature. The effects of Christian rhetoric on human behavior can be seen in how possessions were to be allocated: landowners ought to redistribute their wealth to the poor through alms and legacies and by this means, luxury was 'transformed into charity' (Roche 2000: 72). This principle was a moral justification of the consumption of the rich that furthered the life of the poor. However, people during the Enlightenment adopted a new view on society, aiming at interest and utility instead of the redistribution thought. The significance of the intellectual discourse regarding luxury issues needs also to be put in connection with the development of the public sphere and the importance of the salons for circulating socio-economic ideas.

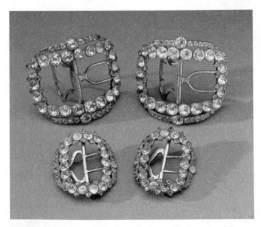

Figure 12:2. Silver German knee and shoe buckles as example of luxury goods, 1770s. (Source: Hallwyll Museum, Stockholm; photographer Samuel Uhrdin).

Parisian Public Sphere

In her study of the *salonnières*, Isabelle Brouard-Arends sustains that the 'opening towards the public sphere, besides the sociability, had also the consequence that the "*l'homme de lettres*" became, through his writings, a man of action, a militant writer' (2001: 100).[9] Voltaire's poem is a clear political statement on the human right to luxury. Enlightenment philosophers were publically concerned about the political apparatus and the rights of the individual in it. The salon[10] was the place to debate ideas as it permitted a sociability that was hardly possible in a strict court milieu. Habermas reminds us that there was barely a great writer in the eighteenth century who had not submitted his ideas in the salons first (1991: 34). It is therefore important to emphasize the structure of the salons, which paved the way for a debate climate such as the one regarding luxury.

So what was happening in the eighteenth century that allowed the public expression of these delicate moral, political, and economic issues? When the rigid structure of the court did not allow any free expression, the tradition created by Mme de Rambouillet in the seventeenth century transformed the salon into a territory for literary, political, and economic reflections. Habermas traced the circumstances surrounding this social development as follows:

> The bourgeois avant-garde of the educated middle class learned the art of critical-rational public debate through its contact with the 'elegant world'. This courtly-noble society... separated itself,...more and more from the court and became its counterpoise in the town. The 'town' was the life center of civil society not only economically; in cultural-political contrast to the court, it designated especially an early public sphere in the world of letters whose institutions were the coffee houses, the *salons*, and the Tischgesellschaften (table societies). (1991: 29–30)

The 'militant' attitude that characterized Enlightenment thinkers is clearly present in Voltaire, who demonstrates a union of the subject with the object. We have seen the clear account of how both self and society can benefit from material culture. This development is also part of the 'civilizing process' that included a mixture of idealism and materialism. Rosalind H. Williams implies that the consumption habits have to be understood in an ideological context:

> To many enlightened thinkers of the eighteenth century, it seemed self-evident that enlightened consumption—patronage of the arts, the vivacious conversation of the salons, collection of paintings and books—was a necessary means to the advancement of civilization.... In the eighteenth century the idea of civilization referred both to a general social and political ideal and, more narrowly, to a comfortable way of life reserved for the upper classes. (1982: 38)

From being an unmistakable element of aristocratic circles, this comfortable life is now explicitly part of a wealthy middle-class existence. The public, i.e., the visitors of the salons, was constituted by a miscellaneous class affiliation where the bourgeois, as intellectuals or wealthy or even both, are actively contributing to the social discourse. There is an openness about issues concerning individual beliefs and, more specifically, individual freedom. It is worth stressing that the luxury debate was the concern of the middle class, a development that shows an interesting transition of social behavior. Roche states that

> luxury was a form of usurpation which contributed to the confusion of ranks; because nobles required to spend ever increasing sums in order to maintain their rank were being led into ruin; and because the legitimacy of luxury encouraged and confirmed the power of the 'new men' who became scapegoats for aristocratic and Christian criticism. (1998: 563)

The luxury debate of the eighteenth century was, first of all, a debate initiated and animated by these 'new men' who were constantly increasing and confirming their social power and at once becoming a threatening factor for the traditional ruling class. A new meaning was created where both the definition and the experience of materiality would not reside in the ancient social heritage of the aristocracy but in a modern taste of pleasures. It is also clear that a social mobility was taking place as power concentrated in Versailles shifted to Paris, where the acquisition of the *hôtels* developed the commerce in the city.[11] Paris became the center of luxury consumption where the clients consisted of aristocrats and the newly wealthy bourgeois. Material progress that came along with new riches and cultural acquisitions contributed to an increased similarity in clothing habits; however, this was primarily a Parisian phenomenon while 'the countryside remained for some time in the world of scarcity and reuse, and rural people continued to make their own thread and cloth' (Roche 1998: 558–60). The city was the space for commercial and economic prosperity and therefore vital for the defenders of luxury like Voltaire. But it was also the place for corruption and dissociation from the natural as it was represented by Rousseau.

The Tragedy of Separation

In his prize-winning *Discours sur l'origine et les fondements de l'inégalité parmi les hommes* (*Discourse on the Origins of Inequality*), published in 1754 and 1755, Rousseau (1992) develops his philosophy of the 'original man' in order to understand the sources of inequality, human needs, and the foundations of the body politic. The discourse is a harsh criticism of the idea of civilization generating materiality, desires, and luxury goods. Rousseau argues that people have lost the immediate contact with nature and henceforth found comfort in material goods. The methods used in mines to find precious metals and minerals are denounced as vicious practices that kill workers every day. The pursuit of luxury has no other function than to deprive people of their liberty and, for Rousseau, 'it is itself the worst of all evils in any state whatever, whether large or small, and in order to feed the crowds of Lackeys and miserable people it has created, it crushes and ruins the farmer and the Citizen' (1992: 77–78).[12] But why is luxury itself so harmful for humanity?

In his *Discourse* Rousseau distinguishes between two sorts of inequality: the natural/physical and the moral/political. Natural inequality consists of differences in age, health, and physical strength while moral inequality comprises of different privileges like wealth and power that rich people can enjoy on behalf of the others (1992: 18). Luxurious lifestyles belong to the latter since it creates a 'master and slave morality',[13] which increases inequalities in society. This is responsible for creating the distance between, on one hand, different social groups, and, on the other hand, individuals and nature. Jean Starobinski in his essay about Rousseau describes the philosopher's criticism as an expression of losing the original transparency: 'Civilized society, by constantly increasing the distance between itself and nature, obscures the immediate relation of one mind to another: loss of the primordial transparency goes hand in hand with alienation in the world of material things' (1988: 24).[14] The loss of 'transparency' derives from the social progress that has denied the natural and the immediate. In effect, this progress is not merely denying but also obstructing human beings from living the balance that first existed with the world. The original innocence and inherent sensations are lost and humans are increasingly defined according to *created* social values, to artificial ideals and principles. Thus the process of civilization has alienated people from nature and from themselves. They have moved away from the truth in nature and become part of the social lie that culture and progress generate. 'Everything that comes from Nature will be true' writes Rousseau (1992: 19). In accumulating knowledge, the human taste has lost its primordial state. Instead of finding a way to return to the first innocence, where unconsciousness and equality existed, humans constantly seek to distinguish themselves from fellow beings. The meaning of civilization in Rousseau's discourse is connected to an increasingly commercialized society. Luxury represents artificialness, materiality, and technical development and is therefore regarded as an element of social disorder. The state has changed man's nature and made him a slave to his belongings and to his hard work; possessions and work take freedom and joy:

> Savage man and civilized man differ so much in this regard that the state that constitutes the supreme happiness of one would reduce the other to despair. While the savage breathes only repose and freedom, wants only to live and remain idle,…the Citizen always active, sweats, agitates himself, torments himself incessantly in order to seek still more laborious occupations. (Rousseau 1992: 98)

At this point, we need to consider the relationship between consumption and liberty. Voltaire, as a partisan of luxury, defended the human right to material pleasure and the importance of luxury goods to economic welfare. He becomes the spokesman of the freedom of consumption. But does this lead us to understand Rousseau's arguments against material culture are repressive and archaic? Answering yes oversimplifies the complex Rousseauian arguments, so closer examination is necessary.

In Voltairian meaning, luxury is fundamental for its social benefits since the rich consumes what the poor produces and liberty lies accordingly in the working and consumption possibilities. Prior to the eighteenth century, comfort was limited to the elite, court, and aristocratic circles. Economic growth of the middle class was due in part to their increased uptake of important political and administrative posts, and the introduction of new materials like cotton, sugar and tea; these changes paved the way for growth of ambition and for new addictive behaviors. The availability and variety of goods undermined social hierarchies, and the demand for luxury commodities impacted on both economic growth and socio-cultural debates. This change of attitude toward consumption was also sustained by a change of attitude toward education. The modern society believed in the power of educating citizens since 'education would liberate them' (Roche 1998: 425). Jean Marie Goulemot posits that the 'Enlightenment was nothing more than an innovation in educational techniques: letters, dictionaries, and philosophical tales were all new ways of educating the public' (1989: 387). The public took part in the debate on culture, commerce, and economic welfare. Liberty was then defined in terms of an educational and intellectual climate where the public, represented by the world of letters, expressed new ideological ideas.

Rousseau's criticism against a commercial society can be viewed in the light of the political and economic impact of a city-based and growing bourgeois public sphere. While Voltaire championed the town as the luxury space where commerce and industries prospered, Rousseau rejected the town's progress and the sociability of the salons. This 'realm of the mask and fine words' (Roche 1998: 444) did not fit in the Rousseauian philosophy since it represented a society within a society. The age of separation in the idea of the salon is incompatible with the vision of unification that characterized Rousseau's thinking. If the concept and the activity of the salon were not appealing to Rousseau, then were other kinds of social activities more appropriate?

Throughout the eighteenth century there was nostalgia for the community and social exchange, such as popular festivals (Goulemot 1989: 375). At festivals people were both actors and spectators, Rousseau aligned festivals with nature and happiness:

> Entertainments which close up a small number of people in melancholy fashion in a gloomy cavern, which keep them fearful and immobile in silence and inaction, which give them only prisons, lances, soldiers, and afflicting images of servitude and inequality to see. No, happy Peoples, these are not your festivals. It is in the open air, under the sky, that you ought to gather and give yourselves to the sweet sentiment of your happiness. (Rousseau 2004: 343)

On the other hand, the theater, like the salon, ruptures on two levels: there is a separation of the individual from the immediate natural contact and separation of people from each other. The theater was hostile to social values; it was a private space available solely for the cultivated elite, whereas popular events embody the public open space. This idea complements the Rousseauian attack against material prosperity that is built upon separation and inequality. At the core of the consumer's society producers and consumers are no longer united. Commodities and goods have established a duality between the subject and the object. Moreover, where Voltaire made an intimate link between consumption and liberty, Rousseau chose to place the latter in the union of people and condemned luxury because it artificially segregated people from the natural and from their fellow human beings. Luxury generates power that is used to control people, creating inequalities in society:

> Luxury, impossible to prevent among men greedy for their own commodities and the esteem of others, soon completes the evil that Societies began; and on the pretext of keeping alive the poor who should not have made so, luxury impoverishes everyone else, and depopulates the state sooner or later. (Rousseau 1992: 78)

Rousseau's quest for liberty from all forms of materiality can also be seen in this refusal to wear 'stockings, a wig, and a sword' and Goulemot points out that Rousseau's 'withdrawal from Paris society, and his break with Diderot and the group around the Encyclopedia… was a deliberate decision, the beginning of his commitment to philosophy. The road to truth passes by way of social and moral asceticism' (1989: 389). The truth for Rousseau is to be found in an undisturbed harmony between inner self and nature. The way to truth claims a detachment from the world and from the subject and the object. It is only in accord with the truthful nature that moral values can be reached so as to erase social disparities. This quest for the truth is declared in the first lines of Rousseau's *Confessions:* 'I have entered upon a performance which is without example, whose accomplishment will have no imitator. I mean to present my fellow-mortals with a man in all the integrity of nature; and this man shall be myself' (Rousseau 2006: book 1). For Rousseau the town is the place of corruption and endless desires; therefore the ideals of civilization and the culture of Paris' salons can never achieve a naturalized society. The town is a scene of privilege and has a 'lower tax burden' (Roche 2000: 34) and in that, takes part of the separation act. Hence, Rousseau invites people to leave their possessions and desires in town and go back to their first innocence:

> You who can leave your fatal acquisitions, your worried minds, your corrupt Hearts, and your unbridled desires in the midst of Cities; reclaim—since it is up to you to, your ancient and first innocence; go into the woods to lose sight and memory of the crimes of your contemporaries. (1992: 79)

Society built desire in people's soul, making them dependent on false appearances. By losing themselves in materiality, people have lost the contact with their conscience; by embracing progress, they have denied the natural. For Rousseau, luxury is the bitter fruit of a denaturalized civilization.

Conclusion

The luxury discourse of the Enlightenment can be linked to the dichotomy between nature and culture or nature and civilization. Nature is represented either as barbaric or as a source of human values while civilization becomes progressive or provocative of a vicious consumer society.

When Voltaire speaks to our five senses, Rousseau's rhetoric addresses our heart and conscience. While the former evokes the good effects of material culture, the second warns about its harmful effect on society. Voltaire's thought is representative of the needs of a stronger middle class, claiming the rights to aristocratic consumer behavior. His discourse reflects changes in society, like new wealth, increased expenditure on clothing, and the importation of luxurious (and habit forming) foreign goods. Equally, the development of a public sphere, represented by the activities of the salon and the spread of education, permitted ideological debates on the new social conditions and their outcomes for humanity. The moralist Rousseau, on the other hand, deplores a society of cupidity and elitism. He denounces the enslavement of material objects and industries. By approaching mankind's origin, he reminds readers of the innocence lost in the civilization. And when he evokes poverty, he reaches the heart and conscience of the reader in an attempt to re-experience the original state. But this return to nature can only take place by denying the materialistic world. Rousseau's philosophy is built upon a twofold pillar since it refuses the order of society that refuses nature, it is 'the negation of the negation' (Starobinski 1988: 23). Voltaire's derogatory meaning in his letter to Rousseau—'One acquires the desire to walk on all fours when one reads your work'—can be amusing, but in fact Rousseau's rhetoric reached a large audience.[15] That said, it is the Voltairian ideology that triumphed. What we experience today is just an acceleration of consumer habits launched by the eighteenth century's civilization process. However, when today's luxury debate focuses on fashion brands and miscellaneous products, the enlightenment discourse found its arguments in the human experience.

References

Alliance Biblique Universelle (1983), *La Bible: Ancien et Nouveau Testament,* Netherlands.

Aristotle (c. 350 B.C.E.) *Nicomachean Ethics,* The Internet Classics Archive, http://classics. mit.edu/Aristotle/nicomachaen.4.iv.html. Accessed 9 February 2012.

Berg, M. and Eger, E. (2003), *Luxury in the Eighteenth Century: Debates, Desires and Delectable Goods,* New York: Palgrave Macmillan.

Berry, C.J. (1994), *The Idea of Luxury: A Conceptual and Historical Investigation*, Cambridge: Cambridge University Press.

Brouard-Arends, I. (2001), 'Qui peut définir la femme de lettres? De la salonnière à la femme de lettres, intégration et exclusion, une dialectique complexe', in Roger Marchal, ed., *Vie des salons et activités littéraires: de Marguerite de Valois à Mme de Staël*, Nancy: Presses Universitaires de Nancy, pp. 95–103.

Coquery, N. (1998), *L'hôtel aristocratique. Le marché du luxe à Paris au XVIIIe sièle*, Paris: Publications de la Sorbonne.

Elias, N. (1982), *The Civilizing Process: State Formation and Civilization*, Oxford: Basil Blackwell.

Goulemot, J. M. (1989), 'Literary Practices: Publicizing the Private', in Roger Chartier, ed., *A History of Private life III: Passions of the Renaissance*, Cambridge, MA: The Belknap Press of Harvard University Press, pp. 363–95.

Habermas, J. (1991), *The Structural Transformation of the Public Sphere: An Inquiry into a Category of Bourgeois Society*, Cambridge, MA: MIT Press.

Hellegouarc'h, J. (2001), 'Salon du XVIIIe siècle: problèmes de sources', in Roger Marchal, ed., *Vie des salons et activités littéraires: de Marguerite de Valois à Mme de Staël*, Nancy: Presses Universitaires de Nancy, pp. 29–37.

Mandeville, B. (1970), *The Fable of the Bees*, Harmondsworth: Penguin Books.

Morize, A. (1909), *L'apologie du luxe au XVIIIe siècle et « Le Mondain » de Voltaire*, Paris: H. Didier.

Perrot, P. (1995), *Le Luxe. Une richesse entre faste et confort XVIIIe–XIXe siècle*, Paris: Éditions du Seuil.

Roche, Daniel (1998), *France in the Enlightenment*, Cambridge, MA: Harvard University Press.

Roche, D. (2000), *A History of Everyday Things: The Birth of Consumption in France, 1600–1800*, Cambridge: Cambridge University Press.

Rousseau, J.-J. (1965), Lettre 139, in R.A. Leigh, ed., *Correspondance complète de Jean-Jacques Rousseau*, vol. 2, Geneva: Institut et Musée Voltaire, pp. 92–93.

—— (1992), *Discourse on the Origins of Inequality (Second Discourse): Polemics and Political Economy* (trans. Judith R. Bush et al., ed. Roger Masters and Christopher Kelly), Hanover, NH: University Press of New England.

—— (2004), 'Letter to d'Albembert and Writings for the Theatre', in Allan Bloom, Charles Butterworth and Christopher Kelly, eds, *The Collected Writings of Rousseau*, vol. 10., Hanover, NH: University Press of New England.

—— (2006), *The Confessions of J.J. Rousseau*, The Gutenberg Project, http://www.gutenberg. org/files/3913/3913-h/3913-h.htm. Accessed 1 February 2012.

Scott, Katie and Cherry, Deborah, eds (2005), *Between Luxury and the Everyday: Decorative Arts in Eighteenth-Century France*, Malden, MA: Blackwell.

Starobinski, J. (1988), *Jean-Jacques Rousseau: Transparency and Obstruction*. Chicago: University of Chicago Press.

Twitchell, J.B. (2002), *Living It Up: Our Love Affair with Luxury*, New York: Columbia University Press.

Voltaire (1736a), 'Le Mondain', in *Oeuvres complètes de Voltaire*, http://fr.wikisource.org/ wiki/Le_Mondain. Accessed 23 October 2012.

——— (1736b), 'Sur l'usage de la vie pour répondre aux critiques qu'on avait faites du Mondain', in *Oeuvres complètes de Voltaire*, http://fr.wikisource.org/wiki/Le_Mondain#Sur_l. E2.80.99usage_de_la_vie. Acessed 23 October 2012.

——— ([1901), 'The Worldling', in *The Works of Voltaire: A Contemporary Version, Vol. X, The Dramatic Works, Part II (The Lisbon Earthquake and Other Poems)* (trans. William F. Fleming), New York: E.R. DuMont, 1901, pp. 84–88, http://oll.libertyfund.org/index. php?option=com_staticxt&staticfile=show.php%3Ftitle=2240&Itemid=27. Accessed 10 October 2012.

——— (2006), 'Luxury', in *Voltaire's Philosophical Dictionary*, New York: Carlton House, pp. 200–202, The Gutenberg Project, http://www.gutenberg.org/files/18569/18569-h/18569-h.htm#Luxury. Accessed 10 October 2012.

Williams, R.H. (1982), *Dream Worlds: Mass Consumption in Late Nineteenth-Century France*, Berkeley: University of California Press.

Notes

1   In book IV of the *Nicomachean Ethics*, Aristotle makes the distinction between the prodigal and the liberal man: 'he is liberal who spends according to his substance and on the right objects; and he who exceeds is prodigal' and 'a "prodigal" means a man who has a single evil quality, that of wasting his substance; since a prodigal is one who is being ruined by his own fault, and the wasting of substance is thought to be a sort of ruining of oneself, life being held to depend on possession of substance' (Aristotle c. 350 B.C.E.: book IV).

2   According to Christopher J. Berry, luxury was for the Romans 'a political question because it signified the presence of the potentially disruptive power of human desire, a power which must be policed' (1994: 63).

3   This transition concerns Paris and not rural areas. Roche states that 'the countryside remained for some time in the world of scarcity and reuse, and rural people continued to make their own thread and cloth' (1998: 560).

4   This conceptual study does not investigate consumption activities of the eighteenth century, nor the use of luxury items. Investigations of this kind can be found in Coquery (1998), Roche (2000), and Scott and Cherry (2005).

5   'Civilizing Process' is the term used by Elias (1982) to describe the evolution of social manners associated with changes in consumption.

6   My reading of Voltaire's poem is based on the French original version since the translation into English has lost some important details. Both versions will figure next to each other so as to clarify the analysis.

7   *'J'ai chanté la jouissance des plaisirs purs et permis,…je ne veux que vous apprendre l'art peu connu d'être heureux.'*

8 I agree with André Morize's introduction (1909), where he suggests that the moral consciousness of the seventeenth century was individualistic and Christian while that of the eighteenth century was preoccupied with social utility.

9 My translation. The original quotation is: '*L'ouverture vers la sphère publique, outre la sociabilité, a aussi comme conséquence que l'homme de lettres devient, par ses écrits, un homme d'action, un écrivain militant*' (Brouard-Arends 2001: 100).

10 The term 'salon' did not have the same connotation in the eighteenth century as it has today. At the time, it was used to designate the reception hall and it is not until the end of the century that it received the meaning it has today. Terms like '*assemblée*', '*compagnie*', '*société*', and especially '*cercle*' were frequently used to indicate this sort of activities (Hellegouarc'h 2001: 29).

11 See Coquery (1998) for the development of boutiques and commerce around the *hôtels* in Paris.

12 Originally, Rousseau, did not feel 'the animosity toward high society' and he was 'an apologist for luxury', according to Roche. His conversion took place on the road to Vincennes where he definitely took position against material production and civilization (Roche 1998: 571–72). Moreover Rousseau, at first, admired Voltaire's work and in December 1745 wrote him a letter asking him humbly to examine a piece of music even though he not worthy of Voltaire's attention (Rousseau 1965: 92–93).

13 The reference here is to Nietzsche's expression from his book *On the Genealogy of Morals*.

14 Starobinski uses the term 'transparency' to describe the natural state in which human beings are completely exposed to the world.

15 Between 1750 and 1759, there were 363 books published on economics, while there had only been 67 published between 1730 and 1739 in France, likewise, the number of academies offering prize competitions on economic topics were 21 compared to 9 earlier (Roche 1998: 572).

Chapter 13

The Devil of Fashion: Women, Fashion, and the Nation in Early-Twentieth-Century German and Swedish Cultural Magazines

Andrea Kollnitz

'The Devil of Fashion' ('Der Modeteufel') is the title of a cover caricature on the 9 November 1921 issue of the German political satirical magazine *Simplicissimus* (Figure 13:1). It opens a volume wholly devoted to fashion. The striking image on the cover combines outrageous colors of almost expressionist vigor—a gaudy pink square forms the background to a naked woman with a bright yellow body and surrounding yellow soap bubbles. But is this a 'real' woman? A closer look reveals her human body is distorted by diabolic features. Her demonstratively protruding and rounded bottom boasts a long, curling tail, her feet are hooves, her ears are pointed, and two small horns grow from the top of her forehead. Finally, an enormous black mane of hair floats from her head, ending in a contour that reminds one of licking flames. With her eyes closed, this 'devil of fashion' seems dreamily absorbed in blowing into her pipe and surrounding herself with soap bubbles containing (her) fashion dreams. In the yellow bubbles we find erotically exaggerated examples of historical dress: medieval female dress with a protruding belly, rococo male fashion boasting tightly dressed calves, a robe *à la française* with an enormous panier and a wholly exposed bosom, early-eighteenth-century male pantaloons emphasizing the crotch, a Renaissance knight with a bulging bottom, and finally, a contemporary flapper of the 1920s showing long, slim, naked legs. Under the image, a subtext gives us yet more information: 'God made men, but I have made them take themselves seriously' ('*Gott hat den Menschen nur geschaffen, aber ich habe ihn dazu gebracht, sich ernst zu nehmen*'). What messages are being conveyed by the cover illustration of this issue of *Simplicissimus*, one of the most respected international cultural magazines of the time and one known for its wit and artistic quality? Firstly, we understand that fashion is undeniably of great importance.

Secondly, the caricature tells us that fashion belongs to women and conspicuously affected men. It is furthermore connected to seduction and dangerous and immoral behavior. Fashion, or its alter ego 'woman', is insincere (the subtext), unrealistic (the soap bubbles), ungodly (the devil), and thus beyond eternal values. The devil as a close and dangerous companion to the female fashion victim has been a recurring marker of fashion criticism ever since the medieval period and its catholically charged moral discourse (Ribeiro 2003: chapter 3). Furthermore, the body of the main figure and the bodies in the soap bubbles are aggressively oversexualized. Fashion thus is not only superficial and insincere—it is immoral and physically dangerous. But who or what is endangered? Is it manhood at large, male or female manhood or contemporary German society? A little detail in the analyzed image gestures to one area of importance, the devil/woman's black hair; her hair can be considered more than an effective and dramatic contrast to the bright background, it can

Figure 13:1. 'The Devil of Fashion' ('Der Modeteufel'), cover caricature, *Simplicissimus* (9 November 1921).

be linked to a woman from a certain geographical area and culture. The black hair connotes a *femme fatale* of Latin origin, a foreign woman with dangerous characteristics—a blonde woman would have been almost unthinkable in this diabolizing context. Fashion thus is not only metaphorized by a female devil, it is analogized to a type of *foreign* woman, a type that might be considered antithetical to German or Germanic national identity in mental as well as in physical disposition.

Antithetical visual constructions of national and gender identity in fashion caricature and illustrations are the focus of this chapter. It explores the interwoven discourses and tropes of foreignness, femininity, and national identity as *embodied* in fashion caricatures and illustrations distributed by four German and Swedish cultural magazines from the 1910s and 1920s. Earlier research on fashion caricature has identified the late nineteenth century as the period in which fashion caricature came to an end due to increasing democratization and the global acceptance of fashion as a consumption object of great economical importance

(Rasche and Wolter 2003: 24). This chapter shows that fashion caricature had not lost its potency well into the 1910s and 1920s. It had, however, become another kind of caricature, a kind that was no longer directly focused on the changes in fashion and fashion itself. Fashion is here rather used as a metaphor, a powerful instrument of cultural politics and a far-from-harmless carrier of national symbolism during an era of revolutionary political changes.[1]

The Swedish magazines *Saisonen* (1916–1925) and *Strix* (1897–1924) and the German magazines *Jugend* (1896–1940) and *Simplicissimus* (1896–1944) were popular and widely read. In all of them, images of modern women (and less frequently men) in conspicuous fashion were a recurring and obviously decisive feature. They can be interpreted as a visual discourse performing and negotiating not only fashion, but also national identity, modernity, and gender in front of a large national audience. My choice of German and Swedish materials for this study is related to their being interlinked by the negotiation of a common Germanic identity during the period, an identity building that demanded demarcations not least toward outlandish southern or western European influences. In both countries nationalism and differentiation were of unsurpassed urgent (cultural-) political concern during the first decades of the twentieth century, a period of strong modernizing and transnationalist movements. As I have shown in my art-historical dissertation on the construction of Swedish art identity in art criticism on German and Austrian modernism, the antithetical polarization between 'North' and 'South' is common in both German and Swedish cultural discourses. Foreign and most often French 'feminine' influences were regarded as both inspiring and threatening to Swedish and German (or Germanic) 'masculine' identity (Kollnitz 2008: chapter 3).

Cultural-historical narratives are traditionally built on polarizations between different regions and regional styles and aesthetic national differences. They have created ideals of 'genuine' expressions and essential aesthetic identities.[2] In addition, national differences in fashion, linked to political power and cultural competition among the empires and courts of Europe, have become commonplace.[3] One of the strongest examples of this is the antagonism between the French and the English instigated by Louis XIV's aggressive international promotion of French fashion. From the seventeenth century onward French influence in England and English influence in France provoked an ongoing debate between different aesthetic and moral opinions about the ostentation and ornament of French (or generally outlandish) fashion. French effeminate decadence situated British fashion as more natural, practical, and virile. As Peter McNeil writes: 'To the English speaking world, fashion was virtually synonymous with the French, whose ability to create ingenious trifles in every aspect of design simultaneously repelled and attracted the English' (McNeil 2005: 177). The condemnation of French sartorial exaggeration and excessive luxury reached its climax in the French Revolution, which saw French elitist power and aesthetics replaced by bourgeois rationalism and democratic thought, even in clothing. Earlier opposed as a symbol of the French aristocracy, the ostentatious fashion of the *ancien régime* was then made a visual sign of feminine artificiality and weakness; in contrast, British fashion was posited as measured and practical.[4] Even today British tailoring is considered the epitome of quality male clothing while French couture 'is' for women (Rocamora 2009: xiii).

Practicality versus elegance, controlled and natural masculinity versus exaggerated and stylish femininity—these binaries resonate in the Swedish and German discourse constructing 'Frenchness' in the early twentieth century. As fashion has been constantly attacked for its superficiality, artificiality, and connection with feminine vanity, French style maintains its position as a feminine aesthetic in fashion. The alleged femininity of French style is ambivalent, though: inferior in a politically and nationalistically charged rhetoric—superior and an unsurpassable model of artistic creativity in fashion (Kollnitz 2008: chapter 3). This ambivalence is obvious not least in modernist lifestyle magazines that often combine fashion reports and art criticism.[5]

The French as a Model—Examples from *Saisonen,* 1916 and 1918

The Swedish upper-class lifestyle magazine *Saisonen, magasin för konst, nyheter och moder* (*The Season, a Magazine for Art, News and Fashion,* 1916–1925) reported on modern cultural events in art, fashion, and theater. Its name reflects a 'French' focus that is evident also in the French expressions that permeate the text.[6] The front covers and numerous fashion reviews inside the magazine show that fashion is one of its main concerns. Illustrations of the latest fashions compete with photographs of aristocratic and high society Swedish women in a section called 'Youth and Beauty in Stockholm's High Society'. Thus modern fashion signifying modernity and high society portraiture signifying tradition are contrasted and combined visually and ideologically in the covers as well as in the contents. The fashion reports by 'Comtesse G.'—a pseudonym connoting Frenchness as well as aristocratic status—meld both fashion news and fashion history to France and Paris. The article 'The First Spring Fashions' opens with a homage to France 'the country of all beautiful fashions', unequalled in its feeling for style and rarely leaving the realm of good taste ('Comtesse G.' 1916: 11). To support her statement, Comtesse G. refers to historical French fashion tropes as 'Louis style' and 'Pompadour' and uses illustrations of historical French costumes from different periods. Other descriptive metaphorical references come from French art such as 'Manet hat', 'Watteau hats', 'Nattier blue'. This linking of French fashion to its cultural heritage and French art icons shows the hegemonic position of French culture and aesthetics in Swedish discourse. It can be compared to a similar rhetoric in contemporary art-criticism which promotes French art by referring to its old masters and calling it 'masterly', 'devoted to beauty', 'tasteful', and 'refined' (Kollnitz 2008: chapter 3). While Comtesse G. sees modern textiles 'in all their grace as very characteristically French' ('Comtesse G.' 1916: 22), the art historian Axel L. Romdahl talks of the heaviness in German art which 'never can reach the relieving ease of French art' (1914: 33).

A look through different issues of *Saisonen* shows that beauty, refinement, and even elegance are perceived as recurring and self-obvious features of French fashion and painterly style. All of those characteristics shape a national character of French aesthetics and fashion as connected to femininity. Not only is French style associated with feminine virtues but French fashion itself is considered as adequate for and naturally connected to women. Linguistically, this becomes obvious when women are called '*élegantes*' while men are called 'gentlemen' (*Saisonen* 1916, 3: 50). All the reports on male fashion in *Saisonen* use 'gentlemen' (the English term) and refer to English phenomena such as 'Oxford cloth' and 'London tailors'.[7]

The description and interpretation of French fashion in terms of national character, however, does not only concern Frenchness itself, but demarcates Swedish national identity in comparison to its French model or 'Other' (Kollnitz 2008). An interesting dilemma becomes obvious in the following example where Comtesse G. indirectly both praises and rejects French influences on Swedish women. She first explains Swedish women's less sophisticated style of dress by referring to the colder climate. There is obviously a practical excuse and positive reason for resisting the elegance of French fashion. On the other hand, the writer complains that Swedish ladies are unoriginal because they 'stubbornly keep to the same color combinations [inspired by Paris]. After having met fifteen in a line on Strandvägen, you get indigestion and keep seeing red hats during the rest of the day' ('Comtesse G.' 1918: 69) On one hand, Comtesse G. states the superiority of French fashion over Swedish, while on the other hand she criticizes Swedish women's subdued attitude to Parisian influences. She critiques Swedish mentality and taste, which is considered less refined, less versatile, and less courageous than the French. It is bound to conformity and yet it suffers from being too easily influenced and without integrity. This corresponds to the rhetoric in contemporary art criticism that constructs Swedish art identity as less wild and audacious than its artistic counterparts and models from abroad (Kollnitz 2008). Swedish modernist discourse on fashion and the arts shows a recurring ambivalence in recommending and appreciating the inspiration by outward influences and simultaneously criticizing a lack of national self-esteem and demarcated national identity.

The promotion of Swedishness in the context of French fashion models can finally be exemplified by comparing two cover illustrations from *Saisonen* (issues 4 and 12 in 1918). The former shows a fashionably dressed and conspicuous young lady sitting in a café by herself. She has shingled, short blond hair contrasted to a widely brimmed black hat and is wearing lipstick that matches her scarlet red dress, a voluminous white fur collar and white gloves. Even though cafés were numerous in Stockholm, the café scenario links to Paris and its public spaces and amusements where the modern fashionable woman could enjoy and stage herself as independent and self-conscious. At the same time, the woman is blonde and thus a Swedish version of an otherwise Parisian or cosmopolitan feminine icon. Still more 'Swedish' appears the fashionable model on the latter cover, which shows her steering a leaning sailing boat in headway movement. The landscape—possibly the archipelago of Stockholm—and the boat—possibly an elegant Swedish skerry cruiser—as well as the 'sailor's' clothing with its practical simplicity and combination of sporty white and bright blue details connote Swedish national identity. While the technique and linear composition of the illustration seem inspired by French fashion illustrators (such as Georges Lepape), the motif is clearly Swedish. Fashionable French elegance is here transformed and translated to Swedish conditions and presents an ideal image of a feminine (yet Nordic), practical, sporty, and nature-loving woman to the Swedish magazine reader.

Fashion as Decadence—Examples from *Strix*, 1916 and 1922

The satirical Swedish magazine *Strix* (1897–1924) puts (French) fashion into a more conspicuous role. *Strix* is focused on class conflicts—a crucial matter in the beginning formation of a social-democratic Swedish identity. These class differences are visualized by contrasting clothing and drawing styles. We find crudely drawn peasant figures in shapeless, simple, 'primitive' clothing where drawing and clothing style interact in creating an image of ugliness and inferiority. Their crudeness becomes still more obvious in combination with representatives of other classes; for example, conservatively dressed bourgeois women as school teachers and upper-class ladies. The conservatism and power position of bourgeois women is connoted not only by their restricted traditional and socially adequate dressing but also by the controlled, rather naturalist and academic style used to depict their identities. Finally, a contrast to both above-mentioned categories is created by a type of woman who can be visually identified by a more modernist graphic style and her conspicuously modern fashionable appearance.

Most striking is the contrast between an old ugly peasant woman with a rather distorted face and in formless clothes visited by her fashionable daughter wearing a modernist gown patterned with huge black circles reminiscent of creations by Sonia Delaunay (*Strix*, 1 November 1922). The two characters are opposed even by their height and age (a short, crouching old woman and a tall, slim young woman) but they reveal their family bonds by having the same nose and profile. This drawing is one of several about the alienation between provincial and urbanized identities within the same family which was a vehement problem in contemporary Swedish society. As Agnés Rocamora shows, contrasts between city and rural areas are common even in the contemporary discourse on Paris which was perceived as the capital of fashion in contrast to the uncultivated 'province' (2009: 9–11). Similarly, Swedish media connected taste, cultivation, and fashionable appearance to city and intellectualism while province and rural population were kept in 'primitive' outsidership, not least expressed by their unfashionable clothing.

Apart from demarcating outrageous clothing patterns and modern extravagancy, as in the example above, the illustrators of *Strix* express the exotic appeal of the fashionable girl or woman by a number of other recurring signifiers. Most obvious is the exaggerated black eye makeup of young waitresses and shop assistants and certain ladies. One drawing shows an extremely black-eyed shop assistant addressed by a stout elderly gentleman who wants to be shown some stockings. The girl lifts her skirts and shows her own legs dressed in aggressively black tights—a gesture connected with sexual invitation that was already present in eighteenth-century fashion culture (*Strix*, 19 April 1916). The 'black eyes' and black hair—not least in combination with black tights hidden under a proper bright dress—give an impression of French physiognomy and Parisian pleasure life: the Swedish shop girl embodies the *Parisienne*. From 1850 onward the figure of the *Parisienne* became an international icon as a woman of exquisite taste, fashionable appeal, and beauty, showing and enjoying herself on the boulevards and in the night life of Paris; she combines upper-class exquisiteness, lower-class practicality, and moral liberty.[8] Jennifer M. Jones emphasizes the 'intrinsic link between fashion, frivolity, Frenchness and femininity' established in the eighteenth century (2004: 2–3). Paris' female inhabitants embodied by the *Parisienne* and its less distinguished counterpart the *grisette* are admired icons; at the same time they warn of female liberty and metropolitan decadence and are as such repeatedly depicted in *Strix*. This link between Swedish city-life and Swedish women showing off their fashionable appearance in public and the *Parisienne* becomes possible not least because the latter was considered a supranational figure, not bound to French citizenship. Any foreign woman might come to Paris and turn into a *Parisienne*. As Agnés Rocamora states, '*La Parisienne* is impervious to borders because Paris itself, according to discourses on the French capital, is borderless, open to all' (2009: 101).

Like Paris and other modern cities, Stockholm had its places of fashionable display. Several caricatures show the waterside promenade of the Strandvägen in one of the richest parts of Stockholm, as a place of forbidden rendezvous between modern fashionable girls and ugly elderly gentlemen (Figure 13:2). The visual contrast in those images consists of extreme silhouettes with tiny waists and seductive poses in the fashionable light-footed girls and their physical opposite, the heavy-limbed elderly upper-class gentleman trying his luck in vain. A more aggressive critique of the fashionable woman and her demoralizing effect on national society is communicated by images showing pairs of women in movement. In extravagant dress and wearing delicate shoes, they quickly and self-consciously move through the city, their conversation is about cheating on their husbands or exchanging their boyfriends for superficial reasons (*Strix*, 30 August 1916). One recurring marker of contrast is shoes: the unrealistically slight, high-heeled female shoes that can hardly be expected to provide support for walking and the broad, formless, but solid shoes of the traditional male provide one of the most striking examples of a critique of modernity that is strongly connected to physical characteristics. These physical characteristics and practices metaphorize modern flux, lightness, and fickleness against traditionalist stability and stagnation.

Another example of modern unpredictability and movement is the ridiculously overdressed mother giving advice to her elegant daughter who is about to travel to Stockholm. In their conversation the word 'change' simultaneously connotes change of trains, change of partners, and change of clothes (*Strix*, 10 May 1916). One new woman's quick exchange of partners is metaphorically connected to the equally female habit of quickly and superficially changing a fashionable outfit. Feminine unreliability expressed through fashion and fashionable manners makes one of the main messages in this series of recurring images, but their meaning is more than just a comment on modern women. It is about national insecurity under the impact of modern influences, metaphorically connected to the rise of the emancipated new woman and the dangers of speedy changeability expressed through excessive and ruthless

Figure 13:2. Caricature, *Strix* (5 July 1916).

fashion consumption. National authenticity is at stake. The matter is dealt with still more sharply and sarcastically in the context of fashionable and thus superficial male citizens. Those occur repeatedly in the shape of young men depicted as indecent upstarts robbing the elder generation of their money and pretending to be superior. Thus there are several versions of conspicuously dressed and silhouetted young men from the aristocracy showing off not only their modern style but also their stupidity on the promenade of Strandvägen (*Strix*, 22 February 1922). For example, one pair of aristocratic friends stands watching a ship at the pier and sincerely wonders: 'How in heaven have they managed to push the anchor through that tiny hole?' Modern style and vanity are expressed by suits with marked waists and extensive coat-skirts. Shiny waxed hair, sometimes with decoratively formed whiskers, shows under small promenade straw hats. Most conspicuous though are the high-heeled shoes many of the men wear. Not only do the men's feet mirror those of their female counterparts, but they also contribute to a very affected body pose: producing a pushed out stomach and a sway-back that is still more emphasized by the coat-skirts. Even in the performances of decadent male populations, superficial character and sexually seductive aspects of urban fashion play the part of morally undermining socially destructive forces.[9]

However, a final observation demonstrates a crucial ambivalence inherent in the fashion discourse constructed in *Strix*: while the modern woman and her fashion seem to endanger the status quo and undermine conservative national virtues, they simultaneously enhance the beauty and validity of Stockholm as a growing cultural metropolis with continental habits. Fashion as a cultural quality marker is evident in illustrations of beautifully dressed 'Parisian' girls that accompany sentimental poems called 'Chansonette', 'Papillon Bleu', etc. (*Strix*, 21 March 1917). Thus the imagery in *Strix* presents and emphasizes the beauty of French aesthetics while elsewhere warning about its decadent effects on Swedish morals.

Germans and '*Parisiennes*'—Examples from *Jugend*, 1900

An ambivalence in the experience of modern and Frenchified fashionable women and men is also evident in the German magazines *Jugend (Youth)* (1896–1940) and *Simplicissimus* (1896–1944), both published in Munich. German cultural-political relations to France were more aggressive and oppositional compared to Sweden's generally quite affirmative gaze at France as a style-model. Although a stylistic model in art and fashion during long periods of German cultural history, France became enemy to Germany in the Franco-Prussian War (1870–71) and even more so after World War I. By then the German cultural elite became seriously involved in the national project and focused on a German identity rather than French superficial beauty.[10] In 1900 though, French and Parisian culture were still admired as they promised modernity and renewal, ideals that mirrored the ambitions of *Jugend*.

In *Jugend*, symbolist and naturalist images from German nature and culture, such as idyllic Alp landscapes and Germanic mythological heroes, intermingle with more modern Impressionist drawings of metropolitan Parisian life and leave an amazingly manifold visual impact. Romantic drawings of 'innocent' German youths dressed in simple, timeless clothing— as a dreaming young girl leaning against a tree or a shepherd boy lying in the grass—are often directly followed by so called 'Parisian images', a *feuilleton* of far more dynamic drawings presenting contemporary Paris and its pleasure life (*Jugend* 35 [1900]: 589f; *Jugend* 36 [1900]: cover and 605). Those drawings with titles like 'Champs Elysées', 'Jardin de Paris', or just 'Parisian images', can be interpreted as a visual reportage of 'what's going on' in Paris.[11] 'Paris' is presented as an obvious icon of modernity and expressed by predominantly *Parisiennes* in fashionable dress and elegant makeup, often suggesting their belonging to the demi-monde.[12] In 'Jardin de Paris' three Parisian ladies of doubtful profession gaze at the spectator in an alluring way. All three are wearing voluminous hats and heavy eye makeup. Two of them grasp the cloth of their fashionable dresses, thereby emphasizing the form of their hips and exposing their legs and high-heeled shoes. Their lavish clothing has the contrasting colors of white and black, combined with scarlet red details. Though exotic and seductive, these

Paul Rieth (München

Wespentaille

„Woaßt, Hias, mir derfts net g'hör'n, mir bleibats in de Händ'!"

Figure 13:3. 'The Wasp Waist', Caricature, *Jugend* 31 (1900).

women emanate a notion of aggressiveness and menace—not least as they are directly shown after the image of a shepherd boy with closed eyes playing his little flute on a peaceful Alp meadow full of sleeping sheep. In accordance with the role of Paris as the internationally known 'city of pleasure' during most of the nineteenth century, *Jugend* puts the modernity, fashions, and dynamic lifestyle of Paris into an almost romanticizing but also disturbing contrast to the nature, traditions, and people of provincial Bavaria and Munich (Rocamora 2009: 18f). Parisian ways, women, and fashion definitely play the role of the 'Other' but are included in the modern and national spirit of 'life' that *Jugend* seeks for its readers.

Contrasts between modernity and tradition become more ambivalent in the magazine's caricatures. In 'The Wasp Waist' two peasants in typical South-German folk costume (short leather trousers and feathered hats) gaze at a fashionable lady who is passing by quickly. Reacting to her tiny corseted waist one of them says: 'If she were mine, I would keep her in my hand' (Figure 13.3). The question is who we are to laugh at: the provincial peasants keeping to their old-fashioned views on women as property and unfamiliar with modern values or the extravagance and unnatural dress of the modern woman that deforms the laws of nature and tradition. Again city and province are opposed by the means of contrasting dress and physiognomic types. The passing woman can be interpreted as a German counterpart to the Parisian *passante de mode*, a fashionable passer-by in the streets of Paris and a romanticized fugitive female version of the male *flâneur*. She connoted unavailability and the poetry of the modern elusive beauty, especially when shown from behind as is done in the caricature in *Jugend* (Rocamora 2009: 129-35). The caricature's title, furthermore, indicates the aggressiveness connoted by the image of a wasp as analogy to the modern fashionable woman. Another drawing with an ambiguous message shows a slim, fashionable lady gazing at a stout peasant woman in folk costume: when she comments on the peasant's 'breast and awful hips', her male partner insinuates that she is just envious (*Jugend* 41 [1900]). Both of these images contrast fashion and traditional clothing, and they also oppose two body types which are of metaphorical significance for the nation: a modern/cosmopolitan/unnatural body connoting affectation and artificiality and a traditional/national/natural body, less beautiful but stronger, healthier and—presumably—more motherly.

French Fashion as National Danger—Examples from *Simplicissimus*, 1921

The image of women and their (French) fashions carried a still more striking national importance in the sarcastic caricatures appearing in *Simplicissimus* in the 1920s. At this time Germany was suffering from the economic misery caused by the excessive financial burden placed on it by the treaty of Versailles (1919), which had ended World War I. Germany was ordered to pay reparations to the victorious Entente nations, including France, which laid the groundwork for continued German hostility toward France. One highly dramatic and aggressive example is a cover which says 'Off with French Luxury!' (*Simplicissimus* 11 [1921]). The image shows a muscular, blonde German man in simple grey workers' clothes kicking a black-haired, elegantly dressed woman carrying a pile of French luxury products. The French woman's tiny pointed feet and shoes are high up in the air while the brutal male's comparatively large feet, in their clumsy shoes, both kick her bottom and meet the ground. The printed sub-text reads: 'We have our own liquor to drown our worries'. Antagonism between the sexes is a powerful rhetorical trope and consistently repeated in the political and cultural debate concerning German-French relationships from the nineteenth century to the 1930s. Germanic virility and seriousness is opposed to French or Latin feminine weakness and disposition for superficial, purely sensual concerns.[13] In the above-mentioned drawing, the feminine image of France as a national disturbance is still more confirmed by the connection to French fashion and luxury products undermining German values and economic national strength.

Reconsidering the image presented at the chapter's beginning, (French) fashion and its destructive potential become strikingly obvious in the cover to *Simplicissimus*'s special issue

Figure 13:4. Cover, *Simplicissimus* (9 November 1921).

on fashion (Figure 13:4). Though not outspoken, the 'devil of fashion' could be interpreted as French and when looking into this issue dedicated to fashion we find more hints and complaints on the French. A caricature called 'Terrible!' ridicules German women in desperation because of the interrupted import of French fashion to Germany.[14] On the opposite page, a drawing labeled 'Money Hyenas' shows two bony women desperately exploiting a fashion boutique. In the subtext, the readers are told that Germany is an ideal country because '[t]he fashion is French, the textiles English and the prices are heavenly'. The bitter irony in this statement is directed at the weakness and lack of integrity that makes the Germans blindly open to all sorts of influences from abroad. German women's consumption of international and imported fashion is linked to superficial and hysterical behavior far from political responsibility and with tendencies which weaken the national forces.

Conclusion

My analysis of fashion-related images and texts in Swedish and German cultural magazines from 1900 to 1922 reveals the importance of fashion as part of an ideologically charged visual culture. In *Saisonen* French fashion is considered a model as well as an oppositional 'Other' to Swedish fashion and identity. In *Strix*, *Jugend*, and *Simplicissimus* satirical figures of modern, conspicuously dressed women during and after World War I can be interpreted as tools in a war *against* women enacted on the visual and conceptual premises of fashion. Those women and their fashionable physiognomy are furthermore used as metaphors for a perceived feminine aesthetics which both weakens and simultaneously ennobles the nation and its culture. In Swedish and in German discourse, fashion—embodied by (foreign) women and less often men—plays the part of a both seductive and aggressive force antagonizing tradition, political integrity, and national economy. But while obviously endangering an ideal of firm and autonomous national identities, French fashion and fashion as such are also evaluated as enhancing the beauty and refinement of national cultures. Foreign fashion influences are perceived as both distorting and inspiring aesthetical production and the aesthetical self-performance of national societies on their way into modern life.

References

Anderson, Benedict (1991), *Imagined Communities: Reflections on the Origins and Spread of Nationalism*, London: Verso.

Breward, Christopher (1994), *The Culture of Fashion: A New History of Fashionable Dress*. Manchester: Manchester University Press.

Bushart, Magdalena (1990), *Der Geist der Gotik und die expressionistische Kunst*, München: Schreiber.

'Comtesse G.' (1916), 'The First Spring Fashions', *Saisonen*, 1, pp. 11–15.

Facos, Michelle and Hirsh, Sharon L., eds (2003), *Art, Culture and National Identity in Fin-de-Siècle Europe*, New York: Cambridge University Press.

Holleczek, Andreas and Meyer, Andrea, eds (2004), *Französische Kunst, deutsche Perspektiven, 1870–1945. Quellen und Kommentare zur Kunstkritik*, Berlin: Akademie Verlag.

Jones, Jennifer M. (2004), *Sexing la Mode: Gender, Fashion and Commercial Culture in Old Regime France*. Oxford, New York: Berg.

Kollnitz, Andrea (2008), *Konstens nationella identitet. Om tysk och österrikisk modernism i svensk konstkritik 1908–1934*, Stockholm: Drau förlag.

McNeil, Peter (2005), 'The Art and Science of Walking: Gender, Space and the Fashionable Body in the Long Eighteenth Century', *Fashion Theory: The Journal of Dress, Body & Culture*, 9.2, pp. 175–204.

Rangström, Lena (2008), *Lions of Fashion: Male Fashion of the 16th, 17th, 18th Centuries*, Stockholm: Livrustkammaren Atlantis.

Rasche, Adelheid and Wolter, Gundula (2003), *Ridikül! Mode in der Karikatur 1600–1900*, Berlin und Köln: SMB-DuMont.

Ribeiro, Aileen (1984), *Dress in Eighteenth-Century Europe, 1715–1789*, London: Batsford.

—— (2003), *Dress and Morality*, London, New York: Berg.

—— (2005), *Fashion and Fiction: Dress in Art and Literature in Stuart England*, New Haven, CT: Yale University Press.

Riegl, Alois (1901), 'Kunstwollen', in *Die spätrömische Kunstindustrie nach den Funden in Österreich-Ungarn*, Wien: Österr. archäologisches Institut.

Rocamora, Agnés (2009), *Fashioning the City: Paris, Fashion and the Media*, New York: I.B. Tauris.

Romdahl, Axel L. (1914), 'Konsten på Baltiska utställningen II. Utländsk konst', *Göteborgs Handels- och Sjöfartstidning*, 25 May.

Smith, Anthony D. (1994), *National Identity*, Reno: University of Nevada Press.

Steele, Valerie (1988), *Paris Fashion: A Cultural History*, New York: Oxford University Press.

Stern, Radu (1992), *Against Fashion: Clothing as Art, 1850–1930*, Cambridge, MA: MIT Press.

Vinken, Barbara (2005), *Fashion Zeitgeist: Trends and Cycles in the Fashion System*, Oxford: Berg.

Wölfflin, Heinrich ([1929] 1932), *Principles of Art History: The Problem of the Development of Styles in Later Art*, New York.

Notes

1 On the impact of cultural production on the nation and its 'imagined community' see. e.g., Anderson (1991), Smith (1994), and Facos and Hirsh (2003).

2 Classical concepts constructing geographical polarizations in art history are, e.g., Riegl (1901) or Wölfflin ([1929] 1932).

3 For a historical survey of these interrelations see, e.g., Breward (1994) and Ribeiro (1984).

4 Barbara Vinken (2005) claims this shift from fashion as a platform of class conflict to fashion as an arena of gender-conflict. See chapter 1, 'What Fashion Strictly Divided'.

5 Modernist art is strongly connected with fashion, concerning the fashion-design created by artists, the total artworks of, e.g., Kandinsky and the Ballet Russes in Paris and its dependency on modernist costumes and the common aesthetic theories advancing abstraction and other visual modernist innovations (e.g.. the art of Sonia Delaunay). See, e.g., Stern (1992).

6 All translations from Swedish and German to English are my own.

7 The polarization between French and English can already be found in the antithetical relationship between seventeenth-century British masculine Puritans or 'Roundheads', with their shaved heads, and the morally suspect and ostentatious 'Cavaliers', with their curly wigs and feminine attributes influenced by French fashion. See Ribeiro (2005), chapter 3 'Sermonizing Dress'. After the French Revolution, the English textile industry was permanently identified with the production of highly qualified male fashion and became an indicator of a sober, practical, and controlled style, as opposed to the exaggerated elegance of French fashion.

8 On the *Parisienne* see Steele (1988), pp. 68–75. In particular, the figure of the '*grisette*', a Parisian working-class girl romanticized in French literature and art in the late nineteenth century, fits into the image of black-eyed women and girls depicted in the Swedish magazine *Strix*.

9 French fashion was considered an effeminate and endangering force even earlier in Swedish history, when the Swedish court was accused of over-consuming outlandish French fashion and thereby weakening its virility. See Rangsström (2008).

10 On antithetical constructions of German versus French national character in German art discourse, see Holleczek and Meyer (2004).

11 Paris as a source of novelty is iconic in art discourse that often describes Paris as 'the source of new art'.

12 On the significance of the demi-monde for fashion and its revolutionary potential, see Vinken (2005), p. 17.

13 Not least is German art-critical rhetoric that developed during and after World War I, which used those antitheses to demarcate German art and expressionism as 'stronger' than French. See, e.g., Holleczek and Meyer (2004) and Bushart (1990).

14 The German fashion system and its fight for national integrity during the early twentieth century is discussed in Stern (1992).

Chapter 14

Rome: Eternal City of Fashion and Film

Eugenia Paulicelli

After World War II, the city of Rome experienced a cultural rebirth. Images of destruction were almost as they had appeared in the film *Roma città aperta/Rome Open City* (Rossellini, 1945). Rome reconstructed itself, once again becoming a cultural destination of choice. As an intrinsic aspect of this cultural reimagining, fashion had a great impact in constructing and reshaping postwar Rome.

It was through the marriage of fashion and cinema that Rome began to project an image of glamour, art, and beauty. Italy's reconstruction, and especially the status that Rome acquired as a fashion city, were facilitated by the movie industry and the presence of the Cinecittà Studios. Later, the crucial 1950s and 1960s—years of the postwar 'economic miracle'—were defining times for the Italian capital in the larger global economy (Crainz 2005a). The identity of Rome was also shaped through American mediation; in this process, popular culture, fashion, film, photography, and tourism played crucial roles.

Fashion was then in the forefront in telling the complex story of how different systems of cultural mediation (film, journalism, art, architecture, etc.) made critical contributions to our understanding of cities. More importantly, it is vital to evaluate the complex mechanisms by which a city is textualized in different discourses, whether geographical, imaginary, or touristic. In her 2009 book, *Fashioning the City: Paris, Fashion and the Media*, which explored the mechanisms supporting the image of Paris as a fashion city, Agnès Rocamora emphasized the importance of both the imaginary and the lived dimensions of the city (Rocamora 2009: 123; Breward 2004).

The present article sets out to unravel the fabric that constitutes Rome as a fashion city, and the perception of its haptic and optical dimensions through cinema. Fashion has an important role in the process of modernization during periods of great cultural, political, and economic transformation. Recent scholarship has been crucial for a critical and deeper understanding of fashion and its 'many direct points of contact with the study of a city' (Gilbert 2006: 6).

In the context of fashion, Rome was not the sole competitor in the race to be considered capital of style. Competition with other fashion cities, most notably Florence, was rife. After World War II, before Rome and Milan had established themselves as centers of fashion, it was from Florence that Italian fashion had been launched nationally and internationally. In addition, Turin could boast an important first: that of being Italy's first fashion capital during the fascist regime. It was in Turin that the biannual fashion shows were established around 1932 (Paulicelli 2004). Despite the fascist regime promoting hatred toward France, Italy's fashion capital was located geographically and culturally close to Paris—the world fashion capital. After World War II, Florence became Italy's fashion capital in 1951 with the 'Sala Bianca' shows. After Florence, it was Rome—the 'Eternal City'—which became the center for *alta moda*—high fashion. With its significance couched in a history clearly visible in its architecture and style, Rome became the theater on whose stage some of the most influential images of Italian style and *la dolce vita*—the sweet life—were forged and transmitted to the world via the powerful medium of global cinema.

Rome, then, will be considered as a city and as a trope that came into being during the boom years following World War II. David Gilbert, paraphrasing the geographer John Agnew, has noted that fashion takes an active role in 'spatialising the world—dividing, labeling and sorting it into a hierarchy of places of greater or `lesser' importance' (Agnew 1998: 2; quoted in Gilbert 2006). Although Agnew is writing about the present, the principle he elaborates holds good for several historical periods, and identifies why and how fashion contributes to the weaving of the narrative and identity of a city. This mechanism has become especially visible in the last twenty years, as fashion has become increasingly powerful. The high visibility enjoyed by fashion designers, brands, spokespeople, celebrities, and fashion events—where new collections are presented—all emphasize the seductive quality of fashion, as well as its role as a motor of economic growth (Zukin 1996: 13). The notion of being a 'fashion city' has become a competition between cities that seek to gain visibility in the geography of consumption and tourism through their 'cultural industries' (Gilbert 2006). Because of the digital revolution, the importance of this process has accelerated and reached global recognition. The mechanism of fashion as a driver of the economy manifests itself in different historical phases and comes to the fore during the periodic processes of modernization or great transformations of nations, as was the case for Italy during the economic boom of the 1960s. These years also witnessed a shift in cinematic and aesthetic ideals. It is for these reasons that 'multiple modernities' can be observed within the narrative of Rome.

David Harvey identifies fashion as one of the strongest vehicles through which cities acquire a mark of distinction that is, in turn, transformed into capital that attracts tourism and other business (Harvey 2001). Following Harvey's theory, we see that it was in the postwar boom that Rome gained a great deal of 'symbolic capital'. Rome has played a crucial role in the foundational myths of the Italian nation. It has been vital to a Eurocentric vision of the world where Christianity is seen as a superior form of religion and civilization. Rome has occupied a special place in both Italian and global history since the days of the ancient Roman Empire. For Old Europe, Rome had represented the *'fulcro metafisico'* ('metaphysical fulcrum' [Sloterdijk 2002: 163]). Rome was seen as a site of 'universal history', a narrative that has been retold in different historical epochs. For instance, Mussolini invoked ancient Rome in his propaganda to legitimize his Fascist regime. Rome and its images have also grown in the experiences and memories of many travelers and visitors.

The new Italian identity that emerged from the postwar boom, as well as the emergence of Rome as capital of chic, was epitomized most tellingly and memorably by Federico Fellini's

1960 film *La Dolce Vita*. Fellini's film is a frequent starting point when considering Italian style. Today, a glance at the sales catalogue of many high-end American department stores demonstrates that Italian style is still subject to the tropes explored by Fellini in *La Dolce Vita*. Despite Milan's status as the global fashion city, which emerged in the late 1970s and 1980s, Rome is still seen as the place for *alta moda*, high fashion, in contrast to the *pret-à-porter* (ready-to-wear) aesthetic of Milan. The competition, however, among Italian cities for the mark of distinction as fashion capital is still fierce and ongoing.

The aforementioned Sala Bianca fashion show was the initiative of Giovani Battista Giorgini, who in 1951 gathered Italian couturiers and journalists, along with American and European buyers from prominent department stores, and launched Italian fashion on the global scene. The show took place in Florence, but in keeping with its image as cultural capital of the country—or indeed, the world—most of the designers and fashion houses that showed there were based in Rome. Giorgini was well aware of the richness, beauty, and attractiveness of Florence, the quintessential Renaissance city so loved by foreign visitors; he therefore organized several parties following the shows, staged so as to emphasize the splendor of the past and the city's architecture. An example was the party organized at Palazzo Vecchio on 25 January 1953, in which Giorgini evoked the wedding of Eleonora di Toledo and Cosimo de Medici in 1539. For the foreign press and buyers, Florence—and Italy with it—became an unforgettable sartorial, cultural, and personal experience of the type so often romanticized in literature and cinema. Wearing Italian, especially Roman, fashion meant wearing Italy's culture, its breathtaking artistic heritage; or, in other words, wearing and embracing the country and its unique and beautiful cities.

In the early 1950s, along with women's fashion, men's fashion—whose sartorial elegance was epitomized by Brioni's 'Roman style'—was also presented at the Sala Bianca. Launched as a brand in 1952, Brioni's 'Roman style' was, in the early 1960s, given even greater exposure by the continental suit that had already launched in the late 1950s, as illustrated by Marcello Mastroianni in *La Dolce Vita* (Reich 2004). Italy has had an important role in tailoring men's fashion the world over, following a well-established sartorial male tradition in Naples, Milan, and especially Rome. The Neapolitan suit was to make a sartorial revolution insofar as its cut had the effect of softening the male jacket, as has been vividly exemplified in a recent documentary *O'Mast*, made by Gianluca Migliarotti in 2011.

It was the encounter between Italy and the United States that launched Italian fashion on a global scale, and it was cinema that provided the fashion industry with a high enough profile, an increasingly international shop window, for promoting and publicizing Italian designers' creations to the world.

This had been the case since the early 1950s, albeit on a smaller scale. In Rossellini's *Viaggio in Italia/Voyage to Italy* (Rossellini, 1953), Ingrid Bergman's wardrobe—and star persona—were refashioned and glamorized in the Roman couture style by the Rome-based Fernanda Gattinoni fashion house. Hers was one of the *maisons*—houses—that, along with that of the Fontana Sisters, was already in place immediately after the war. The artisanal know-how of Italian fashion couture as displayed in the creations of Brioni, Simonetta, the Fontana Sisters, Fabiani, Galitizine, Shubert, and others found its industrial channel in the United States. The skills and bravura of the American ready-to-wear industry were well known, as was the talent of the industry in adapting and translating European aesthetics and styles into American terms. Italian fashion was particularly welcome because it effortlessly combined elegance, color, and sophistication with ease and comfort. For instance, in 1960, Emilio Pucci was celebrated for shirts and clothes that were ideal for traveling: they were easy to pack and resistant to wrinkles. The May 1960 issue of *Harper's Bazaar* reported that Pucci's 'miraculous packable silk jersey only takes up the space of a handkerchief in a travel case and never needs to be ironed' (Anon 1960: 15).

Since the end of World War II, Americans, including those involved in the film industry, spent more and more time in Italy—especially Rome—filming in the Cinecittà Studios and transforming the city into what became known as 'Hollywood on the Tiber'. Fashion houses such as the Fontana Sisters (located in Piazza di Spagna) and Fernanda Gattinoni (near Via Veneto and strategically close to the American embassy and Rome's nightlife) were instrumental in establishing the relationship between glamour, cinema, and the city. The Hollywood stars populated the Roman fashion houses not only because this is where they got the costumes used in their films, but also because they had discovered that Italian couture was elegant and stylish (Figure 14:2). Above all, their ateliers were a uniquely warm and friendly environment. Micol Fontana recalled that the *salotti da prova*—fitting rooms—were like intimate parlors, where stars chatted about their personal lives while being fitted for their outfits. The process of making a dress was also an occasion for personal conversations between dressmaker and client (Personal interview with author, 2000; Cimagalli 1991).

This casual warmth often meant knowing the secrets of the body shapes and measurements of the stars, even while fashioning their public image and style. This is also another important and affective side of fashion and its relationship with embodiment. The Fontana Sisters, for example, made Linda Christian's wedding dress when she married Tyrone Power in Rome in 1949—a dress that became famous worldwide after featuring on the cover of *Life* magazine. In fact, the Fontana Sisters claimed both that the idea of the label 'made in Italy' was glamorous and that their international fashion fame truly began when the Hollywood star advertised their creations in the media and popular press. The same happened for male fashion and lifted the fortunes of Roman tailors, such as Brioni and Caraceni, who dressed Tyrone Power for his wedding. Italian fashion designers capitalized on the fame and glamour of their clients—American Hollywood stars such as Audrey Hepburn, Ingrid Bergman (Figure 14:3), Ava Gardner (Figure 14:1), Gregory Peck, and Cary Grant—and used them as vehicles to elevate the increasingly international status of Italian fashion.

The Fontana Sisters created a dress called 'Roma antica' ('ancient Rome') for Ava Gardner, one of the American ambassadors of Italian fashion who was invited to Grace Kelly's wedding in 1956. The increasingly hegemonic role played by Rome and the city's designers in the dictating of what was fashionable also led to changes in men's fashion. In fact, a different image of masculinity was taking shape, thanks to a suit that was gradually softening its armor-like stiff edges, instead embracing the body with soft fabrics and sartorial fineness of detail. Several examples can be seen in the cinema of the period.

The 1950s and 1960s were a vibrant time to be in Rome. The city was a magnet that attracted both foreign and Italian filmmakers, a locus of a creativity that revitalized design, fashion, and the arts in general. Rome as a city—and as an idea—became an ongoing 'dream spectacle', a promised land for visitors from abroad and from the Italian provinces who hoped to play a part on the city's stage. These characters can be seen in Fellini's movies, where costume plays a key role in the process of fashioning and doubling, and in the *mise-en-abyme* of identity.

In *Lo sceicco bianco/The White Sheik* (Fellini, 1951), Fellini proves to be ahead of his time by grasping the impact of a growing media culture and the effect *fotoromanzo* (comic-strip story) characters have on provincial young women like Wanda, the protagonist of the film. The *fotoromanzo* was a romantic type of literature that appeared in 1947 and enjoyed a huge boom during the 1950s and 1960s. The protagonists, often women of modest means, followed their dreams and fantasy that, for the most part, involved the pursuit of a male protagonist. Fellini's Wanda represents the quintessential reader of *fotoromanzi*. She goes to Rome on her honeymoon, but instead of spending time with her husband, a banal, petit-bourgeois, provincial stereotype, she seeks out her real hero, a character in the *fotoromanzo* she avidly devours each week: the White Sheik (played by Alberto Sordi). Wanda is offered a role in the making of the latest *fotoromanzo*, dresses in exotic costumes, and ends up playing the part of the Sheik's love-slave. Parallel to Wanda's search for a world of fantasy is her husband Ivan's quest to maintain a façade of bourgeois respectability and participate in the ritual audience of newly married couples with the Pope. In *The White Sheik*, Fellini focuses on the nuances and meanings of dress in its emotional and social impact, relating it to the world of appearances, rituals, and religion, all the time blurring the boundary of the sacred and the profane. Later, in *La Dolce Vita* (1960), Fellini has Sylvia (Anita Ekberg), who is visiting the city, dress in a priest-like outfit (an idea Fellini got from the Fontana Sisters' 1955–56 winter collection, the '*pretino*' that was worn by Ava Gardner. Elsewhere in *La Dolce Vita*, Fellini treats 'religious miracles' as media events and as pretexts for the fabrication of new heroes. In both their theatrical and everyday rituals, dress and appearance in *The White Sheik* tell the story of the development of a new Italian identity, suspended somewhere between fantasy and glamour on the one hand, and petit-bourgeois hypocrisy and decorum on the other. The final shot sequence of *The White Sheik*, centered on the dress etiquette for papal audiences, is emblematic. The detail of the black tulle *veletta* (veil), a customary accessory for women in the presence of the Pope, underlines the petit-bourgeois masquerade of the newly married couple.

In the Rome of the postwar boom years, fashion and film found the ideal place to focus their 'magnifying lens' on reality. Similar to the process described by Rohdie in his comments

Figure 14:1. Ava Gardner, American actress. Rome, 10 December 1953. Photographer Giuseppe Palmas, Courtesy of Roberto Palmas and the Guiseppe Palmas Photographic Archive.

on Fellini's work, it is the process of that lens's 'deformation' that helps to emphasize the representation as opposed to simply its form. Images can be seen as 'forms that, like grammar, are machines for the production of whatever utterances' (Rohdie 2002: 115). Fashion and film are powerful mechanisms that communicate meanings and emotions, each drawing sustenance and power from the other. As fashion historian Christopher Breward posits, 'if fashion can be said to be cinematic in its social and visual effects, then cinema is also

Figure 14:2. Sophia Loren, Italian actress, Frederico Emilio Schuberth, Italian fashion designer. Rome, 6 June 1955. Courtesy of Roberto Palmas. Giuseppe Palmas Photographic Archive.

very clearly a primary product of the aesthetic and technological processes of "fashioning"' (Breward 2004: 132).

This idea of place and its imaginary stories, theatricality and performance are particularly evident in a 1961 photo shoot called *Rome Loves Ford/Ford Loves Rome*, published in the American *Harper's Bazaar*. Here the two Rome-based fashion houses of Fontana and Gattinoni are represented, along with two red suits in which the color red is associated with Rome—an early edition of the 'Valentino Red' of more recent years. The models are two Roman aristocrats described in the captions. The Fontana Sisters' 'easy suit decision' and Gattinoni's buttonless jacket over a pink satin blouse matching the jacket's lining were copied by David Crystal for the Saks department store in New York City.

It is even more significant, in terms of these mechanisms for fashioning identity, to consider Rome in 1960, the first year the modern Olympic Games were held in the city. The Olympic Games projected a modern and appealing image of Rome as an emerging

Figure 14:3. Ingrid Bergman, Svedish actress - Rome, 14 April 1956. Courtesy of Roberto Palmas. Giuseppe Palmas Photographic Archive.

city where a newly gained modernity co-existed with a classical past. The Games were a global event that exported an image of Italy and Italian fashion to the American market. In the same year of the Olympic Games, Emilio Schuberth opened his new atelier in Rome, (Figure 14:4) and Princess Irene Galitzine (Figure 14.5) launched her 'pigiama palazzo' style. American photographer William Klein's book—*Rome + Klein*—contains a photo shoot of a party that was set up by American *Vogue* to celebrate Galitizine's collection of 'Palazzo pyjamas.' In his sarcastic commentary accompanying the photos, Klein notes the cachet of

Figure 14:4. Anna Magnani, Italian actress, Frederico Emilio Schuberth, Italian fashion designer, Rome 28 March 1960, Schuberth boutique opening. Courtesy of Roberto Palmas. Giuseppe Palmas Photographic Archive.

Roman aristocracy at the launch of a sophisticated and seductive Italian look that again went hand in hand with the city's architecture: beautiful palazzi and gardens. The neologism—pigiama palazzo—created to launch Galitizine's alternative evening wear evokes the place for beautiful glamorous parties taking place in 'palaces':

> Present are several authentic noblemen and women, among them on the left, la principessa herself.... But that was not enough, we needed at least a duke or two, a marquis, a viscount, and other patricians. Where to get them? Cinecittà was not far away so central casting could help us out. (Klein 2009: 46)

Klein's fashion photographs, which he describes as 'almost private jokes', were able to capture the playful side of fashion and costume and marry it to what Rome as a city and a stage had to offer. In the section 'moda' ('fashion'), the author comments: 'A Roman composite: classic architecture (a Titian or something), a waiter delivering coffee, and top model, Simone Daillencourt, striding in a Capucci dress. What more could you ask for?' (Klein 2009: 45). This photograph epitomizes the different ingredients that make Rome unique and appealing to the international eye. Much like Fellini, whom he visited in Rome, Klein calls attention to the very form of photography while reinventing the art of fashion photography. In focusing on certain details, bringing together the city and its settings, passers-by, models, nuns and priests, writers and artists, true and fake aristocrats, he calls on the ability of the image to 'magnify' reality. This is what Rohdie describes as happening in Fellini's films. In his essay on the obvious and the obtuse, Barthes explores this concept further. In the essay, Barthes distinguishes the 'obvious meaning' of a sign (which responds to the logic of communication or the 'simple' act of decoding a message) from its 'obtuse meaning' (Barthes 1985: 54–55). Barthes relates the obtuse meaning to the notion of *sens supplementaire*, which gives an imaginative openness to any kind of text, visual or verbal. In this vein, Klein also commented on how the interplay of images produces an excess of meaning (Barthes's 'obtuse') that takes the viewer elsewhere, allowing them to migrate and to make new associations—*sens supplementaire*—in which other images and meanings are encountered. As a result, the boundaries of the image are called into question, while fantasy and dreams are triggered through processes analogous to those in fashion. This idea captures the fundamentals of the changing times, the many faces of Rome, and, above all, its theatricality: Rome as a stage setting is as real as the 'real' Rome.

The culmination of pastiche, bricolage, and excess of this process can be seen in Fellini's film *Roma* (1972). Throughout the film, Rome appears as an incredible costume parade where the ghosts of the past, and especially those of Fascist Italy, punctuate the story and the myths of the present. Borrowing from Marx's 1852 pamphlet *The Eighteenth Brumaire of Louis Bonaparte*, as elaborated in Walter Benjamin's theory of history, we may say that 'the specters of history' in Fellini's *Roma* come back like a Freudian return of the repressed—all dressed up in self-parading garb. In the beginning of *The Eighteenth Brumaire*, Marx refers to the idea of repetition in history:

Hegel says somewhere that, upon the stage of universal history, all great events and personalities reappear in one fashion or another. He forgot to add that, on the first occasion, they appear as tragedy; on the second, as *farce*.... Thus did the revolution of 1789–1814, drape itself successively as the Roman Republic and the Roman Empire; and thus was it that the revolution of 1848 could find nothing better to do than to parody by turns 1789 and the revolutionary traditions of 1793–1795. (Marx 1926: 23–24, emphasis added)

Figure 14:5. Irene Galitzine, princess and fashion designer, Rome, 5 November 1960. Courtesy of Roberto Palmas. Giuseppe Palmas Photographic Archive.

Fellini's *Roma* exemplifies, in cinematic terms, this complex mechanism of citation of the past—a mechanism that is also inherent in fashion. The tragedies of Italy's Fascist past reappear in Fellini's film, refashioned as grotesque farce. Benjamin, writing in the late 1930s in the midst of the triumph of Nazi Fascism in Europe, elaborated on Marx's notion of history in connecting his 'theses on the philosophy of history' with his commentary on fashion with its 'tiger's leap' in the *Arcades Project*: 'The French Revolution…evoked ancient Rome the way fashion evokes costumes of the past. Fashion has a flair for the topical, no matter where it stirs in the tickets of long ago; it is a tiger's leap into the past' (Benjamin 1999:263). In Fellini's *Roma*, there is a conflation of both these theories: through the grotesque and the excessive, Rome as a dream, spectacle, and a trope engender an explosion. The revolutionary trace is cinematic language and the language of clothing is masquerade. Both visually and theoretically, the fashion shows in Fellini's films, *Roma* in particular, are precursors of the extreme fashion shows by Alexander McQueen and John Galliano, with all their distinct features of contradiction, sickness, beauty, excess, and the clownesque. With these comes fragility; the ephemeral nature of the 'now' time in fashion—not to mention the ineluctability of death (Evans 2003).

In Fellini's *Roma*, the apotheosis of this aesthetic process can be found in the ecclesiastical fashion catwalk, an episode tellingly situated between the whores' fashion parade in the Fascist brothel and '*the festa of noiatri*' (the feast of us all). A sense of death and decay is present in the ecclesiastical fashion show, where parody reaches its highest degree. In the fashion show, elements of theatricality, intricate dress, color, and texture, typically associated with the elaborate rituals of the Catholic Church, are revisited with a surrealistic turn. At the same time, the fashion show, a variation on the cinematic, conveys a haptic and optical experience of clothing and fabric replete with silk, laces, light hats and veils, exquisite attention to detail and workmanship, crystals, beading, glitter, and sequins that cover the bodies of the unusual models. Before the rapt audience, the Pope himself appears on the catwalk at the end of the show. The human models become machines, robotic forms by which clothes walk by themselves, empty of human bodies. Costumes become independent forms, images, where dressing up calls attention to the very process of illusionism, distortion and representation that are an integral part of reality and its construction. The ecclesiastical fashion show, set in Rome and performed by Roman representative of both Church and aristocracy, ultimately erodes the separation between audience and spectacle. It corrodes the borders of image and identity, self and otherness. Indeed, as Rohdie notes:

Fellinian images are at a border between desire and reality, the subjective and the objective. They seem to be reflected, the image of an image, or more precisely projected, as if they are what we wish them to be while the distance between the wish and a view that Fellini imposes of their 'reality' is the source of their mystery, their grotesqueness, their self-parody. It creates a fascination because no image, no sight is ever stable. (Rohdie 2002: 9–10)

Similarly, the narratives surrounding the different tropes and images of a city like Rome are in a constant flux, never stable. In *Roma*, Fellini announces the end of an era and the self-parody of institutions, spaces of leisure and consumption, and icons representing the city's 'identity': the Pope appearing in a fashion show, Anna Magnani playing herself and going back home, the semi-orgiastic feasts of food and people out in the street, and, of course, even Fellini himself. *Roma*, and the crucial role that costume and fashion play within its narrative, is emblematic in its blurring of the boundaries between the lived, real Rome and the imagined, fantasized Rome. Both cities, however, carry equal weight. Film and fashion shows, as they appear in Fellini's *Roma*, are signifying machines that textualize cities and countries. With their magnifying lenses metamorphosing reality, fashion and cinema transform representation of cities while exposing their most intimate and hidden truths.

References

Anon (October 15, 1960), '*Vogue*, "Rome Loves Ford, Ford Loves Rome,"

Barthes, Roland (1970,1985), "The Third Meaning: Research Notes on Several Eisenstein Stills" in *The Responsibility of Forms: Critical Essays on Music, Art, and Representation*, trans. Richard Howard, Berkeley: University of California: 1985.

Benjamin, Walter ([1955] 1973), *Illuminations* (trans. Harry Zohn), London: Fontana/Collins.

――― (1999), *The Arcades Project* (trans. Howard Eiland and Kevin McLaughlin), Cambridge, MA: Belknap Press of Harvard University Press.

Bordwell, David (1999), *On the History of Film Style*, Cambridge, MA: Harvard University Press.

Breward, Christopher (2004), *Fashioning London: Clothing and the Modern Metropolis*, Oxford: Berg.

Breward, Christopher and Gilbert, David, eds (2006), *Fashion's World Cities*, Oxford: Berg.

Bruzzi, Stella (1997), *Undressing Cinema: Clothing and Identity in the Movies*, London: Routledge.

――― (2002), 'Desire and the Costume Film: *Picnic at Hanging Rock, The Age of Innocence, The Piano*,' in Graeme Turner, ed., *The Film Cultures Reader*, London: Routledge, pp. 246–67.

Church Gibson, Pamela (2006), 'New Stars, New Fashions and the Female Audience: Cinema, Consumption and Cities, 1953–1966', in Christopher Breward and David Gilbert, eds, *Fashion's World Cities*, Oxford: Berg, pp. 89–106.

Cimagalli, Dino (1991), *Micol Fontana. Specchio a Tre Luci.*, Nova Eri Edizioni Rai: Turin.

Crainz, Guido (2005a), *Storia del miracolo italiano. Culture, identità, trasformazioni fra anni cinquanta e sessanta*, Donzelli: Rome.

――― (2005b), *Il paese mancato. Dal Miracolo economico agli anni ottanta*, Donzelli: Rome.

Dyer, Richard (1988), *Stars*, London: British Film Institute.

Evans, Caroline (2003), *Fashion at the Edge*. New Haven, CT: Yale University Press.

Giddens, A. (1991), *Modernity and Self Identity*, Cambridge: Polity Press.

Gilbert, David (2006) 'From Paris to Shanghai. The Changing Geographies of Fashion's World Cities', in Christopher Breward and David Gilbert, eds, *Fashion's World Cities*, Oxford: Berg, pp. 3–32.

Harvey, David (1999), *The Condition of Postmodernity*, Oxford: Blackwell.

—— (2001), *Spaces of Capital: Towards a Critical Geography*, London and New York: Routledge.

Klein, William (2009), *Rome + Klein*, New York: Aperture.

Marx, Karl (1926), *Eighteenth Brumaire of Louis Bonaparte* (trans. Eden and Cedar Paul), London: George Allen & Unwin Ltd.

Paulicelli, Eugenia (2000), "Personal Interview with Micol Fontana" (July)

—— (2004), *Fashion Under Fascism*, London: Berg.

Paulicelli, Eugenia and Clark, Hazel, eds (2009), *The Fabric of Cultures: Fashion, Identity, Globalization*, London: Routledge.

Paulicelli, Eugenia and Maraldi, Antonio, eds (2010), *1960, un anno in Italia: Costume, cinema, moda e cultura*, Cesena: Il Ponte Vecchio.

Reich, Jacqueline (2004), *Beyond the Latin Lover: Marcello Mastroianni, Masculinity, and Italian Cinema*, Bloomington: Indiana University Press.

Ribeiro, Helena C. (2009), 'Made in America: Paris, New York, and Postwar Fashion Photography', in Paulicelli and Clark, eds, *The Fabric of Cultures: Fashion, Identity, Globalization*, London: Routledge, pp. 41–53.

Rocamora, Agnès (2009) *Fashioning the City: Paris, Fashion and the Media*, London: I.B. Tauris.

Rohdie, Sam (2002), *Fellini Lexicon*, London: British Film Institute.

Settis, Salvatore (2004), *Futuro del classico*, Turin: Einaudi.

Shinkle, Eugenie, ed. (2009), *Fashion as Photograph: Viewing and Reviewing Images of Fashion*, London: I.B. Tauris.

Sill, Barbel (2009), 'Stardom and Fashion: On the Representation of Female Movie Stars and Their Fashion (able) Image in Magazines and Advertising Campaigns', in Shinkle, Eugenie, (2008), ed., *Fashion as Photograph: Viewing and Reviewing Images of Fashion*, London: I.B. Tauris, pp. 127–40.

Sloterdijk, Peter (2002), *L'ultima sfera. Breve storia della globalizazzione*, Rome: Carocci.

Steele, Valerie (2003), *Fashion, Italian Style*, New Haven, CT: Yale University Press.

Turner, Graeme, ed. (2002), *The Film Cultures Reader*, London: Routledge.

White, Nicola (2000), *Reconstructing Italian Fashion: America and the Development of the Italian Fashion Industry*, Oxford: Berg.

Zukin, Sharon (1996), *The Cultures of Cities*, Oxford: Wiley Blackwell.

List of Contributors

Patricia A. Cunningham is a fashion and textile historian at The Ohio State University. Publications in fashion history include *Reforming Women's Fashion, 1850-1920: Politics, Health, and Art* (Kent State University Press, 2003) and *Twentieth-Century American Fashion* (Berg, 2005), as well as numerous articles and chapters in books ranging from fashion in the works of William Hogarth, eighteenth-century men's dressing gowns, and 1930s BVD swimwear. Titles with a popular culture focus include *Dress and Popular Culture* (Bowling Green State University Popular Press, 1991) and *Dress in American Culture* (Bowling Green State University Popular Press, 1993), as well as essays on polyester as an American icon, fashion as popular culture, and 'fashion television'. *Fashioning America*, a history of twentieth-century American fashion, is to be published by Greenwood Press in 2014.

Joseph H. Hancock, II is Associate Professor in Fashion, Product, Design & Merchandising at Drexel University, Philadelphia. He has a twenty-year retailing background, having worked for The Gap Corporation, The Limited, Inc., the Target Corporation, and continues to do publishing and merchandising consulting work on an international level. His research addresses aspirational fashion branding and experiential retailing, as well as men's fashion and lifestyles. Among his numerous publications are his books *Brand/Story: Ralph, Vera, Johnny, Billy and Other Adventures in Fashion Branding* (Fairchild, 2009) and *Fashion: A Global Perspective* (Fairchild, 2014). He is the editor of the forthcoming *Journal of Fashion, Style, and Popular Culture* (2013) and is the president of the Popular Culture Association/ American Culture Association (2013-2015).

Toni Johnson-Woods is a Senior Research Fellow at the University of Queensland. She was the inaugural president of the Popular Culture Association of Australia and New Zealand (2009-2012) and is the co-editor of the *Australasian Journal of Popular Culture* and chair of the Australasian Popular Culture area of the Popular Culture Association of America. She has written dozens of articles and edited several books on popular culture in fashion, literature, and television; her latest book (edited with Amit Sarwal) is *Sold by the Millions: Australian Bestsellers* (2012). Forthcoming is *Shanghai Street Style*, edited with Vicki Karaminas (Intellect 2013).

Susan B. Kaiser is Professor of Women and Gender Studies, Textiles and Clothing, and a member of the Cultural Studies Graduate Group, at the University of California at Davis.

Her research and teaching interface between the fields of fashion studies and feminist cultural studies. Recent and current research addresses shifting articulations of masculinities; issues of space/place (i.e., rural, urban, suburban); and possibilities for critical fashion studies through popular and political cultural discourses. She is the author of *The Social Psychology of Clothing* (1997) and *Fashion and Cultural Studies* (forthcoming), and over 90 articles and book chapters in the fields of textile/fashion studies, sociology, gender studies, cultural studies, popular culture, and consumer behavior. She is a fellow and past president of the International Textile and Apparel Association, and was the first Nixon Distinguished Professor/Lecturer at Cornell University. She is currently organizing a critical fashion studies working group in the University of California system.

Vicki Karaminas is Associate Professor of Fashion Studies and Associate Head of the School of Design at the University of Technology, Sydney, Australia. She is the president of the Popular Culture Association of Australia and New Zealand (2012-2015), the Chair of Fashion, and the Chair for Subcultural Style and Identity for the Popular Culture Association/American Culture Association. Her book publications include *The Men's Fashion Reader* (Berg, 2009), *Fashion in Fiction: Text and Clothing in Literature, Film and Television* (Berg, 2009), *Fashion and Art* (Berg, 2012), and *Queer Style* (Berg, 2013, forthcoming). She is the co-editor of *The Australasian Journal of Popular Culture* and is on the editorial boards of *Fashion Theory: The Journal of Dress, Body & Culture, Film, Fashion and Consumption; Critical Studies in Men's Fashion*; and *Fashion, Style and Popular Culture*. Forthcoming is *Shanghai Street Style*, with Toni Johnson-Woods (Intellect, 2013).

Andrea Kollnitz is Associate Professor at the Centre for Fashion Studies at Stockholm University, Sweden. After studies in the humanities at Vienna University and the Academy of Applied Arts, Austria, including German, English, Scandinavian languages, literature and graphic design, she studied art history at Stockholm University and was awarded her PhD in art history in 2008. Her current research projects concern nationalist fashion and art discourse, *avant-garde* artists and their fashion performances, modernist women artists and their fashion production, among other topics. She is the co-editor of a forthcoming international collection on fashion and modernism, *Modernism och mode,* which will be published in Sweden.

Alphonso D. McClendon is Assistant Professor in the Department of Fashion, Product, Design & Merchandising at Drexel University, Philadelphia. His area of research is the visual and behavioral representation of jazz and African-American aesthetics that influence fashion and popular culture. Conference papers have included 'The Role of Elitism in Jazz Dress', 'Fashion, Colonialism and the Color Line', and 'The Subversive Representation of Jazz'. McClendon's archival research has been conducted at the Schomburg Center for Research in Black Culture, the Institute of Jazz Studies, and the Archives Center at the National Museum of American History. He has over a decade of menswear design, development, and management experience, having worked for VF Corp., Nautica Enterprises, and Phillips-Van Heusen. McClendon holds an MS in Fashion Design from Drexel, and a BS in Accounting from North Carolina A&T State University. He is currently working on *Fashion and Jazz*, forthcoming from Berg Publishers.

Ilya Parkins received her PhD in Social and Political Thought from York University (Toronto) and is Assistant Professor and Coordinator of Gender and Women's Studies at the University of British Columbia, Okanagan Campus. Her research on fashion, feminist theory, and modernist culture has been published in periodicals and collections including *Australian Feminist Studies*, *Time & Society*, *Women's Studies*, and *Biography*. She is the co-editor, with Elizabeth M. Sheehan, of *Cultures of Femininity in Modern Fashion* (University Press of New England, 2011) and is the author of a book on fashion designers' self-representations: *Poiret, Dior and Schiaparelli: Fashion, Femininity and Modernity* (Berg, 2012). Her current research analyzes women's figuration as 'unknowable' in transnational Western beauty discourses of the early twentieth century, with a particular focus on periodical culture, beauty manuals, and celebrity.

Eugenia Paulicelli is Professor of Italian and Women's Studies at Queens College and the Graduate Center of the City University of New York. She co-directs the interdisciplinary concentration in Fashion Studies and coordinates the new track in Fashion: History, Theory, Practice within MALS (MA in Liberal Studies). Among her recent publications are: *Fashion under Fascism: Beyond the Black Shirt* (Berg, 2004), *Moda e Moderno. Dal Medioevo al Rinascimento* (*Fashion and Modernity: From the Middle Ages to the Renaissance*) (Meltemi, 2006, editor), *The Fabric of Cultures: Fashion, Identity, Globalization* (Routledge, 2009, co-editor with Hazel Clark), *1960, un anno in Italia: Costume, cinema, moda e cultura* (Cesena: Il Ponte Vecchio, 2010, co-editor with Antonio Maraldi), and a special issue of the journal *Women's Studies Quarterly*, WSQ on Fashion (co-editor with Elizabeth Wissinger), to be published by CUNY Feminist Press: New York in December 2012. She is completing two books: *Film and Fashion: Italian Style* (Continuum Press, 2014); and *The Fiction of Fashions in Early Modern Italy From Sprezzatura to Satire*.

Anne Peirson-Smith is Assistant Professor in the Department of English, City University of Hong Kong. She teaches and researches fashion culture and communication, popular culture, public relations, advertising and branding and is currently researching youth fashion style in Southeast Asia. She has published various articles on the Cosplay phenomenon and youth style following completion of a large-scale Hong Kong government-funded research grant and is working on a book for Intellect on this subject. She has also recently co-authored a book, *Public Relations in Asia Pacific: Communicating Beyond Cultures* (Wiley, 2009). In addition, she is on the editorial board of the new *Journal of Fashion, Style and Popular Culture* (Intellect) and is the co-editor of a special issue on 'fashion branding' for *Fashion Practice: The Journal of Design, Creative Process and the Fashion Industry*.

Andrew Reilly is an Assistant Professor and Program Chair of Apparel Product Design and Merchandising in the Department of Family and Consumer Sciences at the University of Hawai'i, Mānoa. His primary area of research connects sexual identity to self-presentation, specifically researching body image among gay men as it relates to internalized homophobia and sexual behavior. His secondary line of research examines the local retail market in Hawai'i with attention paid to Hawaiian shirts and fragrances. Dr. Reilly is co-editor of *The Men's Fashion Reader* (2009, Fairchild Books) and is currently working on a second book on the social-psychological aspects of dress. He was the chair of the annual meeting of the International Textile and Apparel Association meeting in Honolulu in 2012.

Nancy A. Rudd is Associate Professor in the Department of Consumer Sciences at The Ohio State University. Her teaching and research interests lie in the area of appearance and human behavior, with emphasis on culture, body image, personal aesthetics, and socially responsible advertising and promotion. She teaches both undergraduate and graduate courses, advises honors students, and directs masters' and doctoral students in their research. She has studied body image for 20 years, focusing on the perceptions, attitudes, and behaviors of diverse groups of people; she has published articles in a variety of professional journals and has co-authored a textbook. She has won outstanding teaching awards in her college, and has received grants for curriculum development, research, and outreach. She serves as chair of the university Body Image and Health Task Force, and is a member of the University Wellness Collaborative.

Marvin J. Taylor is Director of the Fales Library and Special Collections at New York University. He holds a BA in Comp. Lit. an MLS from Indiana University, and an MA in English from NYU. He has held positions at Indiana University and Columbia University. Taylor has been at the Fales Library since 1993. In 1994 Taylor founded the Downtown Collection, which contains over 12,000 printed books and 15,000 linear feet of manuscripts and archives. He is editor of *The Downtown Book: The New York Art Scene, 1974-1984* (Princeton University Press, 2006.) In 2003 he began the Food Studies Collection at NYU, which now holds more than 55,000 volumes and is the largest of its type in the country. He has recently edited *101 Great Cookbooks: 501 Great Recipes* (Rizzoli, 2012). Taylor continues to write about downtown New York, English and American masculinities, and queer theory.

Paula von Wachenfeldt is Assistant Professor and Director of Studies at the Centre for Fashion Studies, Stockholm, and holds a PhD in French literature. Her research interests focus on cultural and literary studies of French society, as well as the development of luxury and fashion, particularly during the early modern era. Von Wachenfeldt has previously published studies on the role of fashion in literature and the socio-cultural representations that fictional narratives reveal. Presently, she is the initiator and co-editor of a Swedish anthology on luxury that examines the changes that took place in the use and conception of luxury in the nineteenth century. She is a member of the editorial board for the international journal *Fashion, Style and Popular Culture.*

Louise Wallenberg is Associate Professor and the Director of the Centre for Fashion Studies at Stockholm University and has been involved in its establishment and development since its start in 2006. She has a background in film studies and gender studies, and received her doctorate in 2002 from the Department of Film Studies at Stockholm University. Her research areas cover fashion and early cinema; early and late queer cinema; Hollywood cinema and trans-cultural flows of dominant fashion in the 1950s; and queer expressions in mainstream cinema. Her most recent publications include *Designing Desirable Men* (2010); *Buggering Freud and Deleuze: Towards A Theory of Queer Masochism* (2010); *Straight Heroes with Queer Inclinations: Male Film Stars in the Swedish 1930s* (2009); *Transgressive Drag Kings, Defying Dildoed Dykes: A Look at Contemporary Swedish Queer Film* (2009); and *Mannequin in Red: Death in a Couture House* (2008).

Index

*Note: italicized page numbers refer to
photographs, illustrations, or
diagrams.*

A

aesthetic dress, 193–4, 195–9, *197, 199*, 200,
  201, 202–4
Albert Nobbs (film), xi
All My Children (TV), 157, 159, 169n1
American Apparel (brand), 148
Another World (TV), 158, 159–60
appearance. *See* dress; fashion; style
Aristotle, 209, 222n1
As the World Turns (TV), 158, 160
Australia
  colonialism in, 57–8, 64–5nn3–4
  gothic atmosphere of, 55–8, 61
  popular culture studies in, xv
  pulp fiction publishing in, 91, 101n1
  as *terra nullius*, 57–8, 64n3
  wildlife of, 65nn5–6

B

Barneys New York, 9, *10*
Barthes, Roland, 34, 70–1, 175, 254
beauty, standards of
  in dress reform. *See* aesthetic dress
  historical descent of, 90–1
  in modeling, 75–6, 80
  in soap operas, 157, 159–60, 164–6
Beauvoir, Simone de, 30, 42–3, 44
bebe (brand), 75
Benjamin, Walter, xii, 34, 47n7, 106, 117,
  254, 246
Bergman, Ingrid, 247, 248, *252*

Birds, The (film), 139, 153n1
bikinis, 93
black leather jackets
  in film, 125–6, *128*, 128–9
  in gay culture, xiv, 123, 125–7, 133
  history of, 124–5
  in punk style, 127–9
Black Light Angels (comic), xiii, 51, 52, *53*,
  55–63, *56, 58, 59, 60, 62*
Blade Runner (film), 55
book covers, *92, 94, 95, 96, 97, 174*, 178
  design of, 89, 99
  as marketing strategy, 89, 90, 99
  as paratext, 89–90
  semiotic analysis of, 90, 92–100
  See also cover girls; pulp fiction
Bourdin, Guy, 144
'brand-Gaga'. *See* Lady Gaga
branding, xiii, 3
  of cities, 245, 246, 252–4
  of fashion, 3, 6, 41–2, 80, 82, 176
  of fashion designers, 105–6,
    111–2, 115–6
  of genre fiction, 89, 90, 99, 175, 178–9
  individualized strategies in, 6–7, 80
  linkages in, 7–9, *8*, 80
  of musicians, 3. *See also* Lady Gaga
  as narrative, 3–5, 6–9
Brando, Marlon, 125–6, *128*, 128–9
breast augmentation, 37–9, 40
bricolage, 54, 254
Brown, Carter, 91, *95*, 99, 101n5
burlesque, 90–1
Burton, Tim, 61
Butler, Judith, 98

C

Calderone, Jo, 16–8, *17. See also* Lady Gaga
Calvin Klein (brand), 75–6, *77*, 79
camp, 5, 12
Carangi, Gia, 78–9, 82
Cave, Nick, 54–5
Chanel, Coco, 204
cheesecake art, *95*, 96, *96*, 101n4
chick lit, xiv, 173, 175, 177–9, 186–7
civilization process (18c.), 210–1, 214–6,
        218–20, 222n5
Clark, Larry, 78, 81
class status
    dress as signifier of, 71, 80–1, 89, 92–100,
        129, 183–4, 213–4, 216, 232–3
    in fiction, 40, 89, 92–100, 183–5
    luxury goods as, 210, 213–4, 215–6
clothing. *See* dress; fashion; style
colonialism, 57–8, 64–5nn3–4
comics, xiii, 51, 52, *53*, 55–63, *56*, *58*, *59*,
        60, *62*, 249
commodity fetishism, 111
consumption
    of brands, 6–9, 15–6
    of fashion, 51, 148, 177, 178, 179–81,
        182–3, 185–7, 213–4, 215
    of genre fiction, 175, 177–81, 186–7
    as identity formation, 51, 80–1, 148,
        178–81, 185–7
    as liberty, 217–8
    of luxury goods, 179, 211, 212, 213–4, 215
contextual flexibility, 26, 28, 30, 39–42
Council of Fashion Designers of America,
        the, 69
Countdown (magazine), 51–2, 55
cover girls (pulp fiction), 89, 101n3
    'dangerous dames', 91, *96*, 97, *97*, 98
    'demure dames', 91, *92*, 92–3, 97, 98
    'hillbilly hoydens', 90
    historical inspirations for, 90–1
    'hoochie coochie mamas', 91, *97*, 97–8
    'playmate pals', 91, 93–7, *94*, *95*, *96*, 98, 99
crime fiction. *See* pulp fiction

cross-dressing, xi, 12, 16–8, *17*
Cruising (novel/film), 123
cultural anxiety, 26, 33–6, 116, 232–5, 237–9

D

DADT (Don't Ask/Don't Tell) policy, 14–5
Davis, Miles, 69, 71, 73, 74–5
Days of Our Lives (TV), 158, 160, *161*, *162*,
        163, 165
Dekker, Carl, 91, *95*
Delsarte, Francois, 202–3
Depp, Johnny, 52
Derrida, Jacques, 153n4
designers. *See* fashion designers
detective fiction. *See* pulp fiction
Devil Wears Prada, The (novel), 173, *174*,
        178, 179–86
dingo, 52, 58, 65n5
Dior, Christian, 92, 97
Don't Ask/Don't Tell policy, 14–5
Dowd, Maureen, 177–8
drag performance, 12, 16–18, *17*
dress
    aesthetic, 193–4, 195–9, *197*, *199*, 200,
        201, 203–4
    as class signifier, 71, 80–1, 89, 92–100, 129,
        183–4, 210, 213–4, 216, 232–3
    as concealment/camouflage, 71–3
    cross–dressing, xi, 12, 16–8, *17*
    definition of, 25–6, 70–1
    in fiction, xi, 25–6, 31, 35–42, 89, 92–100,
        173, 175, 176, 178–87
    and identity, xi-xii, 51, 100, 183–5
    in Scripture, 209
    as strategy, 9, 11, 12–14, 15–16, 26, 39–42,
        43, 183–5
    See also fashion; style; *names of articles/*
        types of clothing
dress reform, xiv
    aesthetic, 193–4, 195–9, *197*, *199*, 200,
        201, 203–4
    classical influences in, 195, 199, 202, 203
    exhibitions of, 195–9

lectures on, 200, 202–3
dress studies, xii-xiii, xv, 34, 80–1, 137–8,
    141–4
drug use, xiii, 69–75, 78–81, 82–3, 143.
    See also heroin chic
Drummer magazine, 123, 129
Duncan Quinn (brand), 137, 142
Dyer, Richard, 150

E
Elle (magazine), 75
Eurythmics (band), 16, 18
Evans, Caroline, 34, 41, 105, 106, 109,
    117, 178
evening gowns, 94–6, *96, 97*

F
fashion
    as academic subject, xii–xiii, xv, 34, 80–1,
        137–8, 141–4
    advertising for, 69, 75–8, *76, 77,* 79–81, 82,
        137, 141, 142, 144, 147–8, 176
    anxiety in, 34, 35–6, 80, 116, 232–5,
        237–9
    branding of, 3, 6, 41–2, 80, 82, 176
    caricatures of, 227–9, *228,* 232–8, *236, 238*
    as class distinction, 71, 80–1, 183–4, 210,
        213–4, 216, 232–3
    in comics, *53, 55, 58,* 58–9, *59, 60,* 61–2
    as communication, xi–xii, 70–1, 80–1
    consumption of, 51, 148, 177, 178, 179–81,
        182–3, 185–7, 213–4, 215
    definition of, 25
    and drug use, 69–73, 75–6, 78–83. *See also*
        heroin chic
    in fiction, xi, 25–6, 31, 35–42, 173, 175,
        176, 178–87
    in film, xi, xv, *27, 28, 29,* 41–2, 47n9, 51,
        90, 125–6, 143, 245, 246–51, 256–7
    and gender, xi, 15, 176, 227–8, 229–30,
        231, 233–5, 237–9
    and health, 195–6, 202–3
    and identity, xi–xii, 51, 100, 183–5

journalism of, 175–6, 186, 230–2. *See also*
    fashion magazines
lectures on, 200, 202–3
in modernity, 105–11, 116–8, 230, 233–5,
    237, 241n5, 245, 246
as narrative, 3–5, 70–1, 82–3, 183–5, 246
and nationalism, xiv–xv, 105, 107–8, 110,
    112–4, 117, 227–38, 249
novelty in, 81, 105–6
pornography as, 144–6
recycling of forms/trends in, 3–4, 34, 106
sexist/misogynist images in, 32, 137,
    141–50, 237–8
time and space transcended by, xii, 34,
    109–10, 117, 246
and tourism, 246, 248, 252–4
fashion designers, *251, 253, 255*
    autobiographies of, xiv, 105–14, 115–8
    branding of, 105–6, 111–2, 115–6
    for films, 28, 41–2, 247–8
    as 'mystics', 109–11
    nostalgia of, 108, 112–3, 114–7
    of reform movement, 195–7, 203–4
    self-branding of, 105–6, 111–2, 115–6
    See also names of individual designers/
        houses/brands
fashion industry
    artistry vs. standardization in, 105, 107–8,
        109–10, 116–7
    dress reform in, 193–4, 199–200, 203–4
    in fiction, 178, 181–6
    French, 105, 107–8, 112–4, 203–4, 229–33,
        235, 236–9, 245–6
    heroin chic in, 69, 75–83, *76, 77*
    Italian, 245–9, 251–2, *253,* 253–4, *255*
    sexism/misogyny in, 137, 141–50
fashionista fiction, 173, 175.
    See also chick lit
fashion magazines, 75, 99, 176, 179–80,
    181, 185, 202, 203–4, 230–2. *See also*
    individual titles
fashion models, 37, 42, 47n9, 256
    for cosmetics, 15–6

and heroin chic, 69, 75–9, *76, 77,* 78–9,
   80, 81
of the Reform Movement, 198–9, *199*
sexual abuse of, xiv, 143, 145, 146–8
See also names of individual models
fashion photography, 34, 78, 81, 144–8, 150,
   251–4
fashion shows, 80, 194, 195–9, 247, 256–7
Fellini, Federico, 246–7, 249, 254–7
feminist critique
   of the fashion industry, 137–8, 142–4,
     148–50
   of fiction, 130, 133, 173, 177–8, 181
   of film, 32–3, 40, 138–40, 141, 148–9
film
   fashion in, xi, xv, *27,* 28, *29,* 41–2, 47n9,
     51, 90, 125–6, 143, 245, 246–51,
     256–7
   in Rome, 245, 246–51, 254, 254–7
   sexism/misogyny in, 32–3, 138–40,
     148–50, 153nn1–2
   See also titles of individual fims
film theory, 137–40, 141–2, 148–9
Finnegan's Wake (novel), 89
flannel shirts, 55
Florence, Italy, 245–6, 247
Fontana Sisters, 247, 248–9, 251–2
France, xiv
   vs. America, 105, 107–8, 110, 112–4
   vs. England, 203, 229–30, 241n7
   epistemological perspective of, 111–2
   vs. Germanic cultures, 230–33, 235, 236–9,
     241nn9–10
   vs. Italy, 245–6
   literary salons of, 210–1, 214–6, 218, 223n10
   luxury discourse in, 211–20, 222n3
   as 'Other', 229–33, 235, 236–9
   Parisiennes in, 233, 235, 241n8
Fritzsche, Peter, 114–5

G

Gabrielsson, Eva, 31–2, 33, 36–7, 47n8
Galitizine, Irene, 253–4, *255*

Gardner, Ava, 93, 248–9, *250*
Gattinoni, Fernanda, 247, 248, 249, 251–2
gay fiction/erotica, 123, 125–7, *127,* 129–33,
   134nn4–6
gay/lesbian/bisexual/transgender (GLBT)
   community, 5–6, 9–10, 11, 14–16,
     18–19, 123–4, 126–7
gender identity, xi, 40, 58–60, 126–7, 130–1,
   132–3, 227–8
gender stereotypes
   in film, 137–40, 143
   in nationalist discourse, 227–8, *228,*
     229–30, 231, 233–5, 237–9, *238*
   of pulp fiction. *See* cover girls
General Hospital (TV), 158, 160
George, Susan, 139, 140, 153n1
Germanotta, Stefani Joanne Angelina.
    See Lady Gaga
Germany, 227–8, 229, 235–9, 241nn13–4
Giorgini, Giovani Battista, 247
Girl Who Kicked the Hornet's Nest, The
   (novel), 26, 35, 43
Girl Who Played with Fire, The (novel), 26,
   35, 36, 37, 38–40, 41
Girl with the Dragon Tattoo, The (film, 2009),
   27, 27–8, 39
Girl with the Dragon Tattoo, The (film, 2011),
   28, *29,* 31, 32–3, 39
Girl with the Dragon Tattoo, The (novel), xiii,
   25, 26, 30–1, 35, 36, 37–8, 40
GLBT (gay/lesbian/bisexual/transgender)
   community, 5–6, 9–10, 11–12, 14–16,
     18–19, 123–4, 126–7
Goffman, Erving, 96
Goldin, Nan, 78, 81
goth, xiii, 51, 52–5, 56–7, 58, 61–3, 64n2
Graber, Louise, 51–2, *54,* 55–63
Grossberg, Lawrence, 47n6
Gucci (brand), 75, *76,* 82, 146, 147

H

H&M (retail chain), 26, 28, 32, 40, 41–2,
   47n9

Habermas, Jürgen, 215
hairstyles, 28, 42
Harpers (magazine), 99
Harper's Bazaar (magazine), 145, 147, 248, 251
Hebdige, Dick, 51
Hedren, Tippi, 139, 153n1
Hello Kitty, 3–4, *4*
heroin chic, xiii, 69, *72*, 75–83, *76*, *77*
HIV awareness, 15–16, 18, 127
Holiday, Billie, 69, 70, 71–2, *72*, 73, 74
Hollander, Anne, 53
'Hollywood on the Tiber'. *See* Rome, film in
Holt, Douglas, 6–7
How the West Was Won (film), 139, 153n2

I
ink. *See* tattoos
Irigaray, Luce, 144
Italy. *See* Florence; Rome

J
Jaffe, Aaron, 106, 115
Jeffreys, Sheila, 141, 145
jewelry, *53*, 92–3, 96, *97*, *214*
Jugend (magazine), 229, 235, *236*, 237, 239

K
Kent, Larry, 91, *94*, *96*, *97*
Kermit the Frog, 10–12
Kierkegaard, Søren, 33–4, 36, 47n7
Klein, William, 253–4
Klimt, Gustav, 200
Koch, Joe, 128–9
Kuhn, Walt, 79

L
La Dolce Vita (film), 246–7, 249
Lady Gaga, xiii, *13*, *17*
   as camp, 5, 12
   causes supported by, 14–16
   criticism of, 3, 16
   GLBT fans of, 5–6, *7*, 9–10, 11–12, 19

self-branding of, xiii, 3–5, 7, 8, 9, *10*, 18–19
Larsson, Stieg, 26, 30–1, 32, 33, 36, 47n8
Lauper, Cyndi, 15, 16
leather jackets. *See* black leather jackets
leathermen, 123–4, 126–7, *127*, 129–30, 134n3
'Le Mondain' (poem), 210, 211–5, 222n6
Lennox, Annie, 16, 18
Liberty, Arthur Lasenby, 197–8, 199–200, 203–4
Lipovetsky, Gilles, 117
Longstocking, Pippi, 31, 42
Loren, Sophia, *251*
Lost Boys, The (film), 51
Loving (TV), 160
luxury, xiv
   criticism of, 179, 216–20, 223n12
   relativity of, 209–10
   social benefits of, 212, 213–4, 217–8

M
MAC Cosmetics, 15–16
MacIntyre, Donal, 143
magazines, xiv, 51–2, 75, 79, *161*, 229
   fashion, 75, 99, 176, 179–80, 181, 185, 202, 203–4, 230–2
   music-related, 51–2, 54, 55, 128–9
   pornographic, 93, 123, 129
   satirical, 227, *228*, 232–5, *234*, 235, *236*, 237–9, *238*
   See also individual titles
Magnani, Anna, *253*, 257
makeup, 4, 10–11, 15–16, 28, 37, 54, 75, 79, 232, 235
Mandeville, Bernard, 211, 212
Mara, Rooney, 28, *29*, 32–3, 39, 40, 42
Marie, Gerald, 143
marketing. *See* branding
Marx, Karl, 254–6
McCall, K.T., 91, *95*
McDowell, Colin, 73, 92, 176
McNeill, Legs, 128–9

McQueen, Alexander, 34, 256
McRobbie, Angela, 175
Men Who Hate Women (novel), 30. *See also*
    Girl with the Dragon Tattoo,
    The (novel)
Millennium Trilogy, The (series of novels).
    See Larsson, Stieg; Salander, Lisbeth;
    titles of individual novels
Miller, Annie Jenness, 198, 200, 202–3
Miss Piggy, 11, 12, 15
Mr. Benson (novel), 123–4, 129–33, 134n5
models. *See* fashion models
modernity, 47n6, 105–11, 114–5, 116–8, 230,
    235, 237, 241n5, 246
Monroe, Marilyn, 96, 99
Moss, Kate, 75–6, *77*, 81
motorcycle gangs, 124–5, *128*, 134n2
MTV, 5, 12, 14, 16, 18
Munch, Edvard, 79
Muppets, The, 10–12
musicians
    drug use among, 69–73
    gothic, 52, 61
    jazz, 69–73, *72*, 74–5, 81
    pop stars, 3, 51–2
    punk, 127–9
    self-branding of, 3
    See also names of individual performers

N
nostalgia, 108, 112–3, 114–7

O
O'Day, Anita, 69–70, 72–3
One Life to Live (TV), 160
Orlando (film), xi

P
Paglia, Camille, 126
paperbacks. *See* book covers; pulp fiction
Paris
    as 'fashion capital', 113, 203, 216, 232–3,
    245–6

as 'Other', 219, 232, 235, 237
    Parisiennes of, 233, 235, 241n8
Parker, Charlie, 73
Passions (TV), 160
PCA/ACA, xv
Peck, Jamie, 146–7
Petty, George, 90
phallogocentrism, 145–6, 148, 153n4
physical culture, 195–6, 198, 202–3
Picasso, Pablo, 79
pinup girls, 90. *See also* cover girls
Playboy (magazine), 93
Poiret, Paul, xiv, 107–14, 115–7, 204
Pre-Raphaelites, 195
Presley, Elvis, 16, 18, 97
Preston, John, 123–4, 129, 132–3
pulp fiction, xiv, 89, 91, *92, 94, 95, 96, 97,*
    99, 101n1, 173. *See also* book covers;
    cover girls
punk, 125, 127–9
Punk (magazine), 127, *128*, 128–9
Purple (magazine), 146

Q
Queen (band), 9

R
Rabbit, Jessica (character), 91, 100
Ramones, The (band), 127, 129
Rapace, Noomi, *27*, 27–8, 30, 32, 35
rape, 28, 30, 36, 140, 153n1
Rasmussen, Rie, 147, 153n5
Reefer Madness (film), 74
reform movement (in dress). *See* dress
    reform
Regis, Paula, 130
Reynolds, Debbie, 139, 153n2
Richardson, Terry, 142, 144–7, 153n5
Roma (film), 254–7
romance novels, 130–3, 134n6, 177, 249
Rome, xiv–xv
    American influence in, 245, 247–8
    fashion in, 245–9, 251–2, *253*, 253–4, *255*

film in, 245, 246–51, 254, 254–7
Olympics in, 252–4
tourism in, 246, 248, 252–4
Rousseau, Jean-Jacques, xiv, 210, *210*, 211, 216–20, 223n12
RuPaul, 15

S
sadomasochism (S/M), 15, 123, 126–7, 129–33, 134nn4–6
Saisonen (magazine), 229, 230–2, 239
Salander, Lisbeth (character), xiii, *27*, *29*
    ambiguities surrounding, 27, 38–41, 43
    anxiety embodied by, 34–6, 43
    body image of, 37–40
    commodification of, 26, 32, 41–2, 43, 47n9
    as feminist, 32–3, 40
    pedagogical implications of, 43–4
    sexuality of, 38–9, 40
    sui generis style of, 25, 26, 31, 46–7n1
Sanrio, *4*
Santa Barbara (TV), 160
Scarlet Letter, The (novel), 89
Schiaparelli, Elsa, xiv, 107–14, 115–7
Schott, Irving, 123, 124, 125, 129, 134n1
Schuberth, Frederico Emilio, 251, 253, *253*
Sedgwick, Eve, 126, 133
self-objectification, 164–6
Sex and the City (TV), 184
sexism
    in fashion, 32, 137, 141–50
    in film, 32–3, 138–40, 148–50, 153nn1–2
shoes, 184, 233, 234, 238
Shaw, Artie, 73
Signet Publishing, 99, 101n5
Simplicissimus (magazine), 227, *228*, 229, 237–9
Sisley (brand), 145, 146, 147, 153n3
S/M culture, 15, 123, 126–7, 129–33, 134nn4–6
Smith, Robert, 52
soap operas
    beauty standards in, 157, 159–60, 164–6

facial scars as plot device in, 157, 159–60, 163, 165–6
    history of, 157–8
    influence on viewers, 163–5
    international, 158
    research on, 159
    See also titles of individual programs
strategic ambiguity, 27, 38–41, 43
Straw Dogs (film), 139, 140, 153n1
Strix (magazine), 229, 232–5, *234*, 239, 241n8
style
    bricolage in, 54, 254
    definition of, 25
    gothic, xiii, 27, 34, 40, 51, 52–5, *53*, *54*, 56–7, 58, 61–3, *62*
    grunge, 55, 61
    heroin chic, xiii, 69, *72*, 75–83, *76*, *77*
    punk, 27, 34, 40, 42, 54, 125, 127–9
    as resistance, 51, 58–9, 62, 100
    subcultural, 34, 51, 54, 61, 63
    See also dress; fashion
subcultures, 34, 51, 54, 61. *See also names of individual subcultures*
Summerville, Trish, 28, 41, 42, 47n9
Sweden, 33, 144, 153n3, 229, 230–5, 239, 241n9
swimsuits, 93, *94*, *95*, 99
Sydney (Australia), 51, 52, 55, 61, 62

T
tableaux vivants, 90, 198
Tasmanian devil, 52, 58, 65n6
tattoos, 28, 30–1, 36–7
television. See MTV; soap operas; *titles of individual programs*
terra nullius, 57–8, 64n3
Tom Ford (brand), 142, 146
Tom of Finland, 125–8, 133
transvestism, xi, 149.
    See also cross-dressing
trousers (ladies'), 195–6, 198, 204
T-shirts, 5, 18, 35–6, 123–4

U

undergarments, 38, 79, 93, 94, *95*, 193

V

Vargas, Albert, 90, 101n2

Venus de Medici (artwork), 199, 203

Venus de Milo (artwork), 90, 199, 202, 203

Victor/Victoria (film), xi

Video Music Awards (VMA), 5, 12, *13*, 14, 16, *17*

Village People, the (band), 123

Vincent, Laurence, 7

Vogue (magazine), 28, 78, 99, 147, 179, 186, 253

Voltaire, xiv, 209, 210, *210*, 211–5, 217–8, 220, 222nn6–7, 223n12

W

W (magazine), 28, 79

White Sheik, The (film), 249

Who Framed Roger Rabbit? (film), 91

Wiener Mode (magazine), 194, 200, *201*, 203–4

Wilde, Oscar, 126, 202

Wild One, The (film), 125–6, *128*, 128–9

Williams, Esther, 93

Williams, Linda, 137

Williams, Rosalind, 215

Y

Yentl (film), xi

Young and the Restless, The (TV), 160

Yves St. Laurent (brand), 141

Z

zeitgeist, xii, 6–7, 187

If you enjoyed this title, please consider subscribing or submitting to...

Fashion, Style & Popular Culture

ISSN: 20500726 | Online ISSN: 20500734

3 issues per volume | Volume 1, 2014

Fashion, Style & Popular Culture is a peer-reviewed journal specifically dedicated to the area of fashion scholarship and its interfacings with popular culture. It was established to provide an interdisciplinary environment for fashion academics and practitioners to publish innovative scholarship in all aspects of fashion and popular culture relating to design, textiles, production, promotion, consumption and appearance-related products and services. Articles related to history, manufacturing, aesthetics, sourcing, marketing, branding, merchandising, retailing, technology, psychological/sociological aspects of dress, style, body image, and cultural identities, as well as purchasing, shopping, and the ways and means consumers construct identity as associated to Fashion, Style & Popular Culture are welcomed.

The journal offers a broad range of written and visual scholarship and includes works done through various methods of research. We welcome conceptual, theoretical and translational applied research in the areas of Fashion, Style and Popular Culture. This journal hopes to stimulate new discussions in the fashion disciplines and to push the envelope of scholarship by welcoming new and established scholars to submit their works.

Fashion, Style & Popular Culture is the preferred journal of the international conference group Fashion in Fiction and is promoted widely at all popular culture regional, national and international conferences.

Principal Editor
Joseph H. Hancock II
Drexel University
jhh33@drexel.edu

Associate Editors
Shaun Cole
London College of Fashion

Patricia A. Cunningham
Ohio State University

Susan Kaiser
University of California, Davis

Anne Peirson-Smith
City University of Hong Kong

Reviews Editor
Jessica Strubel
University of North Texas
Jessica.Strubel@unt.edu

Intellect is an independent academic publisher of books and journals. To view our catalogue or order our titles visit www.intellectbooks.com or E-mail: journals@intellectbooks.com. Intellect, The Mill, Parnall Road, Fishponds, Bristol, UK.